Special Event Production

Butterworth-Heinemann is an imprint of Elsevier
Linacre House, Jordan Hill, Oxford OX2 8DP, UK
30 Corporate Drive, Suite 400, Burlington, MA 01803, USA

First edition 2008

British Library Cataloguing-in-Publication Data
A catalogue record for this book is available from the British Library

Library of Congress Cataloging-in-Publication Data
A catalog record for this book is available from the Library of Congress

ISBN: 978-0-7506-8243-5

For information on all Butterworth-Heinemann publications
visit our web site at books.elsevier.com

Typeset by Charon Tec Ltd (A Macmillan Company), Chennai, India
www.charontec.com

Printed and bound in Canada

08 09 10 11 12   10 9 8 7 6 5 4 3 2 1

Working together to grow
libraries in developing countries

www.elsevier.com | www.bookaid.org | www.sabre.org

ELSEVIER   BOOK AID
            International   Sabre Foundation

Epigraph

Education is a progressive discovery of our own ignorance.

Will Durant
American historian (1885–1981)

Contents

Preface   xiii
Acknowledgements   xv

1   An Introduction to Special Events and Special
    Event Production   1
    1.1   Reasons for Special Events   3
          1.1.1   Religious   3
          1.1.2   Political   4
          1.1.3   Social   4
          1.1.4   Educational   5
          1.1.5   Commercial   5
    1.2   Categories of Special Events   6
          1.2.1   Meetings and Conferences   7
          1.2.2   Expositions and Trade Shows   7
          1.2.3   Celebrations, Ceremonies, and Spectacles   7
    1.3   The Players   8
          1.3.1   Event Manager   8
          1.3.2   Event Planner   8
          1.3.3   Event Coordinator   8
          1.3.4   Event Producer   9
    1.4   The Phases of Event Organization   11
          1.4.1   The Concept and Proposal Phase   12
          1.4.2   The Marketing and Sales Phase   13
          1.4.3   The Coordination Phase   13
          1.4.4   The Execution Phase   13
          1.4.5   The Followup Phase   13
    1.5   The Responsibility Areas of Event Organization   15

2	**Creativity**		**19**
	2.1	What is Creativity?	20
		2.1.1 Characteristics of the Creative Person	20
		2.1.2 Lifespan Development	21
		2.1.3 Social Environments	21
	2.2	The Cognitive Process	21
		2.2.1 Preparation Phase	22
		2.2.2 Incubation Phase	27
		2.2.3 Illumination Phase	29
		2.2.4 Translation Phase	29
	2.3	The External Environment	29
		2.3.1 Quantity Equals Quality	29
		2.3.2 Suspending Judgment	30
		2.3.3 Relax and Have Fun	30
		2.3.4 Continue to Learn	31
		2.3.5 Practice	32
	2.4	Creativity Techniques and Methods	32
		2.4.1 Conceptual Combinations	33
		2.4.2 Analogies	34
		2.4.3 Reversals	35
		2.4.4 Classical Brainstorming	36
		2.4.5 Lateral Thinking	36
3	**Budgeting**		**41**
	3.1	Preparing the Production Budget	42
		3.1.1 Developing a System to Track Expenses	43
		3.1.2 Developing a List of Expense Categories	44
		3.1.3 Researching and Categorizing Actual Expenses	44
		3.1.4 Tracking and Updating Expenses	45
		3.1.5 Handling Contingencies and Unexpected Expenses	46
	3.2	Managing Cash Flow	47
	3.3	Making a Profit	48
		3.3.1 Markup of Supplier Costs	48
		3.3.2 Hourly Fee	49
		3.3.3 Combination Markup and Fee	51
	3.4	Budget Layouts	52
	3.5	Other Financial Considerations	55
		3.5.1 The Employee/Contractor Decision	56
		3.5.2 Event Insurance	56
		3.5.3 Taxes	57
		3.5.4 Workers' Compensation	58

4   Proposals   61

   4.1   What Wins Business?   62
       4.1.1   Creativity   62
       4.1.2   Professionalism   63
       4.1.3   Experience   64
   4.2   Preparing a Winning Proposal   64
       4.2.1   Content   65
       4.2.2   Format   68
       4.2.3   Use of Technology   71
   4.3   Delivering a Winning Proposal   73
       4.3.1   Mail, Courier, or E-Mail   73
       4.3.2   Live Presentation   73
       4.3.3   Timing and Followup   73
   4.4   Ethical Considerations   73
       4.4.1   Copyright and Intellectual Property   74
       4.4.2   Other Ethics Issues   75

5   The Production Team   79

   5.1   Assembling and Organizing the Team   80
       5.1.1   Assembling the Team   80
       5.1.2   Organizing the Team   81
   5.2   Working with the Team: Concept and Proposal Phase   83
   5.3   Working with the Team: Coordination Phase   84
       5.3.1   Running Efficient Meetings   84
       5.3.2   The Producer's Tasks during the Coordination
               Phase   86
   5.4   Working with the Team: Execution Phase   87
       5.4.1   Conflict Resolution   88
       5.4.2   The Producer's Tasks during the Execution Phase 91
   5.5   Health and Safety Issues   93

6   Contract Management   97

   6.1   Definition of a Contract   98
       6.1.1   Elements of a Contract   98
   6.2   What Should be Included in a Contract   99
       6.2.1   Terms and Conditions   99
       6.2.2   Clauses   102
   6.3   Issuing and Signing Contracts   104
       6.3.1   Issuing Contracts   104
       6.3.2   Signing Contracts   105
   6.4   Breaking a Contract   106
       6.4.1   When Does a Breach Occur   106
       6.4.2   What Can Be Done   107

6.5　Resolving Disputes　107
　　6.5.1　Alternate Dispute Resolution　107
　　6.5.2　Small Claims Court　109
　　6.5.3　Litigation　109
6.6　Sample Contracts and Riders　109
　　Appendix A　Simple Producer/Client Contract　112
　　Appendix B　Complex Producer/Client
　　　　　　　　Contract　114
　　Appendix C　Complete Producer/Client Contract
　　　　　　　　with Budget, Schedule, and Change Forms　117
　　Appendix D　Rider to Equipment Rental Contract　125
　　Appendix E　Participant Waiver for Equipment
　　　　　　　　Rental Contract　127
　　Appendix F　Producer/Supplier Contract　130
　　Appendix G　Rider to a Producer/Supplier Contract　132
　　Appendix H　Alternate Producer/Performer Contract　134
　　Appendix I　Alternate Rider to a Producer/Performer
　　　　　　　　Contract　136

7　Risk Management　137

7.1　Theory versus Reality　138
　　7.1.1　Theory　139
　　7.1.2　Reality　141
7.2　Compliance　142
　　7.2.1　General Standards for Workplace Safety　142
　　7.2.2　General Standards for the Safe Design and
　　　　　Use of Equipment　142
　　7.2.3　General Guidelines for the Operation and/or
　　　　　Use of Equipment　143
　　7.2.4　Regulations　143
7.3　Insurance　145
　　7.3.1　The Realities of Insurance and its
　　　　　Relationship to Event Production　146
　　7.3.2　Bringing Event Production to Insurers　147

8　Production Management　151

8.1　During the Event Coordination Phase　152
　　8.1.1　Site Inspection and Venue Liaison　152
　　8.1.2　Site/Venue Layout and CADD　160
　　8.1.3　Production Schedules, Running Orders,
　　　　　and Scripts　162
8.2　During the Event Execution Phase　164
　　8.2.1　Supervising Event Setup　164
　　8.2.2　Running the Event　166
　　8.2.3　Supervising Event Strike　176

Appendix A Sample Event Requirements Form
            for Venue/Site   178
Appendix B Example of an Actual Production
            Schedule for an Awards Show   180
Appendix C Example of a Combined Script and
            Show Running Order   184

9 Event Followup   185

9.1 Following Up with the Production Team   185
9.2 Following Up with the Venue   186
9.3 Following Up with the Client   186
     Appendix A Sample Event Evaluation Form   189

Event Production Toolkit   191
     Master Checklist for Event Production   191
     Glossary of Special Event Technical Production
     Terminology   198

Index   243

Preface

For the past 10 years, I have been giving seminars, guest lectures, and college courses in Canada and the United States on various topics within what has come to be known as the 'special events industry.' Recently, I was asked to re-vamp a new program in event management at Capilano College where I teach near Vancouver, BC, Canada. I quickly realized that there were no relevant textbooks that took event production to the next level of knowledge, a level that universally all attendees at my seminars and lectures had been seeking for a long time. Although many excellent texts have been written, until now there has been nothing that spans the gap between being too technical and thus suitable only for technicians, and being too general to provide enough useful material to make a student 'job-ready.'

This then was my goal in writing these two books. In attempting to achieve this, I have taken the approach that a certain amount of theory and technical background is an essential subset body of knowledge that must be part of the larger set of event management skills that all event producers and event managers should possess. It is not unlike any other profession that requires basic knowledge in a number of core subjects: engineers who study chemistry, physics, thermodynamics, and electrical theory; lawyers who study tort law, criminal law, contract law, property law, administrative law, and civil procedure; architects who study history, design theory, construction technology, materials technology, and environmental technology; doctors who study surgery, pediatrics, women's medicine, and neuroscience; and airline pilots who must understand how aerodynamics and gas turbine engines work in order to qualify as captains. Taking the core courses does not mean they will use them continuously; it simply means they possess a minimum body of knowledge necessary to practice the profession competently. I have thus set out to make these books the logical next step in the evolution of that body for special events.

These books have been designed both as textbooks and as general references for the industry at large. First of all, they are purposely not intended to duplicate the many excellent references that have already been written about the field of event management, where details of the basic responsibility areas may be found. Instead, they concentrate solely on event production. They are not entry level 'how-to manuals' for those who are still trying to decide whether this industry is the right career path; they are for those who have already made that decision and are some years along the path. In these books will not be found basic management theory or simplified explanations of technical equipment, nor will areas more the purview of event managers such as sponsorship, marketing, ticket sales, catering, or transportation. The emphasis in these books is on reality: real-life war stories that prove that even the best producers make mistakes and that is just part of the learning process; real-life production challenges that are intended to place the reader in the position of an actual producer; a continuous stress throughout on the importance of compliance with safety standards and best practices of risk management (note that whenever possible, references to both Canadian and American standards and regulations are applied); and an approach that offers the raw materials but encourages producers to use them to build their own new concepts, rather than presenting the finished ideas on a 'silver platter.'

The two books divide into first the administrative aspects of event production (*Special Event Production: The Process*), following them in the logical order that one would approach event organization, and second the resources used in event production (*Special Event Production: The Resources*), where theory and reality are blended together. *Special Event Production: The Process* only scratches the surface of special event production, concentrating on the general process. The true 'body of knowledge,' the details of all the specific resources used in production, namely entertainment, décor, audio systems, visual presentation technology, lighting systems, special effects, staging, tenting, and other technical resources, can be found in *Special Event Production: The Resources*. However, to give producers a head start, included at the end of *Special Event Production: The Process* is an Event Production Toolkit. This includes a Master Checklist for Event Production incorporating most of the essential steps necessary to ensure a safe and successful event. As well, a glossary of event production technical terms is included with the toolkit that summarizes the meanings of many of the technical terms that can be found in *Special Event Production: The Resources*, although it does not incorporate detailed explanations and photos.

This is a dynamic industry and production, in my opinion, is the most exciting part, the part that I like to say 'causes applause!' I hope you enjoy your journey into learning more about it.

Doug Matthews
November 2006
Vancouver, Canada

Acknowledgements

While books are visible compilations of thoughts and ideas, they are also unseen compilations of encouraging words, suggestions, and contributions from experts, lengthy discussions among colleagues, and occasional sleepless nights.

It is for the encouraging words, suggestions, contributions, and discussions that I wish to gratefully acknowledge the following people.

My publisher, *Elsevier*, editors, *Ms. Sally North*, *Ms. Jane Macdonald* and *Mr. Dennis McGonagle*, and Publishing Project Manager, *Mr. R. Ruskin Lavy*, for having the faith to work with me and to publish not one but two books in an untested area of the special events industry.

My wife, *Marimae*, for her patience and encouragement, not only in the writing of these books, but also as I painfully matured in this industry over the course of 20 years.

Mr. Ben Kopelow, the founder of Pacific Show Productions, and my mentor in the industry, for being hard on me and entrusting a substantial body of knowledge to my care, much of which I pass on in these books.

Ms. Julie Ferguson of Beacon Literary Services, for her extensive suggestions on writing and publishing.

My colleagues in TEAM Net, the Total Event Arrangements and Meeting Network, all of whom are skilled event producers in their own right, for sharing their knowledge and for their numerous contributions to both books.

Mr. Mike Granek, the present owner of Pacific Show Productions, for his willingness to allow me to rummage through old files and photographs in search of interesting content for the books.

The *many contributors* from countries around the globe who have been kind enough to provide photos and to share some of the wisdom gleaned from their years of experience.

All the *employees and subcontractors of Pacific Show Productions* over the years who helped to create some wonderful events.

Everyone else whom I may have missed but for whose assistance I am truly grateful.

Thank you one and all.

AN INTRODUCTION TO SPECIAL EVENTS AND SPECIAL EVENT PRODUCTION

What exactly are special events and what is special event production? How are they related? What is the difference between an event producer and an event manager – or between an event planner and event coordinator for that matter? How are events organized and where in the process does production fit? There are confusing terms in the industry today as well as some misunderstandings about the function of the various players. The goal of this introductory chapter is to make sense of the confusion. However, before we can really explain what special event production is all about, we need to start at the beginning.

By definition, a special event is a gathering of human beings, generally lasting from a few hours to a few days, and designed to celebrate, honor, sell, teach about, or observe human endeavors. This is my personal definition and it is intended to be as all-encompassing as possible. Dr. Joe Jeff Goldblatt, a pioneer in special events, has a similar definition, perhaps more general, when he says 'a special event is a unique moment in time celebrated with ceremony and ritual to satisfy specific needs (Goldblatt, 2002; p. 6).' Getz (1997; p. 4), on the other hand offers two definitions, from each of the event organizer's and the guest's point of view, respectively:

- 'A special event is a one-time or infrequently occurring event outside normal programs or activities of the sponsoring or organizing body.'
- 'To the customer or guest, a special event is an opportunity for a leisure, social, or cultural experience outside the normal range of choices or beyond everyday experience.'

All are equally valid in defining special events as essentially unique and memorable times for people. Often these events are as simple as a birthday party for a child, requiring a few hours – albeit perhaps exasperating hours – of a mother's time to organize. Others – the ones with which we will be concerned in this book – are very large and complex and requiring not just one person but an entire team of specialists to organize.

Celebrations like this are not new. Not long ago, a colleague made a casual comment to me to the effect that special events have been around for at least as long as the world's oldest profession. While we cannot yet relate the two 'professions,' in fact in the archaeological record, prehistoric evidence has been found for celebratory special events, particularly elaborate funeral rituals and monumental building erection and destruction ceremonies, in various locations around the globe. This evidence goes back as far as 60,000 years to Neanderthals and archaic Homo sapiens. Of course, historical records in the form of hieroglyphs and early writing have demonstrated even more extensive evidence of entertainment and religious–political ceremonies across most civilizations: Egyptian, Roman, Greek, Mayan, Khmer, Chinese, and others. Strange as it may seem, however, the 'profession' of special events has really only been present for approximately the last 25 years. It has only been in this time period that the demand for commercially driven special events has been strong enough to enable a growing body of event organizers to actually make a living out of doing what they love.

However, in order to set a course for the next 25 years, like all industries, we cannot operate in isolation. We need to understand who we are and where we have come from, not only to avoid repeating mistakes but also to build on past accomplishments so that we can create more professional and awe-inspiring events in the future. This means we must first explore the past and the common historical reasons for special events in civilizations on every continent. Once we have done this, we will examine the industry the way it is today, looking at the different categories of events, the different jobs involved in organizing events, how event production fits into the overall spectrum of event management, and finally the five phases of event organization.

1.1   REASONS FOR SPECIAL EVENTS

Goldblatt (2002; pp. 8–9) suggests that there are four purposes for special events: celebration, education, marketing, and reunion. While these purposes do indeed encompass much of what we do today in events and present an excellent starting point, upon reflection there appear to be deeper reasons behind most events, particularly historical ones, which in some cases were very clearly non-celebratory in nature. From the distant to the recent past, across all socio-economic strata, I believe that the primary reasons for holding special events can be broken down into five categories: religious, political, social, educational, and commercial. Organizers of any modern-day event would do well to first understand which of these reasons is the primary one for their event. It may not be immediately apparent, but this understanding is critical to getting the correct message across with the event itself. We will examine each of these reasons and how this might work.

1.1.1   Religious

Noted Anthropologist Victor Turner (1988; p. 94) states, 'the major genres of cultural performance (from ritual to theater and film) and narration (from myth to the novel) not only originate in the social drama but also continue to draw meaning and force from the social drama.' By 'social drama,' Turner means the actions of everyday life. In his interpretation, performance is a reflection of what goes on in everyday life. In ancient times, this meant that the success or failure of crops and the health or sickness of individuals were, to the people of the day, almost entirely dependent on gods, shamans, or benevolent kings who had 'direct contact' with the gods. Thus, their special events centered on ritualistic ceremonies designed to appeal to the gods. This was undoubtedly the prime reason for special events in early times. An obvious example in this regard is the ancient Olympics, which began as a religious festival to honor the principal Greek god Zeus.

Even today, religion continues to be one of the reasons for some special events, particularly the affirmation of life events: baptism and confirmation in the Christian religion, bar and bat mitzvahs in Judaism, marriages in all religions, and funerals or memorial services in all societies. Others, like Christmas or Easter events, while certainly extremely important for the believers, are tied more to commercial rather than religious reasons for non-believers. An underlying reason behind some historical religious events has also been to preserve the inter-relationship of king and priest classes (e.g. ancient Egypt), or to affirm the communicative abilities of ancient kings with the gods (e.g. Mayans). Today, the reason is still present in large international religions such as Catholicism that preserve strong ties with a central governing church authority through regulated, common ritual.

1.1.2 Political

Throughout history, politics has been a prime reason for holding special events, in most cases to demonstrate the power of the ruler or ruling class. In ancient times, there are countless examples: military victory parades; gladiatorial combat in the Roman empire designed for public amusement but sanctioned by the Emperor; the public erection ceremonies of memorial monuments by ancient kings (e.g. Mayans, Chinese, and Egyptians); and even public executions right up to the early 20th century in some countries.

Today, politics does not play as large a part in special events; however, it is still present all over the world. Certainly, presidential inauguration ceremonies and coronations are major special events with considerable organizing and planning involved. Political party fundraising dinners and events are obviously political in nature. Not so obvious are other events that have political motivation as the primary, but more subtle reason. An example here might be a dinner organized by a Chamber of Commerce at which the guest speaker is a provincial premier or state governor purportedly speaking about the future business potential for the region. The underlying reason for the event is not the desire of the Chamber of Commerce to communicate good news about business. The reason is to put the premier or governor in a favorable light so that the business community will support him or her in the next election, a political reason.

1.1.3 Social

Reaffirming one's status and membership in social groups has been a reason for special events for at least as long as religion and ritual. As postulated by Turner (1988), performance reflects the social drama. Nowhere was this more apparent than in ancient Roman theater where seating placement and the way spectators acted was a reflection of Roman society in general. As Parker (1999, p. 163) states, 'The theater thus provided a specific place and time for all the dramas of Roman society to be played out, with a full cast of characters, to a complete and representative audience. The Roman consciously used the theater as an embodiment of Rome.' Of course, the theater was not always the venue, and today social events continue with celebrations of common cultural and community ties, including not only some of the life milestone events already mentioned, but also reunions, graduations, and public, non-profit cultural festivals. Examples of these abound, from small community picnics on a national holiday to mega-events such as the annual Carnival in Rio de Janeiro.

1.1.4 Educational

One of the most important historical reasons for special events has long been educational. With literacy rates often almost non-existent in ancient societies, special events provided the only means of educating the populace about their own history and also instructing them about the inherent dangers of not vowing loyalty to the governing body or individual or following the approved societal norms (also a political reason). In comparing Aztec ritual human sacrifices to gladiatorial combat in ancient Rome, Futrell (1997) states, 'For the rulers of the Mexica, Huitzilopochtli's power was a divine parallel to their temporal authority, the hearts of the victims analogous to the tribute demanded by the empire. In addition to the autocratic political rhetoric of the ideology, Aztec rulers manipulated the rituals themselves for political purposes, using the spectacle and blood as a means of impressing, and implicitly threatening, rivals with the power of Huitzilopochtli and the state identified with this deity. For example, Moctezuma II invited enemy leaders to his inaugural celebrations in which the best of their warriors were slaughtered by the thousands, surely a powerful object lesson for those concerned.'

Another example lies in the tradition of 'Potlatch' from the northwest coast native peoples in North America, that was traditionally held to celebrate such events as marriages, the opening of a 'Big House,' the succession of a chief, the raising of a totem pole, and others. Relying on oral and visual history for passing on information to friends, neighbors, and future generations, the Potlatch event was central to their culture. One of the main purposes of the Potlatch was to enlist the support of attendees or 'witnesses' who would be able to validate this history. 'Everyone present is considered to be a Witness, responsible to stay throughout the Potlatch, to hear, understand, and remember the proceedings. The entire community, including children, validates the claim of the Potlatch (Chief Robert Joseph and Rita Barnes, Personal Communication, March 27, 2006).'

In recent times, education as a reason for events has taken on a different context. With the 20th century came improved transportation and communication technology, thus allowing easier movement of people and information within nations and between continents. This lead in turn to the growth of conferences and trade shows that had as their main reason the exchange or presentation of knowledge, in other words an educational reason, but in different form. Scientific, medical, and industry-specific conferences and trade shows have resulted in a burgeoning meetings industry that is worldwide.

1.1.5 Commercial

Due to technological advances in the 20th century, such as air transportation and the Internet in addition to other influences like the cult of celebrity worship, movies, and mass-appeal entertainment, the primary reason for holding special events has now become almost completely commercial.

Thanks to this reason, the special events industry has come into being within the last 25 years. It has provided work and an outlet for the creative energies of many of us.

When considered, almost every event nowadays comes back to having the primary reason for its existence as commercial. An incentive theme night does not have socializing as a primary reason; it has selling the company products as the reason. A Grand Prix auto race event does not have as its primary reason the competition to see who the best driver is; it is there to sell the sponsors' products, whether they are the event sponsor or the individual driver sponsors. A charitable fundraising event put on by a city business mogul is not there as pure philanthropy, no matter what the organizer may argue; it is there to advance the image and hence the sales of the organizer's products or services. A Santa Claus parade is not created for the good of the children; it is created for the good of the sponsors. These are but a minute sample from our industry.

The key point about understanding the underlying reasons for special events, especially commercial, is that it can affect how an event is organized and produced, especially in the choice of resources such as entertainment, décor, and visual presentations. For example, a producer who has been tasked with finding entertainment for a business leader's fundraising event might recommend featuring the leader in a scripted spoken presentation in order to portray that person in a favorable light and give him or her more exposure. If the underlying reason of commercialism were not known, this opportunity might be passed up. An incentive dinner for a corporation's top sales people might, instead of just having buffet stations with interactive entertainment, incorporate some symbols of the company or its products as part of the entertainment, such as souvenir sheets with the company logo or reference to its products on them drawn by a caricaturist, or small products as part of a magician's close-up magic. A post-Grand Prix race drivers' dinner for the media and VIPs might feature an original song or song parody about the race sponsor especially written and sung by a celebrity performer. A souvenir CD handed to all attendees would make this a lasting memory and enhance the image of the sponsor. While some of these may seem obvious, the intent is to emphasize how important it is for producers to dig deeply in order to understand the primary underlying reasons for any event.

1.2   CATEGORIES OF SPECIAL EVENTS

Special events are now so popular that there is an entire spectrum of different categories of events and accompanying specializations of organizers. Depending on which continent one is situated, the categories may be different. Allen et al. (2005; pp. 11–16) from Australia, for example, categorizes events by both size and content, lumping meetings, incentives, conventions, and exhibitions (MICE) into a single category. On the other hand,

Goldblatt (2002; pp. 9–14) divides events into 10 'subfields.' I propose a somewhat integrated approach to this categorization that generally reflects the recognized specializations of organizers, although this does tend to be a moving target as more such specializations continue to evolve. The following are my suggested categories of special events along with the professional designations that are currently available to those who work in them.

1.2.1 Meetings and Conferences

As mentioned in Section 1.1.4, this is now a massive field worldwide. It is a distinct professional specialization, with the designation Certified Meeting Planner (CMP) available through the regulatory body, the Convention Industry Council (CIC). Advocacy bodies include Meeting Professionals International (MPI) and the Professional Convention Management Association. Events that come under this main category include meetings, conferences, conventions, video conferences, Internet conferences, congresses, seminars, symposia, workshops, and retreats.

1.2.2 Expositions and Trade Shows

This category encompasses large expositions, industrial shows, trade shows, professional/scientific shows, and consumer shows. A professional designation for organizers is available, the Certified in Exhibition Management (CEM) designation, through the International Association for Exhibition Management.

1.2.3 Celebrations, Ceremonies, and Spectacles

This category generally corresponds to the various special event organizer designations currently available, including Certified Special Events Professional (CSEP) available through the International Special Events Society (ISES), and Certified Special Event Coordinator (CSEC) and Certified Special Event Manager (CSEM) available in Canada through the regulatory body, the Canadian Tourism Human Resource Council. The Canadian advocacy body is the Canadian Special Events Society. This category is large and can be further subdivided into the following components:

- *Public events*: These include such events as parades, festivals, carnivals, sporting events, concerts, and one-off theatrical presentations. Some of these also have separate professional certifications, such as festivals, with the Certified Festival and Event Executive (CFEE) designation available through the International Festivals and Events Association.
- *Private events*: Arguably the area in which the majority of event producers work, this sub-category includes such events as award shows, corporate dinners, theme events, opening and closing ceremonies, incentive events, fundraisers, social and life events, product launches, and reunions.

Of interest in looking at the overall categorization of special events, is that there is often much cross-pollenization among the categories, in spite of different primary reasons for the events. For example, a large conference may have a separate wrap-up theme dinner for everyone at which there may be entertainment, decorations, and an A-V show. Likewise, a large college reunion may have a small trade show, or an international exposition may include a product launch. Each of these 'sub-events' would have an accompanying reason of its own for being held.

1.3 THE PLAYERS

Because the event industry is so young, terminology is still developing and the titles of 'industry players' often overlap. This leads to confusion and it is one of the general intentions of this chapter and this book to help dispel this confusion. From my experience in the industry as it has developed, the following terms, while not always used consistently, have come to define the people who have a hand in organizing a special event.

1.3.1 Event Manager

This person is the delegated representative of an entity that holds overall ultimate responsibility for the event. This 'entity' could be the owner of the event, such as a company, city, non-profit organization (e.g. trade show, charity, festival, association), or an individual. Usually, the event manager further delegates or sub-contracts other specialists in the areas needed to accomplish the event (e.g. to an event producer). The event manager term is most often used in larger events, such as festivals, or large event marketing events such as major sporting events (e.g. Grand Prix races, Super Bowl, etc.).

1.3.2 Event Planner

This term is sometimes used interchangeably with event manager but tends to refer to a person who plans smaller and more private events such as dinners, weddings, reunions, and similar gatherings. Frequently this is an individual operating independently, and not a company.

1.3.3 Event Coordinator

The term coordinator is sometimes used interchangeably with event manager and event planner, but tends to refer to an individual employed by a larger organization or a venue, who is responsible for bringing together all the event participants to ensure they are working toward the same goal. This person is usually not responsible for the creative side or supplier sourcing, but more for simple coordination duties. Examples can be found in convention centers and arenas that employ event coordinators to liaise with all parties engaged in creating an event.

1.3.4 Event Producer

The term 'event producer' is another one that might be used interchangeably with event manager and event planner, but most often refers to the person responsible for coordinating and executing – and occasionally assisting with creating – the event, particularly the technical side that involves design, scheduling, staging, sound, lights, A-V, entertainment, and décor. In most event situations, the producer is not the event manager but is contracted by the event manager as defined above, who thereby becomes the 'client' of the producer. In situations where the term event manager is not used, the client of the producer may be any one of a number of individuals such as a company owner or internal manager, a 'middle person' (e.g. a destination management company or incentive house representative), an association, or non-profit organization executive member, or just a private individual. Since the producer is the focus of this book, let us look a little more closely at this person.

1.3.4.1 *Skills Required by an Event Producer*

The obvious benefits of advanced – and continuing – education can be found in the skills now required by anyone wishing to pursue a career in special events. The event producer is no exception, and in fact, probably more than any other player, needs to keep abreast of a larger body of knowledge across a greater variety of specialties. For now, let us list the most common and most desirable skills and personality traits.

- *Organizational ability*: A logical mind must keep a myriad of details, times, people, schedules, and tasks in their proper places.
- *Creative ability*: A right brain orientation helps to conceive new ideas, which can be in conflict with the organizational or left side of the brain.
- *Technical interest*: Because of the myriad technical areas coming under the supervision of the producer, at least a general interest of things technical avoids the temptation to keep hands off and simply trust suppliers. The producer must take confident ownership of these areas.
- *Financial acumen*: A working knowledge of financial statements, basic accounting, and budgets is an absolute necessity to effectively manage client budgets.
- *Writing ability*: A concise, creative, and grammatically correct writing style is mandatory.
- *Speaking ability*: A clear, organized, and enthusiastic speaking style is highly desirable for presentations to clients and to production teams.
- *Computer skills*: Familiarity with the most used components of the Microsoft Office suite of software (Word, Access, Excel, and Power Point) is mandatory. Also desirable is familiarity with customer relationship

management (CRM) software such as Maximizer or Act, graphics software such as Adobe Photoshop, computer aided design and drafting (CADD) such as Vectorworks or Vivien, project management software such as MS Project, and finally total familiarity with the Internet, and desirably with Web site design.

- *An ethical and moral grounding*: Because it is not yet fully developed as a 'profession,' the industry still harbors a good many individuals who are ethically and morally irresponsible in their business dealings. A producer who ignores the temptations to follow this path and instead takes the high ground may occasionally lose business but will maintain a sterling reputation which, in the long run, is all one has in a service industry.
- *Personality traits*: In order to deal with the many personality styles and demands of the job, the producer's personality should reflect:
  - a gregarious and outgoing nature;
  - an upbeat, friendly, and positive attitude, even during high stress times;
  - the ability to hide and manage stress and not get upset by it;
  - flexibility in allowing changes to ideas and schedules;
  - a firm and fair management style.

As can be seen, these are widely varying skills and personality traits, a great many of which tend to clash with each other. It is a fine balance and can prove difficult for potential producers who are not used to the constant pressures, late nights, high stress, changing client requirements, and often lower than expected income. The rewards are high in terms of job satisfaction and that often compensates for the other less rewarding aspects.

1.3.4.2   *Habits of Effective Event Producers*

Believe it or not, successful event producers do have much in common with each other. Over the years, I have come to identify several characteristic habits that they exhibit to achieve success. Although not every single producer is the same, here are some of the key habits.

- *Focus*: This is the ability to keep a specific event at the top of one's priority list. It starts with an understanding of the five main phases in the event planning process, discussed in Section 1.4: Concept and Proposal, Sales and Marketing, Coordination, Execution, and Followup. Throughout each of these phases, the particular event must be at or near the top of a daily priority list.
- *Anticipation*: This is the single most important producer habit that should be applied to every phase of the organizing process, but most particularly during the Coordination and Execution phases. It is the ability to visualize the entire event from start to finish and to determine potential problems before they occur. To do this successfully requires a great deal of attention to detail combined with an ear that listens to the 'little inner voice' telling

one to be careful and correct an errant detail before something disastrous happens, in other words an ear that is attuned to intuition.

- *Single-minded purpose*: There cannot be any mixed messages in the minds of any of the production team members. This means that all those team members involved in the event – producer, venue staff, and all suppliers – must understand the goals and purpose of the event passed on to the producer by the event manager or client. The job of the event producer is to ensure that this happens. For example, if an event manager has created a 'Carnival Fun Night,' it is the responsibility of the producer to explain to the production team whether the goal of the event is just for attendees to have fun or if it is to build a sales team. Depending on the interpretation, two entirely different events might result.
- *Ability to devote the necessary time*: Producing events cannot be done piecemeal. Each phase requires a certain amount of dedicated time to complete and it is best to work on each phase all at once. For example, it is better to write a proposal over 5 h rather than over 5 days, before moving on to the next task.
- *Ability to block out interference*: At first glance, this would seem obvious, but in today's harried work environment, it is not as easy as it appears. For example, when writing a proposal where creative thought is required, phone calls should not be allowed to interrupt one's creative time. Instead, an answering service should be used or someone else in the office should take messages.
- *Ability to address challenges*: Everyone gets them, no matter how carefully an event has been planned. The main thing is that one should stay positive and pro-active. The second thing is being fully aware of all the resources at one's disposal and whether they can be used to solve a problem in a timely fashion. Lastly, a producer should not be afraid to say, 'NO!' if trying to make a change will compromise the quality of the event or the producer's reputation.
- *'Show-must-go-on' mentality*: Every member of the production team must have this mindset. No challenge can be too big or too small. Being on time for everything is imperative. Performing in spite of hardships is a given in this business. One must do what is promised when it is promised. Finally, keeping a positive attitude towards all staff and clients brands one as a true professional.

1.4   THE PHASES OF EVENT ORGANIZATION

Before we can effectively understand the event producer's job, we must first understand event organization. It is generally recognized by event management practitioners that there are five distinct phases to the event management – or organization – process. Goldblatt (2002; pp. 36–56) and Allen et al. (2005; pp. 282–285) both have defined these phases in different ways but they are essentially the same. Throughout the event organization process, there are underlying, but ongoing and overlapping event responsibility areas, or tasks. Goldblatt (2002) divides these areas into Event Administration, Marketing, Risk Management, and Event Coordination. Allen et al. divides them into ten 'knowledge areas' rather than 'tasks' by using a project management approach. Herein lies the source of some confusion for persons new to the special events industry: there is not a clear-cut relationship between these tasks and the actual process of organizing the event, although Goldblatt (2002; p. 103) and Allen et al. (2005; pp. 116–125) allude to a relationship. We will attempt to clear up the confusion.

I subscribe to the five-phase model concept of the process, but with slight changes to those models postulated by Goldblatt and Allen et al. These changes, I believe, allow this model to more closely follow the actual tasks (postulated by Goldblatt as the four responsibility areas) that must be accomplished as one goes through the process in logical order. In other words, it clearly ties process and tasks together. Let us now examine each of these event phases and add in the primary tasks associated with each one.

1.4.1 The Concept and Proposal Phase

This phase takes the event from the germ of an idea to the creation of a detailed proposal. The tasks associated with this phase can be further divided into two sub-phases.

1.4.1.1 *Preliminary Research*

In the preliminary research sub-phase, a feasibility study of the event concept is conducted, including a strengths/weaknesses/opportunities/threats (SWOT) analysis to determine if the concept is sound and worth pursuing further. Also part of this sub-phase is a site or venue comparison and selection, often requiring site inspections and detailed analyses. These tasks are all associated with the event administration responsibility area.

1.4.1.2 *Initial Event Design*

In this sub-phase, the first real steps are taken to actually develop the event concept in detail. First, a preliminary program and content are put together. This usually requires the input of key sub-contractors (suppliers) to provide ideas and preliminary costs. Second, a formal budget is prepared based on these costs. Third, an initial creative proposal for the event is written incorporating the coordinated ideas of the event team (i.e. suppliers and staff) and the event budget. All these tasks generally come under the combined responsibility areas of marketing and event administration. This phase ends with the creation of this proposal. It is typically near the beginning of this sub-phase that the event producer will be brought into the picture.

1.4.2   The Marketing and Sales Phase

This phase takes the event from proposal stage to formal go-ahead decision. In this phase, the goal is to sell enough sponsorships and/or tickets to reach the go-ahead decision with sufficient time remaining before the event to allow for detailed coordination. The primary tasks of this phase come under the responsibility area of marketing and include the creation of marketing materials based on the initial event proposal, and the subsequent selling of sponsorships and tickets. Of course, depending on the event, this phase may be skipped entirely. For example, if the event is a private corporate one for which a fixed sum has been budgeted, there is no reason to find sponsors or sell tickets. The event is a 'go' from the beginning and only fine tweaking of the proposal and budget usually remain. Otherwise, this phase ends with the go-ahead decision.

1.4.3   The Coordination Phase

This phase takes the event from the go-ahead decision to the beginning of the actual event setup. It is the most complex and time-consuming phase of the event organizing process, the tasks for which involve risk management (obtaining licenses and permits, assessing risks), human resource management (recruiting volunteers and organizing staff), administration (contracting suppliers, accepting registrations, and reservations), and the commencement of event coordination (production management, contracting caterers, and transportation, etc). This phase ends the moment event setup begins.

1.4.4   The Execution Phase

This phase is the period that includes event setup, the actual running of the event itself, and event strike. From an event management point of view, the responsibility areas and associated tasks involved in this phase include administration (paying suppliers, coordinating volunteers, and staff), marketing (badging, signage, media liaison, onsite registration, and ticketing), risk management (monitoring risks, security liaison), and event coordination (transportation liaison, catering liaison, onsite management, and production management). This phase ends after strike once the venue or site has been returned to its pre-event condition.

1.4.5   The Followup Phase

The final phase in the organization process is that of followup. This phase begins the moment event strike is complete. The responsibility area for this phase falls under event administration and involves paying suppliers, thanking

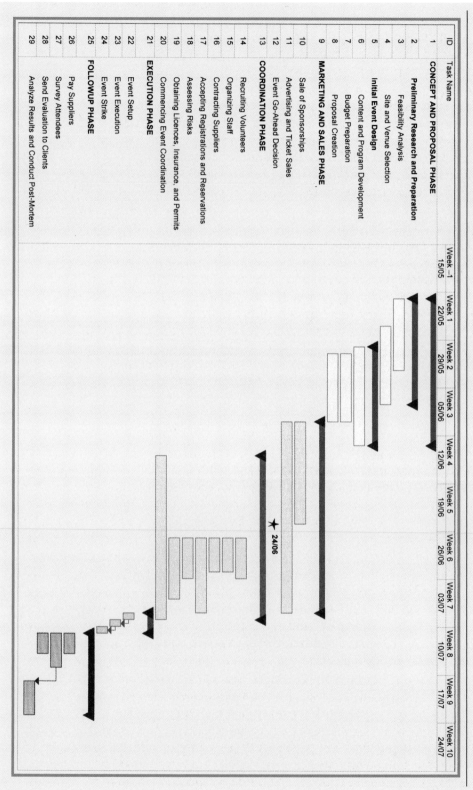

FIGURE 1.1
SAMPLE EVENT TIMELINE

the client and/or participants, evaluating the event through participant or client surveys, conducting an event team wrap-up review meeting, making adjustments for any budget and contractual changes, and analyzing the event's success or failure. It ends once these tasks have been accomplished.

In order to put the organization process into perspective, we have created a theoretical event in project management software (Microsoft Project) and have output a simplified version of a general project timeline (also known as a *GANNT chart*) as Figure 1.1 to assist with understanding the inter-relation of process and tasks. This chart is plotted horizontally as weeks from the commencement of event planning. In this example, each of the event phases is color-coded for easy reference: blue for the Concept and Proposal phase, pink for the Marketing and Sales phase, red for the Coordination phase, green for the Execution phase, and purple for the Followup phase. Likewise, the tasks within each phase are similarly color-coded and reflect the explanations given in this section. As in most real events, there is overlap in tasks amongst the various phases, some of which is shown here. For example, concept development is going on simultaneously with the initial feasibility studies and site selection, ticket sales overlap event coordination, and so on. Neither are all events equal in terms of the time spent in each phase or on each task. The key is to understand what happens and approximately when it happens on the event timeline.

1.5   THE RESPONSIBILITY AREAS OF EVENT ORGANIZATION

Now that we understand how the event organization process is laid out, we need to put all the tasks within the four responsibility areas in their proper place and then relate them to what this book is all about, event production. Table 1.1 gives an overview representing some of the generally accepted key tasks that fall under each of these responsibility areas. One change has been made to Goldblatt's four areas, and that is the Coordination area has been re-named Operations and Logistics in order to avoid confusion with the Coordination phase.

Of course, as already mentioned, not every event will have this exact division of responsibilities because the final organizational structure and division of responsibilities usually end up as personal preferences of the event manager (e.g. some events may have the risk management tasks assigned to event administration, entertainment under a separate programming responsibility area, catering and transportation under event administration, etc). However, this table gives a good indication of the type of division that has proven successful. For further reference, Goldblatt (2002; pp. 112–115), Allen et al. (2005; pp. 121–125), Rutherford-Silvers (2004; pp. 172–176), and Van Der Wagen and Carlos (2005; pp. 165–167) discuss possible organizational structures that may be used for event management, including the above form of *functional* structure.

TABLE 1.1
EVENT MANAGEMENT TASK OVERVIEW

Event Responsibility Area			
Administration	**Marketing**	**Risk Management**	**Operations and Logistics**
Event feasibility analysis (SWOT)	Program development	Assessment and control of risk	Catering
Site and venue selection	Sponsorship acquisition	Creation of emergency plans	Transportation to and from the event site/venue
Financial administration and budgeting	Proposal preparation	Organizing emergency services	Onsite management
Contracting	Promotional material development	Obtaining licenses and permits	Production, including entertainment, décor, lighting, audio, visual presentations (A-V), staging, tenting and temporary structures, special effects, electrical power, HVAC, sanitation and waste management, rigging, fencing, technical direction
Staff selection and training	Advertising	Addressing insurance and liability issues	
Volunteer recruitment, training, and coordination	Web site design and maintenance	Analyzing security needs and obtaining security services	
Event evaluation	Media liaison Signage Registration and badging Ticketing Housing (usually for conferences only)		

Courtesy: Doug Matthews

From this point on in this book, we lay out the chapters as if we were undertaking the organization of an event as event producers. In other words, we integrate what we have covered with respect to the event organization process and the responsibility areas and relate them to exactly what the event producer does and when it is done. Let us briefly outline what each of the subsequent chapters in this book will be covering and how they relate to event production.

- *Chapter 2: Creativity.* This chapter reflects the initial involvement of the event producer in the Concept and Proposal phase in which the event manager must study the feasibility of conducting the event and to do so requires the input of key contractors, specifically the producer, who must submit a creative proposal that incorporates all the technical areas and possibly entertainment and décor as well.

- *Chapter 3: Budgeting.* The producer must accurately budget for the equipment and concepts proposed, again within the Concept and Proposal phase.
- *Chapter 4: Proposals.* This chapter is all about writing an effective proposal by the producer; thus it still lies within the Concept and Proposal phase.
- *Chapter 5: The Production Team.* Moving into Chapter 5, we assume that there are normally no tasks for the producer in the Marketing and Sales phase of event organization. This chapter thus begins the involvement of the producer in human resource management and discusses how to do this with the production team in the Coordination and Execution phases. It parallels the timing of the human resource tasks of volunteer recruitment, training, and staff selection as outlined above for the event administration responsibility area in the same phases.
- *Chapter 6: Contracting.* As shown in Figure 1.1, at the same time as event administration is contracting other suppliers, so too is the event producer contracting technical suppliers during the Coordination phase, as well as contracting with the client (the event manager). This chapter explains how contracting applies to the producer.
- *Chapter 7: Risk Management.* Also paralleling the risk assessment tasks of the event management team in the Coordination phase, the producer must begin to assess any risks associated with the technical production, obtain insurance, obtain associated permits and licenses, and assure compliance with equipment design standards and safety regulations.
- *Chapter 8: Production Management.* This chapter is about coordinating all the production elements as shown on line 20 of Figure 1.1. It begins in the Coordination phase and continues through the Execution phase.
- *Chapter 9: Event Followup.* This chapter explains the producer's involvement in the followup tasks of the event team and of the producer's own responsibility areas.

Once all the tasks have been laid out in logical order in these chapters, we then devote the second book (*Special Event Production: The Resources*) to explaining the theory and background of all the technical areas that may, at some point in time, be the responsibility of the event producer.

PRODUCTION CHALLENGES

1. Describe in your own words the main historical reasons for holding special events and give a modern day example of each.

Continued

PRODUCTION CHALLENGES (CONTD.)

2. Explain how an event producer is different from an event planner, event manager, and event coordinator, and describe some of the tasks that differentiate each of these jobs from the other ones.

3. You have been given the task of preparing and delivering (in person) a major creative proposal for the production of three different incentive events for an important client. Describe the skills you require to complete this task successfully.

4. Explain the difference between the organizational **phases** of an event and the **responsibility areas** of organizing the event.

5. You have been approached by a well-known event manager to act as the producer for a new comedy festival in your city that will take place in multiple indoor venues over a week-long period. You will be responsible for acquiring all the talent and providing the audio, lighting, and staging for all the venues. Since this is a new venture, sponsors must be found. Describe where in the event organization process your input will be needed and what that input will be at each point, assuming that eventually enough sponsors will be found for the event to proceed.

REFERENCES

Allen, J., O'Toole, W., Harris, R. and McDonnell, I. (2005). *Festival and Special Event Management*, Third Edition. Milton: John Wiley & Sons Australia, Ltd.

Futrell, A. (1997). *Blood in the Arena: The Spectacle of Roman Power*, First Edition. Austin, TX: University of Texas Press. Retrieved October 30, 2006, from Questia database: http://www.questia.com/PM.qst?a=o&d=61841987.

Getz, D. (1997). *Event Management and Event Tourism*. New York: Cognizant Communication Corporation.

Goldblatt, J. (2002). *Special Events: Twenty-First Century Global Event Management*. New York: John Wiley & Sons, Inc.

Parker, H.N. (1999). The Observed of All Observers: Spectacle, Applause, and Cultural Poetics in the Roman Theater Audience. In B. Bergmann and C. Kondoleon (Eds.), *The Art of Ancient Spectacle*. Washington, DC: Trustees of the National Gallery of Art.

Rutherford-Silvers, J. (2004). *Professional Event Coordination*. Hoboken: John Wiley & Sons, Inc.

Turner, V. (1988). *The Anthropology of Performance*. New York: PAJ Publications.

Van Der Wagen, L. and Carlos, B.R. (2005). *Event Management for Tourism, Cultural, Business, and Sporting Events*. Upper Saddle River, New Jersey: Pearson Education, Inc.

CREATIVITY

LEARNING OUTCOMES

After reading this chapter, you will be able to:

1. Understand what creativity is and how intelligence, personality, lifespan circumstances, and the social environment influence it.
2. Understand the different phases of the cognitive process of creativity and how perception works in them.
3. Understand and apply different means to improve the creative environment.
4. Understand and apply a variety of techniques to generate creative ideas.

Creativity is a wonderful tool and an absolutely essential one in the special events industry. Invariably, it is the event producer who ends up with the task of creating and designing an event from the ground up, incorporating everything from décor and entertainment to all the technical elements. Producers are constantly being challenged to come up with events that 'surpass last year's,' are 'bigger and better,' and are 'totally different and exciting.' Television, Internet, newspapers, a multiplicity of magazines in all fields, and easy international travel have given people access to other ideas and views of the world like never before, thereby raising their expectations for dramatic, unusual events to unprecedented levels. The producer must rise to this challenge by generating a spark of ingenuity that will launch the event during the Concept and Proposal phase. This chapter will examine how to generate that spark. It will look at what creativity is and the internal

tive thinking, it will propose guidelines to assist in the cre-
. developing the best creative environment), and finally it
of the most popular techniques for encouraging creative

2.1   WHAT IS CREATIVITY?

Many people from numerous entirely different fields have tried to define
creativity and ended up with just as many definitions. Prior to 1950, minimal psychological research was proffered to creativity. However, since then
progress has taken place on four fronts: the cognitive processes involved in
the creative act (i.e. how creative people think), the distinctive characteristics of the creative person, the development and manifestation of creativity
across an individual's life span, and the social environments most strongly
associated with creative activity. We will be examining cognitive processes
in Section 2.2 at length, so will begin by discussing the creative person.

2.1.1   Characteristics of the Creative Person

Classic and current psychological studies break down the attributes of a
creative person into two headings: intelligence and personality.

2.1.1.1   *Intelligence*

The relationship between creativity and intelligence has long been a concern of psychology, particularly with respect to the proximity of genius to
madness. Pop psychology has gone on to identify so-called creative people
with right-brain activity and more logically thinking people with left-brain
activity. Increasingly, however, there is growing evidence that while there
may be some creative personality traits, creativity per se is less intelligence
dependent than first thought. Mackinnon (1962) found no correlation
between intelligence and creativity above an IQ score of 120, and more
recently, Rothenberg and Wyshak (2004) found no evidence for any direct
inheritance of creativity or genius. In fact, although they concede that some
inborn degree of high intelligence must be possessed by a genius, it is far
more likely that being read to by parents will have more influence. Recently,
it has also been shown that the traditional model of intelligence is more
multi-dimensional and can be manifested in specific areas such as painting,
choreography, or psychology (Gardner, 1993).

2.1.1.2   *Personality*

It has been long recognized that creativity is as much a dispositional as
an intellectual phenomenon (Dellas and Gaier, 1970). Recent research has

compiled a profile of creative individuals. They are disposed to be independent, nonconformist, unconventional, even bohemian, and they are likely to have wide interests, greater openness to new experiences, a more conspicuous behavioral and cognitive flexibility, and more risk-taking boldness (Martindale, 1989; Simonton, 1999).

2.1.2 Lifespan Development

The acquisition of creative potential takes place in the early years of one's life. Studies have shown that influencing factors include birth order, early parental loss, marginality, the availability of mentors and role models, and even performance and experience in primary, secondary, and higher education (Simonton, 1987). Interestingly enough, creative potential seems to surface in adverse childhood situations. Culture may also play a part.

The actualization of creative potential takes place throughout an individual's lifetime. At present, studies are inconclusive about how much it continues into later years but it would appear initially that factors are at work that help to maintain creative output and even to promote a resurgence in creativity in these later years.

2.1.3 Social Environments

Rogers (1954) postulated early that creativity is largely influenced by environment. The myth of the lone genius is just that, a myth. Amabile (1996) found that creativity usually appears more favored when individuals perform a task for inherent enjoyment rather than for an external reason, including monetary gain, a time deadline, fear, or competition. Csikszentmihalyi (1990) postulated that creativity requires not only the individual creator in order to be the most successful, but also the presence of a *domain* (i.e. a set of rules and a repertoire of creativity techniques) and the presence of a *field* (i.e. other persons who work within the same domain, such as other event producers, or other creative persons in a similar discipline, like painters, musicians, dancers, etc.).

To sum up this section in simple terms, what this all means is that, irrespective of one's age, intelligence, or personality, the chances of coming up with good ideas for events can be improved by working with creative people in a socially relaxed environment and by using creative idea generation techniques.

2.2   THE COGNITIVE PROCESS

By definition, cognition is the action of knowing, perceiving, and conceiving. It is the very act of creative thinking. How does this happen and what actually takes place in the brain of someone trying to solve a problem creatively, or trying to generate a creative concept? If we can answer this question, we might be better able to simulate the same conditions for ourselves in coming up with creative ideas for events. Fortunately, considerable recent research has been applied to answering the question. Ludwig (1989) theorized that there are four distinct phases to the creative process: preparation, incubation, illumination, and translation.

2.2.1   Preparation Phase

In the preparation phase, a problem is presented and relevant pertinent information is sought out in order to try to solve it. *Perception*, the processing of sensory input, plays an important role in this phase because it determines how the problem is initially interpreted. Many cognitive psychologists hold that, as we move about in the world, we create a model of how the world works. That is, we sense the objective world, but our sensations map to *percepts*, and these percepts are provisional, in the same sense that scientific hypotheses are provisional. As we acquire new information, our percepts shift to account for our new knowledge. Since percepts are functionally critical to the discussion of optical art and visual illusions, we will occasionally refer to examples of optical illusions to assist with explanations. For purposes of this chapter, we will work only with visual perception as it provides for easy illustrations.

2.2.1.1   *Perceptual Organization*

Knowledge and experience are extremely important for perception because they help us make sense of the input to our sensory systems (Foley, 2005). Gestalt psychologists were the first to identify several principles by which people organize isolated parts of a visual stimulus into groups or whole objects (Wertheimer, 1923):

- *Proximity*: The closer objects are to one another, the more likely we are to group them together.
- *Similarity*: We tend to link together pairs of the visual field that are similar in color, lightness, texture, and shape.
- *Continuity*: We see lines as continuing in a particular direction rather than making abrupt turns. Figure 2.1 illustrates how we want to do this in spite of the illusion that the diagonal line is misaligned (it is not). This is called a Poggendorff illusion.
- *Closure*: We prefer complete forms to incomplete forms and tend to mentally close gaps. Figure 2.2 illustrates how we tend to mentally form the letter 'E' rather than just see several unrecognizable lines.
- *Common fate*: We tend to group together objects that move in the same direction. Figure 2.1 also illustrates this.

FIGURE 2.1
POGGENDORFF ILLUSION

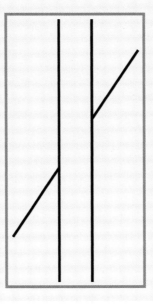

Courtesy: http://www.michaelbach.de/ot/ang_poggendorff/index.html, redrawn by author

FIGURE 2.2
EXAMPLE OF MENTAL CLOSURE

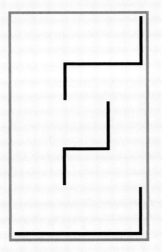

Courtesy: www.eyetricks.com, redrawn by author

FIGURE 2.3

EXAMPLE OF SEEKING SIMPLICITY: THE BLIVET

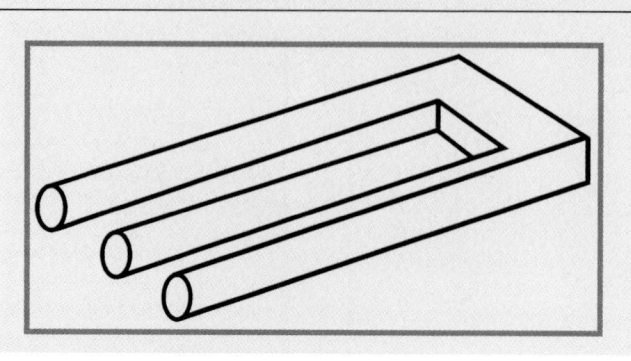

Courtesy: http://en.wikipedia.org/wiki/Image:Blivet.png

- *Simplicity*: People intuitively prefer the simplest, most stable of organizations. Figure 2.3, called a *blivet*, an undecipherable image and optical illusion shows how we frustratingly seek to make simple sense of an impossible object.
- *Figure and ground*: Perception also involves distinguishing an object from its surroundings. Once an object is perceived, the area around the object becomes the background. Some illusions test our interpretation of figure and background such as Figure 2.4 in which the background varies from the red side to the yellow side depending on one's interpretation.

2.2.1.2 *Perceptual Constancy*

Perceptual constancy denotes our tendency to see familiar objects as having standard shape, size, color, or location regardless of changes in the angle of perspective, distance, or lighting. The impression tends to conform to the object as it is or is assumed to be, rather than to the actual stimulus. Figure 2.5 illustrates our perception of brightness constancy, which is our ability to see objects as continuing to have the same brightness even though light may change their immediate sensory properties. We see a checkerboard pattern that seems to have light and dark squares. Our perception of brightness constancy indicates that square A is darker than square B, even though square B is in shadow. In fact, they are both of identical brightness. As with many so-called illusions, this effect really demonstrates the success rather than the failure of the visual system. The visual system is not very good at being a physical light meter, but that is not its purpose. The important task is to break the image information down into meaningful components, and thereby perceive the nature of the objects in view. In terms of the preparation phase of the cognitive process, this means that our brain is interpreting the image as it should; however, it also means that given this new knowledge, our percept can now change to allow for the second interpretation presented by this illusion.

FIGURE 2.4

FIGURE 2.4

FIGURE AND GROUND ILLUSION

Courtesy: www.eyetricks.com, redrawn by author

FIGURE 2.5

ILLUSION TO FOOL BRIGHTNESS CONSTANCY

Courtesy: http://en.wikipedia.org/wiki/Image:Optical.greysquares.arp.jpg

2.2.1.3 *Depth Perception*

This is the ability to see the world in three dimensions. To perceive depth, we depend on two sources of information: *binocular disparity*, a depth cue that requires both eyes; and *monocular cues*, which allow us to perceive depth with just one eye (Foley, 2005). Believe it or not, binocular disparity is effective over a range of less than 3 m (10 ft), and beyond that, we rely on monocular cues to tell us about depth. These monocular cues include:

- *Interposition*: This refers to overlap, or the obvious positioning of nearer objects in front of farther ones.

- *Atmospheric perspective*: Due to microscopic particles of dust, distant objects appear hazy or blurry.
- *Texture gradient*: When we view a surface from a slant, nearer objects seem to have more texture.
- *Linear perspective*: This refers to the facts that parallel lines converge with distance.
- *Relative height*: This cue leads us to believe that below the horizon, objects higher in the visual field appear farther away, while above the horizon, objects higher in the visual field appear nearer.
- *Motion parallax*: This refers to the apparent different rate of movement of objects close to you when compared to objects farther away from you when you are also in motion.

Figure 2.6 is a wonderful example to further explore the preparation phase of creativity. It demonstrates how an artist can rearrange depth perception cues to confuse us into imagining that an object is something it is not, and in more subtle terms, how by moving our viewpoint, we can see an object in an entirely different way. Known as an *anamorphism*, it is an image whose perspective or projection has been distorted in such a way that it becomes visible only when viewed in a special manner. It is sometimes also referred to as a *trompe l'oeil*, a similar illusion that integrates architectural elements.

2.2.1.4   Motion Perception

Our brains perceive motion in several ways. When we move our heads or bodies, we discount the apparent movement of stationary objects as being due to our own movements and not theirs. When objects move, we can either track them by moving our heads or eyes, or we can infer that their motion takes place because they are moving against a stationary background. In both cases, we do this unconsciously. It is also possible to set up a phenomenon called the peripheral drift illusion that creates the illusion of movement in our peripheral vision, as in Figure 2.7, which appears to move in a circular motion when viewed peripherally. It is yet another demonstration of how our brains seek to interpret and to make sense out of the unknown, which is really just the first step in the creative process.

2.2.1.5   The Relationship of Experience and Context to Perception

Recent research has demonstrated that exceptional talents are less born than made (Simonton, 2000; Ericsson, 1996), whether it is in sports, music, or any other endeavor. In fact, it can take upward of at least a decade to achieve world-class performance through extensive practice. It is increasingly evident that the same holds true for creativity. This means that the more we challenge our creativity, the better it is likely to become. Furthermore, every experience is useful because it in turn creates memories of past stimuli that can serve to help us perceive new stimuli. This experience

FIGURE 2.6

EXAMPLE OF TROMPE L'OEIL IN LYONS, FRANCE

Courtesy: http://en.wikipedia.org/wiki/Image:Lyon_Trompe_l%27oeil_velo%27v.jpg

can be considered as a form of context that we can put in our heads as a tool. For some simple examples, look to Figures 2.1–2.7 which can now help us understand similar puzzles we might encounter in the future.

2.2.2 Incubation Phase

The incubation phase is the one in which information and facts are digested and ideas germinated. It is also the phase at the beginning of which

FIGURE 2.7

PERIPHERAL DRIFT ILLUSION

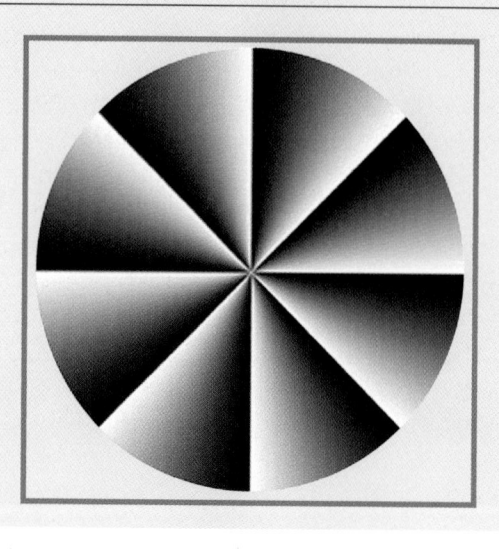

Courtesy: http://en.wikipedia.org/wiki/Image:PDIFaubertHerbert.png

creative perception or *creative cognition* may be introduced and considered. One of the most exciting developments in recent years is the extensive research by Smith et al. (1995) that has proven that creative cognition is a mental phenomenon that results from the application of ordinary cognitive processes. In more simple language, creativity is not a 'mysterious, unobservable process,' or an innate, unlearnable ability, but a set of skills that can be taught and learned by anybody. For the special event producer, this means that new and exciting ideas can be generated through the use of learned skills. According to De Bono (2006), one of the functions of creative perception (cognition) is 'to take an apparently known and fixed situation and then seek to see it differently,' and that is exactly what we want to happen as event producers in this phase. We take the challenge presented to us, say perhaps to generate a novel form of entertainment for a theme event, examine the 'raw materials' we have available (e.g. a number of different performers or acts), and integrate them into a new form using one of the techniques for generating creative ideas, all along influenced by our perception of the challenge as explained in Section 2.2.1. We will be reviewing some of the more popular techniques for generating creative ideas, including some of those proposed by Ward (2004) in Section 2.4.

The incubation phase is one in which most of what goes on occurs in the subconscious mind, where ideas are free to combine and recombine. One is more open to insights in this phase when the external environment is optimum, and we will be discussing how to set up such an inviting environment in Section 2.3.

2.2.3 Illumination Phase

Illumination is a short-lived phase but the one that gets all the glory. It is that moment of insight or discovery, the 'eureka' experience, when the subconscious mind finally spits out a solution to the problem. As in the incubation phase, this occurs most often at times when the mind is in a relaxed state, when one's skills are perfectly matched to the challenge at hand. Everything feels harmonious, unified, and effortless (Goleman and Kaufman, 1992). Psychologists call this state *flow* and more time is spent on it in Chapter 1 of *Special Event Production: The Resources.*

For special events, this is the moment when the award-winning concept appears. It is not necessarily limited to a general idea. It could be as mundanely specific as a new location for a stage, a new combination of performers, a different way to have a multimedia show, or even a creative dinner menu. The main point is that it can happen when external and internal mechanisms gel and it can happen to ordinary people, not just the so-called creative ones.

2.2.4 Translation Phase

Also called elaboration and verification, this phase takes the creative insight of the illumination phase and turns it into reality. It is the idea transformed into action.

For event producers, this phase requires a thorough knowledge of the resources that are available to actually accomplish this transformation. Simple though this may seem, it is not. In fact, it can take years to accumulate such a knowledge base, and it is a continuous learning process. *Special Event Production: The Resources* is devoted to explaining what resources are available to do exactly this.

2.3 THE EXTERNAL ENVIRONMENT

The need for setting the right external environment conducive to facilitating the cognitive process is essential to successful idea generation. We have referred to this need several times, as have many researchers and creativity practitioners. No matter what method is used to generate ideas – and these will be discussed shortly – to be most effective, they should be used in conjunction with some or all of the following proven suggestions for setting up the external environment, most of which can be applied during the incubation phase of the cognitive process.

2.3.1 Quantity Equals Quality

Although there are those who subscribe – with some proof – to the belief that one's first idea is usually the best, in the case of creativity, the first idea usually becomes a lead-in to even more and better ideas as the first idea becomes the building block for the ideas to follow. The point here is that one should not stop at only a few ideas, but rather continue to exhaust all possible avenues of ideas within a given theme, no matter what method is used. Research suggests that creative people make more mistakes than their less imaginative peers. They are not less proficient. It's just that they make more attempts than most others. They spin out more ideas, come up with more possibilities, and generate more schemes. They win some; they lose some (Goleman and Kaufman, 1992).

2.3.2   Suspending Judgment

Nothing kills creativity more than a phrase like, 'If it ain't broke, don't fix it,' or something similar. All those participating in the creative process should understand from the outset that pre-judging an idea can not only cause that idea to be lost forever, but it can also cause its creator to become discouraged with the process and with the detractor. Judgment should not be brought into the creative process.

2.3.3   Relax and Have Fun

After 'playing' and practicing with creativity for some time, one usually finds that the creative process is best served away from the daily work environment, often when the brain is relaxed. Some of the more successful environments and lifestyle inducements to achieve this state are:

- *During sleep*: A pencil and paper or notebook available at all times, including bedside, ensures that ideas will not be lost. Indeed, some of the best ideas come during the relaxed state of 'near-sleep' and this is precisely when ideas need to be jotted down. If the ideas do start to form freely, one should avoid the temptation to force sleep to return and continue with the process until all possibilities have been exhausted in that particular line of thought. This notebook can also be used as a 'dream diary' to record dreams on waking, which in turn can act as catalysts to ideas.
- *During a favorite relaxing activity*: Massage, sauna, shower or bath, meditation, listening to music, and reading are all relaxing activities that tend to free the brain from unwanted clutter and stress. In turn, one is more able to daydream and take ideas to their logical conclusion. Jocelyn Flanagan president of event management company e = mc^2 in Calgary, Canada, uses music to regenerate senses and emotions in her staff so that visuals associated with the emotions and memories begin to appear (Jocelyn Flanagan, Personal Communication, February 22, 2006).
- *During a favorite aerobic activity*: As long as it is not overly strenuous, this is one of the best ways to get ideas flowing. Not only does aerobic activity increase blood flow to the brain, but it also releases endorphins to aid in relaxation, thereby triggering the condition sometimes called

'runner's high.' This can be a powerful opportunity to generate new ideas and work them through to conclusion. Examples are jogging, walking, swimming, and cycling. Activity should be for a minimum of about 30 min or more in order to have enough time to get into a relaxed state and take advantage of it to generate ideas.

- *Maintaining a healthy lifestyle*: In addition to exercise, creativity specialist Linda Naiman recommends eating well, especially vitamin B, and also getting lots of rest, both of which encourage brain activity (Hall, 2004).
- *Having fun*: The 'work' of creativity goes more smoothly in an atmosphere of lightheartedness. Amabile (1996) found that people in companies were more likely to have a breakthrough if they were happy the day before. Researchers also report that when teams of people are working together on a problem, those groups that laugh most readily and most often are more creative and productive than their more dour and decorous counterparts. Joking around makes good sense; playfulness is itself a creative state (Goleman and Kaufman, 1992).

2.3.4 Continue to Learn

Experienced producers understand the importance of keeping up to date on the latest inventions in special events. Like any profession, it has many complex resources (see *Special Event Production: The Resources*) that change very rapidly and good producers stay in touch with the changes. More than the industry resources, however, are unrelated resources that can trigger ideas. Here are some ways to learn:

- *Read*: Browse books, magazines, and newspapers, even ones in unrelated fields, such as old maps or trashy novels, and search for interesting fonts, styles, clothing, or activities. This is another tool found useful for Jocelyn Flanagan for generating ideas.
- *Stay curious*: Every time you visit a store, restaurant, movie, play, go on a holiday, play sports, or engage in almost any activity, look around and take in the environment and the way people interact. Perhaps there is something unusual that can be applied to a special event.
- *Take courses*: One way to keep our minds active is to attend continuing education courses or conference education sessions. There are many in the events industry. Likewise, even courses in other disciplines, especially creative endeavors such as writing, photography, painting, or sculpture will keep the creative juices active. These also provide opportunities to interact with other creative people and to trade ideas with them.
- *Keep records*: This is simply recording all the knowledge and contact information about any of the resources one encounters. Detailed records are immeasurably useful when one is trying to recall what certain technology can do, what performers will fit into a stage show, what specific décor will work in a large room, etc. The best way to keep detailed records is to use good database software such as Microsoft Access, Act,

or Maximizer. All names, phone numbers, e-mail addresses, mail addresses, and capabilities should be kept on file in an easily retrievable format.

2.3.5 Practice

Nothing improves creativity more than practicing it on a regular basis, as we have already mentioned. Producers need to challenge themselves at every opportunity and keep the ideas flowing for *every* event, no matter how small. Like any other skill, creativity needs to be honed or it will be forgotten.

PRODUCTION WAR STORY: LAST-MINUTE CREATIVITY

The high-end event was 2 h from doors opening for dinner. After dinner, a spectacular show combining fire choreography, magic illusions, acrobats, and rhythmic gymnasts would begin with a surprise display of indoor pyrotechnics. The onsite rehearsal was being reviewed by the client who, although she had been told in advance what the show would entail, stated that it could not begin with surprise pyro because all the guests were from New York. Since it was only 3 months after 9/11, she was afraid that they would be terrified and try to duck under tables to escape. Eliminating the pyro entirely would damage the show's flow, not to mention adding extra cost for a service that could not be given. It was time for the creative mind to kick into overdrive.

Now finally amongst the themed décor and in a position to observe the entertainment for the event in context, the producer was able to combine all the sensory input and decided to script a special voiceover to introduce the entertainment that would in essence describe and put into perspective all that the décor and entertainment meant while still allowing for the surprise pyro at the beginning. The event was highly successful and the script actually improved the show because it added more meaning to it. This demonstrated that creativity could indeed flourish when the environment is right.

Courtesy: Doug Matthews

2.4 CREATIVITY TECHNIQUES AND METHODS

Smith et al. (1995) were really the first researchers to prove that simple techniques could be used to generate creative ideas. Since then, seemingly countless experts have purported to own a method that will work the best (at last count 177 on one web site, www.mycoted.com). Some of these methods are complicated and take considerable organizing, making them ill suited for the special event creative situation in which ideas must be generated in a very short timeframe and with minimal organization. Interestingly,

Ward (2004) has put his and his colleagues' theories into practice and refined their original techniques to ones that are very useful. A few others are also well suited to the somewhat restrictive creative environment of event production. These will be reviewed and explained individually. To put our discussion into perspective, these techniques would be injected during the incubation phase of the cognitive process.

2.4.1 Conceptual Combinations

Combination is a very simple method used to modify, extend, or transform stored knowledge. Also known as *Janusian thinking*, it integrates two opposing or disparate concepts. It underlies some of the greatest creative acts in history, including the paintings of da Vinci, the symphonies of Mozart, and the scientific reasoning of Einstein. Taking some simple examples of new word pairings from today's world, it has been used to devise 'mouse pads,' 'sport drinks,' and 'nonalcoholic beer.' The special event world has already come up with some interesting examples of its own. Consider the use of 'flying tables' introduced by Bernie Gaps of Spandex USA (the surprise lowering of dining tables from the ceiling of an event venue – see Figures 2.8 and 2.9), the use of 'tension fabrics' in decorative props

FIGURE 2.8

FLYING TABLES: START POSITION

Courtesy: Spandex USA, www.spandexusa.com

FIGURE 2.9
FLYING TABLES: END POSITION

Courtesy: Spandex USA, www.spandexusa.com

(Transformit, Inc. and Pink, Inc. – see Chapter 2 of *Special Event Production: The Resources*), the invention of 'airtubes' by Doron Gazit of Air Dimensional Design, and the 'living garden' designed by Priscilla Blight of 2nd Nature Productions (see Chapter 2 of *Special Event Production: The Resources* for more details and photos). The possibilities go beyond mere word combinations, and extend to unusual resource combinations. Perhaps a great event could result from combining entertainment as lighting, cooking as entertainment, stage construction as entertainment, sound as lighting, lighting as sound, chairs as tables, guests as workers, and so on. It does not take a giant leap to use these combinations as the first step to something more. Probably one of the greatest examples of combinations in modern entertainment is the world-famous Cirque du Soleil, who combine skilled athletes with story lines, original music, and unusual costuming.

2.4.2 Analogies

An analogy is a comparison of one thing or situation to another thing or situation. Examples of analogies in creative endeavors abound. The analogy of Shakespeare's *Romeo and Juliet* to *West Side Story*, Conrad's *Heart of Darkness* to *Apocalypse Now*, or the solar system to the atom, all demonstrate the concept. In special events, the concept has also been demonstrated. For example, several motivational speakers have capitalized on analogies, such as fighter pilots comparing marketing and sales to a fighter mission or Mt. Everest conquerors and Olympic champions to realizing one's dreams. Another interesting analogy that one of my students revealed during a conference education session was how at a particular resort the hotel housemen had become so efficient at room changeovers, much like a military operation, that the actual room changeover became part of the event's entertainment! This is also an example of an unusual combination. Certainly, other possibilities cannot be far behind for novel events. Analogies can be:

- Close or direct. This means a straight functional parallel (e.g. those dancers dance like Fred Astaire and Ginger Rogers).
- Fantasy. This means coming up with a wild image (e.g. those dancers are like angels flying between clouds).
- Remote or surprising. This comes out of left field (e.g. those dancers are like 'running home on the last day of school' or like 'going to a drive-in movie').
- Personal or component. You become a component in the system (e.g. if you are considering a unique way to get the dancers onstage, think of yourself as the shoe of one of the dancers).

2.4.3 Reversals

The world is full of opposites. Any leader knows that in order to lead well, the leader must learn to follow. Many successful, rich people got there because they once lived poorly. Night turns into day. Winter turns to summer. Problem solving using reversals is a simple and very effective method to get directly to a unique solution if one learns to see things backwards, inside out, or upside down. Here are some ways to do it:

- State the problem in reverse. Instead of pondering the question, 'How do we get more attendees through our gate and avoid lineups,' consider the question, 'How do we get more gates to the attendees?' With minimal thought this could lead to a solution of putting multiple gates farther away from the event site, or perhaps even selling combined entrance/ transit tickets if attendees take buses or the subway to the event.
- Do what everyone else is not doing. For example, if everyone else is producing politically correct events, consider producing a tongue-in-cheek, politically incorrect event.
- Make the statement negative. If, for example, you need to set up all the lights for an event in 2 h, consider what would happen if you did not set

up any lights in 2 h. Where might this lead? Perhaps it would lead to a novel solution of having attendees providing all the lighting using some sort of lanterns they were given as they entered the event.

- The 'What-If' scenario. This takes any number of situations starting with a 'what if' question and applies them to the problem. For example, 'What if we … magnified it, shrunk it, froze it, heated it, rearranged it, eliminated part of it, put it to another use, changed its shape, etc.?' A personalized list can easily be made up for using this method. As an example, how do we solve the rather mundane production problem of ground level dry ice fog being used as a surprise entrance effect, drifting away when the doors open? Let's apply the 'what if' scenario and look at magnifying it (could maybe lead to more fog in the entrance foyer as well), or rearranging it (could maybe lead to putting it in select corners of the event venue at certain times only), or putting it to another use (could maybe lead to using dry ice fog as part of the actual meal service by the wait staff). Obviously, there are many ways to create new approaches to solve the problem.

2.4.4 Classical Brainstorming

This is one of the most common and widely taught methods of generating ideas and is best suited to a group of people, rather than done alone. Basically, the six main steps in a brainstorming session are:

- Define the problem, situation, or goal.
- Give a time limit, with more time available the larger the group participating.
- Shout out solutions and encourage participants to try for unusual ideas.
- Select the five best ideas or answers.
- Use four or five judging criteria such as 'it should be legal,' 'it should be effective,' 'it should be within a certain budget.'
- Score the solutions and keep the best ones.

Encouraging unusual ideas can in itself be a dilemma because the reason the group is brainstorming is to be creative. As a lead-in, participants can approach their suggestions using one of the previous methods such as reversals, what-if scenarios, or combinations.

2.4.5 Lateral Thinking

Popularized by De Bono (1970), this concept is one of the most useful methods to force the mind to think 'out of the box.' In its most basic form, it takes an unrelated thought or item and force fits it back to the related topic in a new and different way. The method lends itself well to either solo or group participation. Similar to brainstorming, the main steps in a lateral thinking session are:

- Define the problem, situation, or goal.
- Generate random input. This is the key difference with this method compared to classical brainstorming, the injection of a random input. This can be through exposure to new ideas from a different field (e.g. science into special events) or from observation of different things or places (e.g. toy stores, restaurants, magazines). It can also be through the formal generation of random input (e.g. the use of a random word found in a dictionary). From these random inputs, new ideas are generated and forced to fit into a solution to the problem at hand.
- Set a time limit.
- Accept solutions and apply judging criteria only after the solutions are in.

Since this method is so different, let's examine what we are really doing. As opposed to brainstorming, we are using an outside influence (random input) to force one to think creatively by: creating new patterns, challenging old patterns and assumptions, provoking and permitting new arrangements of information, and liberating imprisoned information. In other words, we are forcing the brain to perceive more creatively.

By way of example in a special event context, if one is trying to develop some creative ideas for an event that will exemplify a conference theme of 'Striving to Greater Heights in the New Millennium' at a theme dinner, including décor and entertainment, a random word such as 'refrigerator' might be chosen used to force fit an association with the theme in a logical progression. The process might go like this:

- 'Refrigerator' leads to
- 'Cold' leads to
- 'Cold air up high in the atmosphere' leads to
- 'What is up high?' leads to
- 'Planes/balloons/satellites/spaceships' leads to
- 'Looking down on the earth' leads to
- 'Looking down on the past years' leads to
- 'Series of photos' leads to
- 'Close-up aerials changing to satellite photos of earth' leads to
- 'Equating to past performance' leads to
- 'Maybe old time flying machines progressing to modern flying and the space shuttle' leads to
- 'Could reflect in variety of table centers and décor' leads to
- 'Could also reflect in entertainment story and dance' leads to
- 'Could reflect in A-V,' and so on.

The best way to achieve results with this process is to maintain a list of random words, or even a bag of unrelated objects, that can be used as 'idea generators' and starting points for the process of 'force fitting' to get to the idea that will be associated with the event itself, or some component of the event.

The creative process as explained and applied in this chapter is best done in conjunction with an extensive knowledge of resources as has been mentioned, areas of specialization that include entertainment, décor, lighting, audio, staging, tenting, visual presentation technology and special effects, so that once the ideas come, they can be mixed with the various resources at one's disposal and new ideas will flow. *Special Event Production: The Resources* devotes considerable time to explaining how these resources may be used.

PRODUCTION CHALLENGES

1. Your staff would like to know what it takes to become creative. Explain to them what the different influences are in a creative person's life and what type of personality that person is likely to have.
2. Describe to your staff the four phases of the cognitive process and how perception works in them.
3. How can you improve and maintain your knowledge of resources that you use for events?
4. You and several of your suppliers are about to go into a brainstorming session to come up with an event concept that will reflect a theme of 'The Slow Revolution: The Road to Business Success in the 21st Century.' Suggest ways to improve the creative environment for this session.
5. Using the same event theme, describe in detail four different techniques that will help your team to launch creative ideas.

REFERENCES

Amabile, T.M. (1996). *Creativity in Context*. Boulder, CO: Westview.

Csikszentmihalyi, M. (1990). The Domain of Creativity. In M.A. Runco and R.S. Albert (Eds.), *Theories of Creativity*. Newbury Park, CA: Sage, pp. 190–212.

De Bono, E. (1970). *Lateral Thinking – Creativity Step by Step*. New York: Harper & Row.

De Bono, E. (March 11, 2006). Perceptual creativity: seek a new perception, discover new ideas. *Thinking Manager*. Retrieved March 11, 2006, from http://www.thinkingmanagers.com/management/perceptual-creativity.php.

Dellas, M. and Gaier, E.L. (1970). Identification of creativity: The individual. *Psychological Bulletin, 73*, 55–73.

Ericsson, K.A. (Ed.). (1996). *The Road to Expert Performance: Empirical Evidence from the Arts and Sciences, Sports, and Games*. Mahweh, NJ: Erlbaum.

Foley, H.J. (2005). Perception (psychology). *Microsoft® Encarta Online Encyclopedia 2005*. Retrieved March 9, 2005 from http://encarta.msn.com.

Gardner, H. (1993). *Creating Minds: An Anatomy of Creativity Seen through the Lives of Freud, Einstein, Picasso, Stravinsky, Eliot, Graham, and Gandhi*. New York: Basic Books.

Goleman, D. and Kaufman, P. (March, 1992). The art of creativity. *Psychology Today*. ID 1903.

Ludwig, A.M. (1989). Reflections on creativity and madness. *American Journal of Psychotherapy, 43*, 4–14.

Hall, N. (August 24, 2004). The Art of Creativity. *The Vancouver Sun*, B2.

MacKinnon D.W. (1962). The nature and nurture of creative talent. *American Psychologist*, *17*, 484–495.

Martindale, C. (1989). Personality, Situation, and Creativity. In J.A. Glover, R.R. Ronning and C.R. Reynolds (Eds.), *Handbook of Creativity*. New York: Plenum Press, pp. 211–232.

Rogers, C. (1954). Toward a theory of creativity. *ETC: A Review of General Semantics*, *11(4)*, 250–258.

Rothenberg, A. and Wyshak, G. (March, 2004). Family background and genius. *The Canadian Journal of Psychiatry*, *49*, 185–191.

Simonton, K. (1987). Developmental antecedents of achieved eminence. *Annals of Child Development*, *5*, 131–169.

Simonton, K. (1999). Creativity and genius. In L. Pervin and O. John (Eds.), *Handbook of Personality Theory and Research*, Second edition. New York: Guilford Press, pp. 629–652.

Simonton, K. (January, 2000). Creativity: cognitive, personal, developmental, and social aspects. *American Psychologist*, *55(1)*, 151–158.

Smith, S.M., Ward, T.B. and Finke, R.A. (Eds.). (1995). *The Creative Cognition Approach*. Cambridge, MA: MIT Press.

Ward, T.B. (2004). Cognition, creativity, and entrepreneurship. *Journal of Business Venturing*, *19*, 173–188.

Wertheimer, M. (1923). Untersuchungen zur Lehre von der Gestalt II. *Psycologische Forschung*, *4*, 301–350.

BUDGETING

Most special events are all about money.

Before any event is executed, during the Concept and Proposal Phase, event managers must come to terms with the cost of staging the event. Whether it is an outdoor festival for 500,000 people or a simple wedding for 50, there will be a requirement to tally up the anticipated funds available for the event and compare them to the anticipated expenses of putting on the event. The mechanism that keeps these anticipated funds and expenses in check is called a budget and it is budgeting that forms the core of this chapter. In accounting terms, a budget is simply a Profit and Loss Statement that is an estimate of projected revenue, expenses, and net income (profit or loss) for an endeavor, in this case an event rather than a company. In Canada and some other countries, the Profit and Loss Statement is known as an Income Statement, but the term 'budget' still applies.

As part of the budgeting process, an event manager will rely on the event producer to control the production portion of the event budget. It is the producer's role in the budgeting process that we will be discussing in this chapter. In doing the job properly, however, the producer has several concerns, and we will look at them in detail, specifically:

- Preparing the production budget
- Managing cash flow
- Making a profit
- Creating a budget layout
- Considering other potential costs and budget impact items, including how to deal with the employee/contractor decision, insurance, Workers' Compensation, and taxes.

One point that must be made very clear is that our discussion in this chapter centers on the budget for an individual event and not for an individual company. In other words, we are not particularly concerned with expenses that might be incurred by an event producer's company unless revenues or expenses that pertain to the company influence, or are related to, the financial viability of the event itself. The other distinction to be made is that this chapter discusses budgets only from an event producer's point of view in that we do not cover sources of revenue (e.g. sponsorships, ticket sales and such), and we do not include event expenses other than production expenses. Budgeting from an event manager's perspective is covered very thoroughly in other sources (Goldblatt, 2002; Allen et al., 2005; Fenich, 2005; Van Der Wagen and Carlos, 2005).

3.1 PREPARING THE PRODUCTION BUDGET

Why budget? The answer is simple: control. A budget is a living document that compares anticipated revenue with actual revenue, and anticipated expenses with actual expenses. It assists an event manager in keeping control of the event, enabling the shifting of funds when necessary while still maintaining the integrity of the event.

Since in the vast majority of cases the producer works for the event manager, the producer is usually given a portion of the overall event budget with which to work. This portion is strictly on the expense side of the budget and has nothing to do with revenue. In other words, the producer is tasked with spending the portion of the budget assigned to production in the most efficient manner possible in order to achieve the goals of the event.

The event producer normally works on the budget in one of two ways. The first begins during the Concept and Proposal Phase of the event when an event manager comes to the producer and the producer's company asking for a proposal to produce the event, with the producer acting as a contractor. It is at this time that an initial production concept is created and that suppliers of the different resources are contacted for quotes for their services. These quotes are then used to establish a preliminary production budget. This preliminary budget may either be unrestricted to begin, or restricted by a maximum allowable amount given initially by the event manager.

The second way that a producer may become involved is as a member of the event manager's staff. In this case, the producer's work on the budget probably also begins during the Concept and Proposal Phase but is strictly a fact-gathering mission intended to establish a starting point for the allocation of funds within the entire event budget. In other words, there may not, at this point, be any budget amount allotted to event production. In both cases, however, the process of creating the budget remains the same and we will review that process.

There are five key items to establishing and maintaining an accurate production budget: developing a system to track expenses, developing a meaningful list of production expense categories, researching and categorizing expenses, tracking and updating expenses, and handling contingencies and unexpected expenses.

3.1.1 Developing a System to Track Expenses

Because a budget is a living document, it is constantly changing and is in a state of flux from event conception right through event execution. An effective method is needed to keep track of all these changes as they occur and the best method, the one used by most event producers, is a spreadsheet. A spreadsheet has several advantages:

- It enables easy calculation of total costs based on unit costs since this calculation can be done automatically.
- It enables the easy integration of tax calculations.
- It allows for automatic calculations of profit margins.
- It permits easy comparisons of estimated and actual expense line items.
- It minimizes the possibility for errors in calculations.
- It can be separated into individual responsibility areas.
- It can be easily e-mailed to event or production team members and clients, which in turn allows for separate updating for their individual responsibility areas, thus saving time.

Of course, individual event producers have their own preferred layouts. We will be offering some examples with explanations later in this section.

There are software packages within the events industry that integrate budgeting with event scheduling and contracting so that duplication of information in different programs (e.g. MS Access, MS Excel, accounting software) is no longer necessary.

3.1.2   Developing a List of Expense Categories

The production budget demands a continuing effort throughout the event organizing process in order to keep it current. Therefore, it needs to be developed in a way that will facilitate easy access to any line item. Breaking down the expenses into main categories and sub-categories best achieves this. Although every event will have different such categories, here is a sample list of some of the most common production expenses:

- Entertainment and speakers
- Décor
- Special effects
- Staging
- Audio
- Lighting
- Visual presentation
- Sanitation and waste management
- Tenting and temporary structures
- Electrical power
- Rigging
- Fencing and security
- Communication equipment
- Stage management.

Depending on the event, some of these may not be applicable. Also, most of these would be undoubtedly broken down into further sub-categories and line items.

3.1.3   Researching and Categorizing Actual Expenses

This is the most important step in the entire budgeting process. It is the step that most event producers spend their time on. The initial working event budget is created at the very beginning of the planning process, during the Concept and Proposal Phase. To obtain an accurate budget at this early point in the process requires that expenses be estimated as closely as possible to what they will actually be. This in turn requires that as many suppliers as possible be contacted to request current quotes for their responsibility areas, given the general event concept that has been developed by the event manager. Failing this, if either there is insufficient time to contact suppliers (e.g. a tight deadline for an event proposal requested by a corporate client) or if the event concept has not been fully enough developed, then it may be possible to start with a budget based on past experience. For example, if a budget is being drawn up for the second year of an annual event and there are no changes to the requirements, the cost figures for the last event may be used for an estimate with a minor increase equal to the cost of living. Perhaps, for example, there is a need for the same audio system as last year. Last year's costs could be used for initial budgeting purposes with a small increase included; however, it would have to be noted that the final figures would be subjected to confirmation by the actual supplier.

Once quotes have been obtained from each supplier, they should be immediately entered into the budget spreadsheet under the appropriate category and sub-category. For example, if the main production expense is décor, it might be further broken down on a line item basis once the overall quote has been received from the designer. Here, in simplified form, is how it might appear:

Décor	
Table linens	$ 6000
Chair covers	$ 4000
Table centerpieces	$ 5000
Stage backdrop	$ 800
Entrance décor vignette	$ 1000
Room vignette	$ 7000
Lighting for vignettes	$ 3500
Labor	$ 4000
Subtotal décor	$31,300

Quotes from all other suppliers would be entered in the same manner, with more sub-categories created depending on the depth of the quote. It is worth mentioning that common courtesy dictates that the work associated with any quotes that have been solicited from suppliers be either confirmed or cancelled well prior to the event date. Unfortunately, many event producers have a habit of not doing this, thereby leaving valuable rental inventory from suppliers on hold for a date. To help discourage this practice, at least one supplier, Bernie Gaps of Spandex USA in California, has in place a written pricing policy that acts as a sliding scale with better preferred pricing the farther out from an event that an order is confirmed (Bernie Gaps, Personal Communication, February, 2006). It is expected that more suppliers will be following his lead.

3.1.4 Tracking and Updating Expenses

The budget would be a useless document if it were not continuously monitored and updated. Thus, once it is created, any and all changes must be recorded in it. The best way to do this is as soon as any changes occur, it should be entered into the appropriate column and row in the spreadsheet. Ideally, a comment may also be included in a separate column to note the date of change and the reason for it.

Another suggestion that works well based on experience is to use a format that allows for recording changes after contract signing. This is especially good for independent event producers who are contracted to manage the event and obtain their income from supplier markups, rather than as a salaried event producer, because it shows all changes over and above the contract. It is also a good idea to get these post-contract changes approved in writing from a client, and a budget prepared in this fashion allows for easy analysis by the client.

3.1.5 Handling Contingencies and Unexpected Expenses

No matter how well organized an event may be and how experienced an event producer may be, there are inevitably extra costs and unforeseen requirements. The bigger the event, the greater will be the possibility for these costs to creep in. Within the budget, it is therefore wise to incorporate a contingency of some sort.

Event producers may be approaching the event organization process from different viewpoints. One such viewpoint is that of an event producer employed by the event manager or event organization. Another viewpoint may be that of an independent event producer contracted by a corporation or event manager. In each of these cases, the income of the event producer will be treated and calculated in a different way. Because of this, for each of these cases, a budgeted contingency fee will also be calculated differently. Let us look at each case.

In the case of an event producer employed by a festival board of directors, for example, the producer's salary will be common knowledge and there is no need to add any contingency to the salary to cover cost overruns, as the sponsoring organization will do that. The contingency would thus simply be added to the budget as a separate line item. A suggested figure is around 10 percent of the total expense estimates for the event.

In the case of the independent event producer who is a contractor, that person's income is often derived simply as a markup of all supplier costs. If these costs overrun their original estimates, the event producer is in danger of losing money. In this case, a contingency can be built in as an additional hidden amount within a line item, which also includes the event producer's markup, thus eliminating the possibility of losing money. Other ways to add a contingency fee for an independent event producer include simply adding extra hours to the total of billed time if the event producer is using an hourly fee to derive income, or simply adding an extra line item as for the event producer who is an employee. The most common way nowadays, however, is to obtain a sign-off by the event manager or client for any changes to contracted or estimated production expense items, rather than using any contingency at all since this method allows for complete transparency.

3.2 MANAGING CASH FLOW

As business owners know, cash is king. A business, or an event, will not be able to operate if there is insufficient cash available to pay bills on time. Even worse than the inability to pay bills on time is the detrimental effect on the reputation of the event producer or the event sponsoring organization. If bills are not paid on time, not only is there the distinct possibility of legal action against the event producer, but there is also the possibility that any future request for the services of suppliers will go unanswered. A budget, along with the contractual obligations for supplier payments, can be used to assist in monitoring and predicting cash requirements of producers. In the case of cash flow, this section will deal with some areas that are not directly applicable to a specific event. Some of the main ways that cash can be managed by producers to achieve good cash flow include the following:

- Negotiating sufficient deposits. This applies almost exclusively to the independent event producer who is contracted to manage an event by a client. It is very applicable to event producers in the ordinary course of their work as well. Because of the costs that will be incurred by the event producer, including paying all salaries and meeting the contractual deposit obligations of suppliers, sufficient deposits should be demanded from clients and these amounts should be written into the client/producer contract. Current industry norms are in the order of 50–75 percent of the total value of the contract in advance upon contract signing, with the remainder payable either 1 week prior to the event, on the event day itself, or at minimum no more than 1 week after the event. This ensures that there will be enough cash to cover all contracted services.

- Monitoring accounts receivable. Many companies fail to closely track accounts receivable, or money owing as a result of a service or product delivered. Once these accounts are allowed to lapse more than 30 days, the likelihood of being paid decreases quickly. A polite but firm set of increasingly strong requests should be part of the event producer's policies with someone delegated to track the accounts. Invoicing for services or products delivered should be done immediately following that service or delivery and not more than 1–2 weeks should pass without a followup phone call or letter to the outstanding account.

- Negotiating flexible supplier terms. On the other side of the coin, most accountants will advise that accounts payable should be allowed to take the maximum time permissible. For example, if the event producer has contracted with a lighting company to install and operate a lighting system for the event, and the contract allows for up to 30 days after the event before full payment is required, then in order to keep as much cash available as possible, the full 30-day time period should be used up before payment. A word of caution is due here, however. In reality, this can sometimes spell trouble for the event producer if followed to the letter.

Experience has shown that suppliers who are paid promptly by event producers are much more likely to offer discounts, better service, and even longer payment terms when necessary to those event producers for future events, since they know the event producers to be reputable. Far better, in fact, is to have a check in hand at the event to give final payment to the supplier in order to maintain and enhance this reputation. This is particularly true for small suppliers such as individual entertainers who themselves are often operating on the edge of bankruptcy.

■ Considering a loan or line of credit. Most banks will set up loans or lines of credit for established companies that have proven track records of paying bills on time. For independent event producers with established companies, there is a good chance of obtaining them. Loans and lines of credit do cost money, though, and really should only be considered when all other forms of obtaining necessary cash are exhausted.

3.3   MAKING A PROFIT

Producers can earn income either as contractors or as employees. As an employee, a producer does not have to be concerned with profit. However, for an independent contractor, there are two possible methods that may be used to obtain a profit, the supplier markup method and the hourly fee method.

3.3.1   Markup of Supplier Costs

This method is representative of the majority of events for which producers are contracted. The producer is normally the only person in direct contact with an individual supplier and all communication and contracting goes through the producer. The event organization deals directly with the producer and has no dealings with the supplier. In other words, the producer is in an agency relationship with the supplier. There are separate contracts between the producer and each individual supplier and usually a single contract between the producer and the event organization, the producer's client. Because the producer is taking all the risks associated with the contracted delivery of the supplier's services or products and because the producer must of necessity also arrange for payment to that supplier, the producer is entitled to a fee or markup for the service of being a 'one-stop shop.'

The industry norm for markups is in the range of 20–35 percent of the supplier cost. This markup may be calculated in two ways. The first is to multiply the supplier cost by a given markup percentage. For example, if a dance band costs $2000, the producer may choose to markup that amount by 25 percent, or multiply by 1.25 to arrive at a figure of $2500, which would then be the price the producer would quote to the client. The second way to calculate a markup is to divide by a fixed amount. Again, if the band costs $2000 and the producer wishes to make 25 percent (also called the *gross profit*) of the funds available for dance entertainment, then the $2000 must be divided by 0.75 to arrive at a cost of $2666. This number would typically be rounded to the next higher multiple of 5 or 10 for easier working, so that the price charged to the client would be $2670.

There is no right or wrong way to calculate profit in the markup situation. It is simply a matter of preference for the producer in terms of what is needed to survive (i.e. to pay the producer's company bills) and what works the easiest in budgeting. It is important to understand, however, that there is a difference in the end amount. A markup of 25 percent does not yield a gross profit of 25 percent. Again, to illustrate with a simple example, a markup of 100 percent on a $500 cost gives a price of $1000 which yields a gross profit of 50 percent ($500) based on the final price. It really depends on whether the calculation is referenced to the supplier cost or the final price. In the case illustrated in Table 3.1, the method used was division (i.e. gross profit method) and the supplier costs were divided by 0.75.

3.3.2 Hourly Fee

This method is sometimes used by event producers in the following situations:

- When the amount of work is fixed.
- When the work is of a specified duration and event producers can devote their full-time efforts to the task.
- When event producers are hired for their specific expertise and the market will bear their fee, in spite of competition.

To determine what an event producer's time is worth in the simplest manner, the producer should calculate what his or her entire company overhead is worth for the whole year, including personal salary, or salary goal, and divide it by 235 (the approximate average number of working days per year, allowing for 104 weekend days, 11 statutory holidays, and an average 15 working days vacation), then divide the result by 8 (number of working hours per day) to get the final answer. The formula looks like this:

$$\frac{\text{Total annual overhead (including event producer's salary) (\$)}}{235 \text{ (working days per year)} \times 8 \text{ (hours per working day)}} = \text{Hourly fee (\$)}$$

As an example, if an event producer operates as a sole proprietor with only himself/herself to pay, let us consider how this formula would work. If the event producer's total company overhead is $24,000 (e.g. $2000 per month), and the personal salary goal is $50,000 per year, then $74,000 is divided by 1880 to arrive at an hourly fee of $39.36. This, of course, only ensures a break-even situation if the producer works 100 percent of the time, so adding extra may be required, especially if a profit is desired over and above the producer's personal salary. However, if the contract will be for a specified time and the producer will be devoting 100 percent of his/her time to the project during that period, then the fee of $39.36 per hour is both justified and reasonable.

If there is more than one salaried event producer in the company (note that we only use the persons who generate income for the company), then the above formula must be multiplied by the proportional share of each individual producer's salary to arrive at that individual's hourly fee. The actual modified formula is as follows:

$$\frac{\text{Total annual overhead (including company owner's salary) (\$)}}{235 \text{ (working days per year)} \times 8 \text{ (hours per working day)}}$$

$$\times \frac{\text{Specific worker annual salary (\$)}}{\text{Total annual payroll of event producers (\$)}} = \text{Hourly Fee of Specific Worker (\$)}$$

For example, if the event producer's company employs three producers including himself/herself as the owner, and the producer wants to earn $50,000 while paying the other two employees $30,000 each, then the total annual payroll of event producers is $110,000. Let us also assume that the total overhead, including all three salaries, is $150,000. Thus, to calculate the hourly fees for all workers, the calculations look like this:

$$\frac{\$150,000}{1880} \times \frac{\$50,000}{\$110,000} = \$36.27 \text{ per hour for the event producer/owner,}$$

and

$$\frac{\$150,000}{1880} \times \frac{\$30,000}{\$110,000} = \$21.76 \text{ per hour for each of the other event producers.}$$

Once again, however, these numbers are only good if the employees are paid an hourly fee for 100 percent of their time. Herein lies the problem of using an hourly fee as the only method of making a profit. It is dependent on a number of factors:

- *Productivity*: Looking at the example of the event producer operating as a sole proprietor for simplicity, let us examine how productivity affects the hourly fee. Nobody working as a sole proprietor can devote 100 percent of his/her time to a project. There are always other tasks to be accomplished such as banking, marketing and obtaining new business, meetings, phone calls, and attending to a myriad of other details involved with running a company. Likewise, time-wasting activities such as coffee breaks, long lunches, and frivolous conversation constitute non-productive time. These activities can be estimated and a final rough figure calculated that represents the approximate amount of time that is actually productive. Therefore, in the sole proprietorship example, let us assume that the non-productive time is approximately 40 percent of the total time available in the working day. That means that 60 percent of the day is productive. Therefore, to arrive at a more realistic hourly fee we must divide the $36.27 fee by 0.60 which gives us a new fee of $60.45, a fee that now takes into account the non-productive time. Exactly the same calculations can be done for the other event producers as well. It can be seen that too much non-productive time leads to excessive fees that must be charged in order to create enough income to keep the company viable, a logical conclusion.

- *Experience*: Unlike productivity, time in the industry does not translate into a number that will automatically generate an hourly fee equivalent to a specific time or experience level. Generally speaking, the longer a producer has been in the industry, the easier it is to justify a higher hourly fee.
- *Competition*: Similar to experience, what the market will bear is a subjective evaluation. If there are numerous event production companies with lots of experience in a particular market area, then it is going to be difficult to justify a higher fee, no matter how much experience a producer may have. It is far better to control overhead expenses and limit non-productive time in order to achieve desired income levels. Of course, this only confirms the proposition of free enterprise: work hard and get ahead!

How does one estimate the time it takes to plan an event? There are a number of choices. A straight fee can be charged based on a best guess of the total time required, or a running log of time spent on the project can be kept, much like lawyers and other professionals do. It is really up to the individual event producer and the client to agree on the best arrangement.

It should be noted that for event producers who have a vested interest in keeping a confidential relationship with their suppliers (i.e. they rely on their well-deserved and hard-gained body of knowledge in the industry), the hourly or fixed fee method may not work unless there is absolutely no chance that the client will bypass the event producer in going to suppliers directly for future dealings. This is because with the hourly fee method, all supplier contracts are usually between the suppliers and the end client, thus giving the client direct access to supplier contact information.

3.3.3   Combination Markup and Fee

Often, a markup is combined with a fixed or hourly fee. This usually depends on what the work involves. Many event producers do this in circumstances where there is a specified amount of work but the event producer is also expected to take the risk of contracting all suppliers and handling all funds going to the suppliers. It is justified in that the event producer is covering the risks involved. An example might be a producer's hourly fee of $100 plus a markup on supplier services of 10 percent to handle all contracts and payments. The other benefit to this method and to the simple hourly fee method is that it does not result in severely decreased profit should some or all of the event components be cancelled, which could occur with the markup method.

3.4   BUDGET LAYOUTS

As already mentioned, every event producer has a preference for a budget layout, and there is no right or wrong one. However, in order to remain accurate and to give the maximum information possible, most budget spreadsheets include columns for the following, as a minimum:

- Specific categories and sub-categories of revenue and expense items.
- Budgeted costs.

Optional columns may include:

- *Actual costs*: If the budget must compare estimated costs with actual as in the case of a recurring event (e.g. annual festival, fundraising gala), then columns for both budgeted and actual are important. This allows tracking of items that are over or under budget, which can be useful for refining the budget for the following year.
- *Number of units*: This allows for automatic calculations if there will be large numbers of items with unit costs as expenses (e.g. tables and linens, florals, labor at an hourly rate). It can be placed adjacent to the Actual Cost column which may then become the Unit Cost column.
- *Marked-up price*: If the producer is a contracted individual who derives his/her income from markups of supplier costs, then a column that includes the marked up price is useful as a substitute for the Actual Costs column. If the markup is a standard amount, this column can be automatically calculated.
- *Taxes*: Depending on the event producer's jurisdiction, there may have to be state, provincial, and/or federal taxes added to some or all of the budgeted items. Extra columns allow these tax calculations to be made automatically.
- *Comments*: This is useful to make notes about changes as they occur as to reason, date, whether they have been approved, whether the changes are over or under budget, and such.

Let us now examine some sample budget layouts. The first, shown in Table 3.1, illustrates a budget layout for a simple private event with a fixed budget. This would be a typical situation for contracted producers, in that they would not be concerned with event revenue but would be given a fixed budget to work with.

This example is for an event that has an independent event producer contracted by the event organization or event manager to plan the production

TABLE 3.1

BUDGET LAYOUT FOR A SIMPLE PRIVATE EVENT

Item	Cost	Price with markup	Comments
Fixed Budget (i.e. revenue)	**$29,250**	**$39,000**	Fixed budget amount is $39,000, which must include event producer profit. It would be given to the producer by the client as the maximum amount to be spent.
Expenses			
Entertainment			
Dance Band	$ 3000	$ 4000	
6 roving look-alike characters	$ 1800	$ 2400	
Stage show			
– Dancers	$ 1200	$ 1600	
– Magician	$ 1000	$ 1335	
– MC	$ 500	$ 670	
Total entertainment	**$ 7500**	**$ 10,005**	Total of all entertainment
Décor			
35 table centers	$ 1750	$ 2335	
35 table linens	$ 700	$ 935	
350 napkins	$ 1750	$ 2335	
350 chair covers	$ 2800	$ 3735	
Stage backdrop	$ 300	$ 400	
Total décor	**$ 7300**	**$ 9740**	Total of all décor
Technical Production			
Lighting			
Room lighting and table pin spotting	$ 5000	$ 6670	
Stage lighting	$ 3000	$ 4000	
Audio	$ 4000	$ 5335	
Staging	$ 2000	$ 2670	
Stage management	$ 300	$ 400	
Total technical production	**$ 14,300**	**$ 19,075**	Total of all technical production
Total event expenses	**$ 29,100**	**$ 38,820**	Sum of Entertainment, Décor, and Technical Production
Gross profit		**$ 9720**	This is the total event producer profit and represents the difference between the total price with markup and the total cost. The client would be invoiced for $38,820 if a contract were established between the client and the producer.

component of the event given a fixed budget of $39,000, excluding taxes. For his own or his company's income from this work, he would be charging a markup on all supplier costs which would have to be taken out of the $39,000 budget. Some specific items are worth noting. First, the event producer's profit is the difference between the 'Price with Markup' column and the 'Cost' column. Note that a client would typically only see the marked up prices. Second, the price that would be charged to the client is $38,820, $180 under the budget of $39,000 (before taxes, if applicable).

Most producers would subcontract all the entertainment, décor, and technical production to specialist companies and each of these budget amounts would be a contracted item with these companies. Any changes would have to be approved by the producer and also the end client. It is not as likely with this type of small event that there would be major changes or cost overruns as there is less likelihood of other variables causing problems (e.g. weather, larger audience than anticipated, cancellation of headliner, etc.).

It sometimes also helps to add a new row under the final totals that indicates the contract date. This enables the producer to enter any changes to the contracted amounts separately under the original totals as they occur after the contract has been signed with the client, thus making tracking contract changes easier.

Let us now examine a more complicated example of a large public event in which a producer has been hired as a contracted member of the event staff, as illustrated in Table 3.2.

This example is for an event that has an event producer who is on a fixed fee contract to manage the production component of the event. Several important points with this budget are worth noting. First, the budget for this event is also fixed at the outset of planning; however, because of the larger scope of the event, there is much more likelihood that expenses will change due to unforeseen circumstances. This example illustrates how these changes might appear and includes an accompanying explanation in the Comments column, along with a note that indicates that they must all still be approved by the event manager. Second, in this case, there are no markups on supplier costs because the producer has no reason to make an individual profit. The event producer fixed fee contract value is listed as an overall event expense under the Personnel section of the Production Expenses. Third, different from the smaller private event example, is the fact that whatever amount the actual expenses are over or under the budgeted expense, is absorbed by the event organization and not by the producer or the producer's company. Fourth, the Comments column is useful for annotating reasons for changes and differences between budgeted and actual figures. Lastly, neither this example nor the private small event example has incorporated taxes, because every jurisdiction treats them differently. Some add taxes before marking up costs and some do not. See Section 3.5.3.

TABLE 3.2

BUDGET LAYOUT FOR A LARGE PUBLIC EVENT

Item	Budget	Actual	Comments
Production expenses	**$140,000**	**Unknown**	Budgeted amount at the beginning of the event for all production is $140,000. Actual is unknown until after event.
Entertainment			
Headline performers	$ 70000	$ 85000	Changed headliner at last minute
Accommodation for talent	$ 3000	$ 3500	One room upgraded.
Backline equipment rental for band	$ 800	$ 1100	Extra instruments required by replacement headliner
Transportation for talent	$ 2400	$ 3000	One day longer for rental vehicles
Total entertainment	**$ 76,200**	**$ 92,600**	All additional amounts approved by event manager
Technical Production			
Audio	$ 11,000	$ 12,000	Extra staff
Lighting	$ 16,000	$ 18,000	Added lights backstage for visibility
A-V	$ 5000	$ 7000	More complex show with new headliner
Staging and drape	$ 6000	$ 5500	Smaller stage approved by all acts
Total technical production	**$ 38,000**	**$ 42,500**	All additional amounts approved by event manager
Personnel			
Event producer	$ 20,000	$ 20,000	Fixed fee contract. Producer becomes a staff member for the duration of the event.
Technical director	$ 5000	$ 5000	Fixed fee contract
Stage managers	$ 800	$ 800	
Total personnel	**$ 25,800**	**$ 25,800**	No changes. On budget.
Total Expenses	**$140,000**	**$160,900**	Over budget by $20,900. This amount is absorbed by the event organization.

3.5   OTHER FINANCIAL CONSIDERATIONS

Event producers, like most small business owners, often forget or rather choose to ignore, the myriad federal, state/provincial, and municipal rules and regulations that govern the operation of a business. Ignoring these regulations is done at one's peril. The state/provincial and federal governments and various other responsible bodies keep a watchful eye on business owners to ensure that regulations are being followed. With most of these regulations, that watchful eye is concerned with the business owner correctly administering the regulations, which usually means taking and submitting the correct deductions from either individual or corporate income, or charging or paying the correct tax. The manner in which the regulations are followed and the deductions taken can have an effect on the budget of an event.

The most common areas for concern are: deciding whether a worker is an employee or a contractor and thus taking the correct salary source deductions, obtaining event-related insurance, the correct application of taxes, and finally, deciding which employees or contractors are required to have Workers' Compensation Board deductions made. Here is a very brief overview of each of these areas.

3.5.1   The Employee/Contractor Decision

In the events industry, the vast majority of companies are small, independent businesses who act as suppliers to event producers and organizations that manage events. These event producers and organizations are also in themselves small businesses. Invariably, because they are small, all these businesses need to work both with employees and with independent contractors to deliver the services or products they contract. In most jurisdictions, a distinction is made between employees and independent contractors for tax purposes, and failure to understand the differences can result in backdated penalties being assessed by federal, state, or provincial agencies that collect and administer taxes. These penalties can include backdated payroll source deductions that are due if a contractor has been determined to be an employee, such as employment/unemployment insurance, old age pension, other pension plans, Medicare, and federal, state, or provincial taxes.

Before hiring a contractor, an event producer should understand these differences. They distinguish between employees and contractors primarily by the amount of control that is exerted by the employee or payer. Generally, the payer exercises control if he has the right to hire or fire, determines the wage or salary to be paid, and decides on the time, place, and manner in which the work is to be done. Most jurisdictions have detailed guidelines for determining who is and is not a contractor and producers should be familiar with these.

3.5.2   Event Insurance

Since the 'Great White incident,' the club fire in New Jersey in February, 2003, where 96 people died as a result of not being able to escape a nightclub that was engulfed in flames, the event insurance industry has changed. That occurrence, plus September 11, 2001 and a number of other natural disasters, has combined to substantially increase event liability insurance rates to the point that, for many event production companies, the costs are extremely onerous. At this time, astute companies are adding a separate line item into their budgets for liability insurance that is not part of the marked up services they provide. We will discuss more about insurance in our review of Risk Management in Chapter 7.

3.5.3 Taxes

Depending on the jurisdiction in which event management and production companies operate, there will be differing methods of taxing the services provided. Many countries, including Canada, the European Union, and Australia, have federal service taxes (GST, VAT, etc.) that must be added to the cost of any event services provided, and subsequently charged to clients. Sometimes, but not always, these taxes or a part of them may be refundable within a certain time period after the event, but every jurisdiction is different and not all services are treated equally. In addition, some non-profit organizations in these countries are exempt from being charged service taxes if they are clients. Lastly, most service taxes are what is known as *flow-through taxes*, meaning that there is no impact on a company's profit when they are paid or charged. This works because the governments deduct any taxes paid to suppliers from taxes submitted (i.e. charged to clients), thereby resulting in a null effect on income. These federal service taxes are only applicable above a specific revenue level, below which a company usually is not required to register or charge for services. However, most companies in the event production business are above the level and should register. In the United States, there is currently no federal tax applied to event services.

In most countries, there are also state or provincial taxes that may be payable on event services. These are usually applied in one of two ways. The first is for the production company to pay suppliers the tax on goods and services supplied, mark up the gross amount, and charge this amount to the client with no specific tax charged. In other words, the state or provincial service tax ends at one level below the client. The second way to apply the tax is to buy the goods or services from suppliers with no tax paid to the suppliers. This wholesale price is then marked up and the tax is calculated on this final amount and charged to the client. In other words, the tax ends at the final client. Obviously, most of these state or provincial taxes do have an effect on company profit, depending on whether or not the tax is included in the amount marked up. Because every jurisdiction has its own set of regulations that apply to these service taxes, it is highly recommended that event producers obtain an interpretative ruling in writing from their applicable state or provincial governing body that dictates exactly how they should be operating and applying the service tax. See the Production War Story for an example of what can happen when this is not done.

3.5.4 Workers' Compensation

Workers' Compensation is a universal system regulated by individual states or provinces that allows for employees to receive wage replacement payments as well as payment of medical benefits if they sustain a work-related injury. In order to be considered a work-related injury, an injury must be caused by and arise out of the course of employment. In most jurisdictions, a company or individual who works in the events industry is legally required to register with Workers' Compensation if that company or individual is an employer who hires one or more workers and pays them on a full-time, part-time, casual, or contract basis. Depending on the type of work (e.g. office worker, laborer, rigger or technician, entertainer), the company is assessed a rate based on the annual total salary or contract payments of workers covered under Workers' Compensation and on previous claims. These assessments on employers are used to cover the costs of workplace injuries. Even individual subcontractors (e.g. entertainers, technicians) in special events must be covered, and if there is any doubt about whether they have been registered for Workers' Compensation, a certificate of coverage should be provided by them to their client, the event producer. This will ensure that the employer (the producer) will not be liable for back payments of Workers' Compensation assessments if that individual subcontractor is injured on an event. To ensure that some uncovered individual subcontractors are covered, separate allowances may be required as part of the budget.

PRODUCTION CHALLENGES

1. Explain the important points of maintaining a production budget and tracking expenses.
2. Describe the four methods that can be used to maintain good cash flow.
3. Your company marks up supplier costs to earn profit and you like to earn 20 percent of whatever budget a client gives you. If a client requests 100 table linens costing $12 per linen and 1000 chair covers costing $6 per cover, what will you charge your client for the entire package of table linen décor?
4. Your production company employs three event producers plus yourself, the owner. Your annual overhead is $300,000 including all staff salaries but not your salary. You would like to personally make $80,000. Each of the other event producers earns $40,000 annually. Assuming your productive time is 75 percent, what is the **minimum** hourly wage you will have to charge clients to make this much, assuming you will be working 100 percent of your time on contracts?
5. Briefly describe four external concerns that may affect the amount charged a client besides the actual production services you provide.

REFERENCES

Allen, J., O'Toole, W., Harris, R. and McDonnell, I. (2005). *Festival and Special Event Management*, Third Edition. Milton: John Wiley & Sons Australia, Ltd.

Fenich, G.G. (2005). *Meetings, Expositions, Events, and Conventions: An Introduction to the Industry*. Upper Saddle River, New Jersey: Pearson Education, Inc.

Goldblatt, J. (2002). *Special Events: Twenty-First Century Global Event Management*. New York: John Wiley & Sons, Inc.

Van Der Wagen, L. and Carlos, B.R. (2005). *Event Management for Tourism, Cultural, Business, and Sporting Events*. Upper Saddle River, NJ: Pearson Education, Inc.

PROPOSALS

Before a written proposal can be prepared, which occurs in the Concept and Proposal Phase of event organization, producers must have a thorough understanding of the special events industry. In particular, what makes clients respond to ideas in a favorable way and what will make them give business to one company over another? Once this is known, a proposal can be tailored to suit each individual event and client. It should be noted that this chapter deals with proposals for private events and that these are not necessarily suitable for public events or for proposals seeking event sponsorship, although some of the contents may be similar.

From an event producer's perspective, one has to understand that a good proposal is far more than just an impressive list of technical equipment. It also encompasses every aspect of one's professional life and experience, not to mention the creative component described in Chapter 2. In this chapter, we will discuss just what it is that actually wins business, go on to explain how to put a winning proposal together, and end with a short discussion of the various means to deliver the finished product. Most of this information has been taken from Matthews (2004; pp. 49–63).

4.1   WHAT WINS BUSINESS?

It is not only a well prepared written proposal that wins business. That is the first lesson a producer must learn. Although it helps and is the subject of this discussion, it is only part of the overall package that is an event producer's company. What always seem to come to the fore are three-key areas that influence whether or not one will win business: creativity, professionalism, and experience.

4.1.1   Creativity

Creativity is highly important, arguably the most important aspect of winning a bid, but creativity goes beyond the novel and unusual. Having been encouraged to think creatively in Chapter 2, a producer must now rein in the wild ideas and consider external influences and restrictions. This is considered to be a change from what is called *divergent thinking* to *convergent thinking*. If this can be done while maintaining the integrity of those ideas, then there is an excellent chance that the proposal will win a bid. The boundaries inside which the creative concept must live are:

- Does it match the client's vision? Certainly, it may match the producer's vision. However, it will only be a winner if the producer and client see eye to eye on the creative concept.
- Does it fit the client's budget? The real creativity comes in squeezing and modifying the original concept into a meaningful semblance of itself under budget constraints.
- Is it appropriate for the client's guests or for the audience as a whole? A great vision will be great to the audience only if they can relate culturally and demographically to it. For example, too much talking in entertainment will not work for an audience for which English is not their primary language, American comedy may be lost on a British audience even though they do speak English, or lavish décor and an abundance of floral displays probably will not work for a group of male engineers.
- Is it cutting edge? Today's audiences, be they a group of 20-somethings at a summer music festival or guests on an incentive tour, are very aware of the latest in technology and entertainment. Giving them something old or trite will no longer cut it. To win business these days requires stepping out from the ordinary and going beyond what has been done by others.

- Are all risks covered? Every potential risk must be assessed and addressed. Sufficient insurance must be in place and all parties must be cross insured by each other. This is particularly necessary when much of the cutting-edge events involve high degrees of risk these days, whether it is a flying circus act or fire dancers. The event setting is changing and becoming riskier and to be at the leading edge requires an acute awareness of risk.

4.1.2 Professionalism

Professionalism, or from another view, service, is part of the one-two punch along with creativity, that regularly wins bids for special event business. It may seem at first glance to be simple, but there are some rather subtle aspects to professionalism that warrant a closer look.

- *Quality of initial contact*: Are there people with personality at the producer's end of the telephone, or is there just an impersonal voicemail at all times of the working day? Are e-mail inquiries handled and answered promptly and politely? Do the people who answer phones and e-mails do so with knowledge and a friendly manner? The personal touch still wins business hands down.
- *Timeliness of response*: When taking down the details of a request for business or for a proposal, do staff members ask for a deadline date for submission? If not, it should be done. Once that date has been given, it should be treated as a serious deadline, no matter what. If something unforeseeable happens and the proposal cannot be submitted on time, this fact should be communicated to the client before the deadline and more time politely requested. A late proposal with no reason will make the company appear unreliable.
- *Quality of the proposal*: This is the meat of the written proposal and the subject of this chapter. Suffice it to say that every proposal sent out, no matter how large or how small, must be of the highest quality.
- *Followup*: So often, event companies are only too happy to be finished the hard work of generating a proposal and forget to commit to regular followup. This means ensuring that the proposal has reached its destination right after it was sent and it continues with regular followup phone calls or e-mails to check on progress. The more that continuing contact can be maintained with a client, the more they begin to rely on the production company and will see it in a positive light. Of course, too regular a contact might be seen as a negative.
- *Web presence*: These days, an event production company without a web presence is viewed as less professional, less progressive, and less technologically astute than their competitors. In short, there really is no excuse for not having one, even if it is just a simple but tasteful online brochure.

4.1.3 Experience

The last of the trio that helps to win business is experience, although it is much farther down the scale of importance. Given two equally capable companies with strong bids for a piece of business, the more experienced one will have a better chance of winning. What comprises experience and how can it help? Here are some of the variables that may influence clients to choose one company over another.

4.1.3.1 *Time in the Industry*

This is self-explanatory. Obviously, the more time a company has in the industry, the more it is seen to be reliable and capable of handling a client's requirements. It is also considered to be a sign of a good business person who understands what it takes to run a successful company for an extended period of time.

4.1.3.2 *Appropriateness of Experience*

Time in the industry is good, but the special events industry is a diverse one, with many different disciplines. If that time has been spent as an entertainment agency doing no more than booking bands and suddenly the company is thrust into the market to produce full events, all the previous experience is not as meaningful.

4.1.3.3 *Credibility*

This aspect of experience can really be interpreted as, 'How does the rest of the industry and the world view the producer and the producer's company?' It is a reflection of personal reputation and the company's commitment to the craft of event production. It includes:

- *References*: Are there lots of clients who would gladly recommend the production company based on past performance?
- *Awards*: Has the production company been recognized by industry peers with awards applicable to the company's specialization?
- *Certification*: Have any of the producers taken the time and effort to gain industry certification in the form of CSEP (Certified Special Events Professional through the International Special Events Society), or CSEC and CSEM (Certified Special Event Coordinator and Certified Special Event Manager, both through the Canadian Tourism Human Resource Council)?

4.2 PREPARING A WINNING PROPOSAL

What exactly is a proposal in the event production business? The proposal is a marriage of the creative ideas (i.e. the cognitive process we discussed in

Chapter 2) generated after being asked to bid on a project by way of a *request for proposal* or *RFP*, with the producer's knowledge of resources. It is a reflection of the producer's ability to 'put it all together,' and it forms the template for the actual event. By the time the proposal is being written, most of the hard work has been done in conceptualizing the event, including discussing the entire event from start to finish with all suppliers and obtaining from them reasonably firm quotes for providing their products and services. A winning proposal covers all the bases: it is creative; it matches the client's vision and goals; it is unique in presentation; it is timely; and it fits the client's budget. These aspects can be explained in terms of content, format, and the use of technology.

4.2.1 Content

Content is the 'meat' of the written proposal. It includes descriptions and prices of all the services and products that the client may potentially purchase, ideally in as much detail as is required for a clear understanding by the client. Understanding is the key word here, because without it, the producer's vision will never match the client's vision and that must be the goal in a proposal. The main components of content include the following.

4.2.1.1 *Company Background*

A brief company history and biography of the owner(s) may be included to establish credibility. Items that assist with this, as discussed in the previous section, are the time the company has served the industry, a sample of key clients accompanied by references (e.g. either letters, excerpts of letters, or contact names and phone numbers), awards in the industry, and individual credentials if applicable.

4.2.1.2 *Description of Services and Products to be Provided*

This part of the proposal should be very detailed and describe all the resources to be provided. Some of the more common inclusions in this part are:

- Creative description of the entertainment program with short biographies of individual acts or performers.
- Creative description of the décor.
- Brief description and listing of the audio system and its components.
- Brief description and listing of the lighting system and its components.
- Brief description and listing of any visual presentation equipment and its purpose.
- Descriptions and listings of other services such as special effects, staging, tenting, fencing, or waste management if they are the responsibility of the producer.

- Description and listing of services, including estimated costs, not provided by the producer but still required for the production responsibility areas and for which the client may be responsible for paying directly (e.g. rigging, insurance, electrical power hookup, heating or air conditioning, permits and licenses, green rooms, and staff meals).

In terms of the actual language used, imaginative and descriptive language always works, but triteness should be avoided. Conway (2005) advises, 'Please do not say: "As the guests enter they will be greeted by … ." This is so overdone and quite old. Instead, cut to the meat of the proposal: 'To carry out the theme, the entryway will be … .' The goal is for the client to form a mental picture of what will be purchased. Everything written must be perfect from a grammatical and spelling point of view. It should be simple, with minimal use of technical jargon, since most readers will be uninformed about the special events industry. It is best to set the scene for the overall event with a general description to whet the client's appetite and then narrow down to the individual components, with descriptive paragraphs for each major component.

4.2.1.3 *Graphics*

Pictures embedded in the proposal itself, attached to it, or sent as separate e-mail photos are virtually essential nowadays to win business. These pictures can take the form of actual photos of past events the production company has done that are similar to what is being proposed, photos of other events as long as credit is given, sketches by a designer, or even short videos on CD or posted on a Web site. Again, the aim is to form as accurate a mental picture as possible in the mind of the client.

4.2.1.4 *Budget*

Budget and the 'bottom line' are what will usually interest the client the most, although not always. A budget should not be hidden but be in plain view and broken down into as many small components as possible. Although there is no 'right way' for budget presentation, a shopping list format seems to work the best as it allows the client to pick and choose options. This can be achieved either using separate pricing opposite each item that is described, or as a single attached listing of individual items and their price. All mark-ups, labor, and rental or purchase fees should be included for each item if possible, as well as any applicable taxes, so that the bottom line has no surprises.

To summarize, here are two real examples from an actual proposal. The first illustrates how one major décor element was described. The second example is a comparison of two descriptions of an entertainment element.

Example of Proposal Content: Internal Paragraph on a Décor Element

Gold Rush Town:

A reproduction of the BC gold rush town, Barkerville, this 45 ft long street scene fits perfectly against the wall where the ceiling height lowers. Four buildings with a boardwalk in front create the scene. They are: a land and claims office; a two story hotel; a general store complete with gingham curtains in the windows and barrels, wooden crates, old tins and produce displayed on its steps; and a saloon with swinging doors. See below for an example of this street (Note that the actual street may differ somewhat in appearance but all components will be included). $10,500

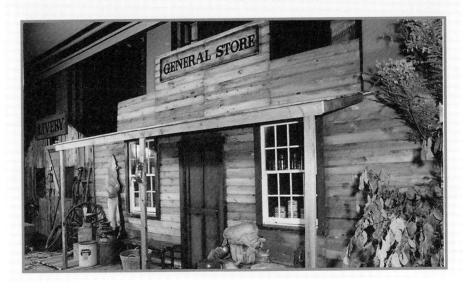

Courtesy: Pacific Show Productions, www.pacificshow.ca – Copyright 2006

    This description indicates that the producer is knowledgeable about the event venue because the exact location for this set piece is stated. A second point is that the description, while not overly 'flowery,' still manages to give a clear picture of what will be provided and allows just enough for the receiver to form his or her own mental image. The price for this décor set piece is also clearly stated. The accompanying photo is intended only to give a reasonable indication of what will be received since the set piece is no longer in existence. Figure 4.2 shows what the client actually received.

FIGURE 4.2

ACTUAL DÉCOR SET RECEIVED BY CLIENT

Courtesy: Wayne Chose Photography and Pacific Show Productions, www.pacificshow.ca – Copyright 2006

**Example of Proposal Content: Comparison of Descriptions
of an Entertainment Element**
These descriptions illustrate the difference between being too minimal with not enough information and no photo, and being just right with sufficient information to justify the cost of the entertainment along with a representative photo (Figure 4.3). Figure 4.4 shows the actual event setup for this entertainment.

4.2.2 Format

Format refers to how the proposal will look physically. Not all proposals are just straightforward written epistles. Some of the considerations and possibilities include the following.

4.2.2.1 *Font*

Standard font for business holds true for special events, and that is 12 point Times New Roman, although 12 point Arial can work, and occasionally a unique style, but only as long as it is very readable and no smaller than 12 point.

FIGURE 4.3

EXAMPLE OF GOLD MINER AND GOLD PANNING

The short version:

Gold panning and miner in costume: $1000

OR

The descriptive version:

Gold Panning: Our authentic miner (see below), in prospector's costume, will show you how to pan for real gold at the old water trough. The gold panning area will be set up as part of the old town, with a functioning water wheel and a trough for panning in. Cost will depend on the amount of gold nuggets that you want to give away. Basic cost is for the miner, plus 100, one-dollar value nuggets. We can add more or larger nuggets at your request. Miner, costume, supplies, and $100 worth of gold nuggets: $1000

Courtesy: Pacific Show Productions, www.pacificshow.ca – Copyright 2006

4.2.2.2   Size and Design

If it is to be a written proposal, will it suffice to be typed on standard 8 ½ × 11 in. paper or does it demand – or does the uniqueness of the event and client demand – something out of the ordinary, such as a square, 8 × 8 in. uniquely packaged booklet? Almost anything is possible with the printing capabilities available now. Does it demand white paper, colored paper, or not even paper at all? It is worth discussing the possibilities with a printer, especially what format works for them, such as converting all Microsoft Word files to Adobe pdf files for easier printing.

FIGURE 4.4
ACTUAL GOLD PANNING ENTERTAINMENT
RECEIVED BY CLIENT

Courtesy: Wayne Chose Photography and Pacific Show Productions, www.pacificshow.ca – Copyright 2006

If it is a long proposal, make it as easy as possible for readers to find pertinent information. Michaels (2004) advises, 'Include a Table of Contents with tabs. At the end of the day, it comes down to basics. If you present a 100-page proposal to five people at a meeting, each one is going to be looking for different information. By sectioning the proposal into tabs, you make it easier for each person to find what he or she needs to make an informed decision.'

4.2.2.3 Cover and Binding

Will it be a loose compilation of papers and photos or a uniquely bound document? What sort of binding: spiral, cerlox, glued, three-ring binder, or something unusual? Will the cover be a reflection of the producer's corporate image or something totally different? It is not a bad idea to have a standard format cover and to get several printed so they can easily be pulled out when needed for proposals.

4.2.2.4 *Uniqueness*

How much 'over-the-top' should the presentation be? Does it warrant an approach that shows off the producer's wild creativity or is the client likely to find that ridiculous? Although creativity is fine, sometimes an overactive imagination can backfire in the corporate world and one must know the client well enough to make a decision as to whether an 'over-the-top' delivery and presentation will work. My company once delivered a proposal for a corporate family beach party in a child's bucket of sand, complete with miniature shovel and beach toys, and the client loved it. On the other hand, we once also went into a presentation with an example of our live entertainment and the client hated it. When in doubt, it is best to err on the side of conservatism.

4.2.3 Use of Technology

In today's business world, and especially in special events where producers are expected to keep up with trends, technology can be an advantage if used as part of a proposal. There are some serious and potentially expensive considerations.

4.2.3.1 *Amount of Effort*

Some technology can be very labor-intensive, such as *computer aided design and drafting* (CADD) drawings. The amount of effort and money spent on it should be proportional to the contract value and a company's chances of winning. Too many bidders for one contract, or contracts of low value do not warrant time and effort wasted on preparing sophisticated technological presentations.

4.2.3.2 *CADD*

Having said that, sometimes a simple two-dimensional CADD drawing of a proposed event space is valuable in proving that a producer knows how to use the technology, knows the venue, and knows how everything fits together. Sometimes, due to the tightness of elements being used in the event (e.g. many tables and stages in a small room), a CADD drawing is essential to ensure everything will fit safely and comfortably. A full color, three-dimensional presentation is extremely impressive but can take an inordinate amount of time to create, thus making it of doubtful value in anything but the most expensive, high profile bids. There are some programs now coming onto the market that make three-dimensional drawing easier and we cover these in more detail in Chapter 8.

4.2.3.3 *CDs and DVDs*

There are now available several excellent home movie-editing programs that can be used for business to make a CD or DVD. In this way, they can be easily mailed, couriered, or even used in a live presentation at a client's office from a laptop computer. Still and moving images as well as slick PowerPoint presentations can be combined with graphics and professional editing to make a winning combination. Again, however, this is somewhat time consuming and may not be worth it for smaller proposals.

4.2.3.4 *Graphics and Photos*

A compilation of photos and graphics in the form of client logos combined with past successful events a producer has done is always a smart move if they are used to enhance the suggested event elements such as décor, entertainment, or A-V. Client logos can be incorporated into PowerPoint presentations and CDs for a customized look.

4.2.3.5 *Use of the Internet*

Many astute producers are now posting proposals for their clients to view on their Web sites, and use a password for client access. As well, a producer's regular Web site, if content-rich, can be used to augment a written presentation with videos and photos, thus saving considerable time in the creation of a unique proposal that must incorporate all these items.

PRODUCTION WAR STORY:
SOME CLIENTS ARE NEVER HAPPY

Initial discussions between a potential client and our company indicated that the client's event would be a very energetic, high-end extravaganza for about 2000 guests in a conference center. The client wanted an entertainment show with cirque acts and unusual, creative décor. Every indication was given that the client was going to work with us. Several days were spent preparing an extensive creative proposal. Upon presentation to him, the client indicated that he had also received two other proposals from competitors that were lower in price but not as creative, and he asked us to rework the numbers. This entailed another day of dedicated time.

A second meeting with the client took place with the revised proposal and the client again said that the competitors had beaten the price but that he really wanted to work with our company. At that point, we called his bluff and stated that we would do no more work without being paid for creative and that the event now had a minimum fee for any work done. We walked out of the meeting and never heard from the client again, but did hear that all the other companies had done the same thing and that the client ended up producing his own show which was much smaller than originally anticipated.

What was the lesson learned? It was one that every independent business person eventually figures out. There comes a time when it is no longer feasible to work on a project, either from a financial point of view or from a 'gut feeling' about the ethics of a client.

Courtesy: Doug Matthews

4.3 DELIVERING A WINNING PROPOSAL

Last but not least in trying to win a bid is to decide how the proposal is best delivered and how one should follow up after it has been delivered. Here are the most common options.

4.3.1 Mail, Courier, or E-Mail

All have their advantages and disadvantages, but nowadays, most producers consider the cost of a courier as minimal compared to getting the business by having the proposal into the client's hands in time, especially when many proposals have a very short lead time in this industry. E-mail is efficient but lacks the ability to show the full extent of the producer's creative mind if a special packaging or physical design has been used. However, it does allow for photo attachments, video attachments, and such.

4.3.2 Live Presentation

Sometimes this can augment a written proposal and for those who are personable, can represent a real advantage in gaining business. It also allows for more conversation and time to get to know the client. Enough copies of the proposal should be prepared for all attendees, samples of décor such as fabric swatches – or a full table setting – can be brought, a taste test can be incorporated if catering is involved, and giveaways can be considered for attendees at the presentation. The goal is to entice and enthuse them by tempting their senses and making them see the producer's vision as much as possible.

4.3.3 Timing and Followup

All proposals should be on time with no deadlines missed unless there is a very good excuse and it is communicated to the client in advance of the deadline. Furthermore, once the proposal has been delivered, the producer's work is just beginning. It requires regular followup phone calls or e-mails to check on progress and ensure that there is nothing more needed by the client. If this persistence is positive but not harassing, the chances of winning should be increased.

4.4 ETHICAL CONSIDERATIONS

Ethics is one of the current hot topics in the special events industry. It is not only hot, it is hotly debated, because whenever the topic arises, there are always people who do not see in black and white but in many shades of gray. There is the constant clash between what is morally and ethically right, and what is good for business. The current business climate requires one to do all that is possible to make money yet be ethically responsible at the same time. Generally speaking, if one approaches business with an ethically responsible attitude, it is hard to go wrong, as this approach will yield more goodwill in the long term, even if it means missing some business in the short term. Because this is a major topic in the industry and it covers a multitude of scenarios, presented here are some general guidelines pertaining primarily to proposals, and the issues surrounding copyright.

4.4.1 Copyright and Intellectual Property

This is probably the most important concern for anyone, especially a producer, who is presenting original creative ideas. Ethically, the client is the one who has the responsibility to behave correctly, but in reality, it seldom happens. That means that the writer of the proposal is the one responsible for protecting copyright.

To begin with – and legally – it is generally agreed that the 'idea' belongs to the person who actually writes and describes the creative concept. Therefore, if the producer is the one who describes in detail how the event will flow and how the décor will look, then the producer is the creator and the 'owner' of the concept. If the designer/decorator designs and describes the room décor, then it is that person who owns the idea. Note that this ownership continues on past the original description and presentation, which means that theoretically, any designs found in a magazine cannot be used by anyone except the original owner unless that person authorizes its use. This, of course, also applies to suppliers. There are two main ways to help prevent copyright theft.

4.4.1.1 *Creative Fee*

The concept of payment for creative work is one that has so far not been widely accepted in the special events industry. Unfortunately, because of intense competition, most clients are unwilling to offer a fee for a creative proposal. If one is preparing an extensive proposal, it is possible to ask for a fee while the client is told that they are free to use the ideas provided the proposal owner is paid for the creation of them (i.e. the proposal owner is selling his or her intellectual property rights). This is not recommended because the client can then get anyone to do the work and the producer or proposal owner no longer has any rights to the ideas. One optional way around this dilemma is to offer to deduct the cost of the proposal from the final cost of producing the event if the producer wins the bid.

4.4.1.2 *Copyright Statement*

A copyright statement acts as a deterrent to clients who may wish to gather original ideas and then use them themselves or get another production company to do the work. A sample statement that my company used with good success, in bold, large font type on a single page either at the end or the beginning of a proposal is the following.

'PLEASE NOTE THAT THE FOREGOING PROPOSAL AND ALL INFOR-MATION IT CONTAINS IS THE CONFIDENTIAL AND PROPRIETARY INTELLECTUAL PROPERTY OF ABC EVENT COMPANY LTD. ALL RIGHTS ARE RESERVED AND NO PART OF THE PROPOSAL OR THE INFORMATION IT CONTAINS MAY BE REPRODUCED, COPIED, USED OR MODIFIED IN ANY WAY WITHOUT THE EXPRESS PRIOR WRIT-TEN PERMISSION OF ABC EVENT COMPANY LTD.

THIS INCLUDES, WITHOUT LIMITATION, THE USE AND/OR MODIFI-CATION OF ANY CONCEPTS OR IDEAS PERTAINING TO ENTER-TAINMENT, DÉCOR OR THE PRODUCTION OF THIS EVENT. INCLUDED IN THIS RESTRICTION IS THE USE AND/OR BOOKING OF ANY OF THE ENTERTAINMENT (ACTS OR PERFORMERS) RECOMMENDED BY ABC EVENT COMPANY LTD. FOR THIS PAR-TICULAR EVENT IF IT IS PRODUCED BY ANY COMPANY OR ORGA-NIZATION OTHER THAN ABC EVENT COMPANY LTD.

ANY BREACH OF THIS RESTRICTION WILL RESULT IN LEGAL ACTION BEING TAKEN TO RECOVER, WITHOUT LIMITATION, ALL COSTS ASSOCIATED WITH THE CREATION OF THIS PROPOSAL AND ALL PROFITS THAT WOULD HAVE COME TO ABC EVENT COMPANY LTD. IF ABC EVENT COMPANY LTD. HAD PRODUCED THIS EVENT.'

© ABC EVENT COMPANY LTD.

Note that this statement may not be enforceable in its entirety in a court of law, but at the very least, it is a strong deterrent to potential copyright thieves. Producers contemplating using a similar statement should have it reviewed by a qualified legal expert.

4.4.1.3   Using Other People's Ideas in a Proposal

This is a constant source of concern in the special events industry. Even though an idea may have been published in a magazine, one cannot assume it is public property, although many people do. Ethically – and arguably legally – it is wrong. The best alternative is to acknowledge it as the other person's work and if the client likes it, state that approval will be sought from the owner to use the concepts. Usually, if the work has been published, the designer will probably allow it or at least part of it, to be used. If there is a special creation like a costume, the designer might insist that the original be used.

4.4.2   Other Ethics Issues

There are several other issues that regularly come up pertaining to ethics in the industry and which sooner or later become of concern when developing a proposal.

4.4.2.1 Obtaining Supplier Contacts

One very serious and continuing problem is that of suppliers and clients trying to short circuit the normal chain of business. For example, it is not ethically right to solicit a supplier's contact information if that supplier is working for another company at the time. A case in point might be a band that a producer sees at a competitor's event. It is definitely not ethically correct to solicit the phone number of the band directly from them. This can be considered similar to a consumer trying to buy clothing directly from a manufacturer instead of shopping in a retail store. The best way to address this potential problem is to have statements that prohibit such solicitation in both the client and supplier contracts (see Chapter 6 for more details).

4.4.2.2 Bidding against Oneself

Producers are occasionally requested to submit a proposal for the same event by more than one client. It is ethically irresponsible to submit a proposal without notifying and obtaining the permission of both potential clients. A good guideline is to inform each of them that there are two requests and to seek permission from the first requestor to submit a bid to the second one. It is usually better to offer to submit a different proposal to the second one only if the first requestor agrees to it. At least this constant flow of information ensures that everyone knows that the producer is ethical. A responsible ethical attitude such as this adds to a company's credibility and serves it well for future business.

These issues highlight a continuing struggle in the special events industry over what Kidder (1995) terms the 'right versus right' ethical dilemma. It is that tough decision that business people often face when there is no obvious law-driven, right versus wrong moral decision. In other words, depending on one's point of view, either decision could be the right one. In the case of copyright, the choice really is a moral decision because there exists a law that protects copyright. However, in other cases such as these latter two, it is a true right versus right decision because there are two ways to solve the dilemma. For example, a producer who finds a new band at an event produced by a competitor might consider that it is his/her duty to obtain as many good acts as possible to offer to clients; however, it is also up to him/her to remain honest in all business dealings, making for two possible 'right' decisions. Kidder (1995) proposes three principles to assist one in making the correct decision in cases such as this: *ends-based thinking* that emphasizes doing what produces the greatest good for the greatest number; *rule-based thinking* that means following only the principle that you want everyone else to follow; and *care-based thinking* that interprets the 'Golden Rule' of doing to others what you would like them to do to you. Although a thorough analysis of each dilemma may never be conclusive, at least the more that one ponders the question and analyzes the possible outcomes to arrive at an answer, the closer to being ethically correct will be the final decision.

PRODUCTION CHALLENGES

1. A potential client has made a request for a large proposal via e-mail to your company with a deadline date and some – but not enough – details. Describe what exactly would be your method of dealing with this potential client in terms of response and contact.

2. You have been asked to prepare a proposal for providing lights, audio, staging, and production management only, for an event. Describe the type of content and format you would use for this proposal.

3. Choreographed jugglers, tightrope-walking live tigers, and a musical comedian are going to be combined for a spectacular event finale. What would you use to best illustrate these acts to the client in a proposal, and what possible ways, in a perfect world, could be used to deliver the concept and proposal?

4. A potential first-time client company has said they will go with you to produce their event, but they want a very creative proposal with CADD drawings and full details. It will take you 3 weeks to develop this proposal. What must you consider in deciding whether to accept this challenge and to protect your creative ideas?

5. A regular and very rich client has seen a wonderful event outlined in a magazine and has asked you to produce the same one. You just happen to know the producer of the event illustrated in the magazine who is a good friend and whom you know will not appreciate her event being copied without substantial remuneration (more than you can pay on our own). What would you do to solve this ethical dilemma?

REFERENCES

Conway, A. (August 22–25, 2005). The write stuff: how to create effective proposals. *9th Annual Event Solutions Idea Factory: Seminar Workbook*. Event Solutions Magazine, p. 168.

Kidder, R.M. (1995). *How Good People Make Tough Choices: Resolving the Dilemmas of Ethical Living*. New York: William Morrow.

Matthews, D. (2004). Proposals that Win Business. In Matthews, D. (Ed.), *Hot Tips for Events That Sizzle*. Vancouver: Total Event Arrangements and Meeting Network (TEAM Net).

Michaels, A. (Winter 2004). Making the Deal – What it takes to propose and present to the big boys. *Canadian Event Perspective Magazine*, 11, pp. 6–7.

THE PRODUCTION TEAM

Event production is more than anything a 'people' business. If one dislikes working with people and taking the good with the bad, then it's the wrong business for that person. If however, one is like the vast majority of event producers who thrive on the adrenalin rush of leading an enthusiastic team to create an unbelievable event experience, then event production is the right place to be.

Several other books do an excellent job of outlining the theory of human resource management for event staff and volunteers, including recruitment, training, the development of policy manuals and job descriptions, compensation, performance evaluation, and recognition (Goldblatt, 2002; Rutherford-Silvers, 2004; Allen et al., 2005; Van Der Wagen and Carlos, 2005). It is not the intention of this book to repeat these explanations but rather to isolate and examine the practical details of managing a real production team before and during an event. In this chapter, we therefore will be dealing with the following topics:

- Assembling and organizing the production team.
- Working with the team during the concept and proposal phase.
- Working with the team during the coordination phase.
- Working with the team during the execution phase.
- Health and safety issues.

5.1 ASSEMBLING AND ORGANIZING THE TEAM

As explained in Chapter 1, the event producer is more often than not a subcontractor to the event manager and is not responsible for recruiting volunteers, hiring and training event staff, writing policy manuals and job descriptions, or evaluating performance. Those tasks are the responsibility of the event manager. Typically event producers are independent contractors who may work alone or who may be part of a larger company, but their job is always focused strictly on working with a temporary team of individual experts to produce and deliver a creative and superbly executed event.

5.1.1 Assembling the Team

The 'production team' is therefore not usually comprised of an event company's staff members, but a number of subcontractors from the various specialties that are needed to successfully deliver the promised event. Occasionally, in a large event production company, a producer may call upon other specialized staff to handle some of the necessary tasks such as writing and monitoring contracts, organizing subcontractor payments, providing onsite technical direction, and providing stage managers; however, this may also be done entirely by the producer if that person is a sole proprietor or has a very small staff.

When and how, then, is the production team assembled? A production company usually enters the picture during the concept and proposal phase of event organization. The event manager, who, as we have previously explained, could be a company represented by an individual, a non-profit organization, a destination management company (DMC), or a host of others, typically approaches one or more production companies and requests a bid for a specific event or events. This request or request for proposal (RFP) as explained in Chapter 4, outlines the general details and budget for the event. It is at this time that the production company names one of its staff as the lead producer for the event. This individual then undertakes to first evaluate what is entailed to put in a successful bid and then decides on the key suppliers who are appropriate for this event. The suppliers further determine themselves which of their staff members – or subcontractors – will be working on the event. These persons, from a variety of suppliers, thus become the production team, under the direct supervision of the producer.

5.1.2 Organizing the Team

The organization hierarchy of the production team will probably resemble Figure 5.1 in concept. By its nature it is a temporary hierarchy and one that is only valid during the production of the applicable event. All other issues, such as the hiring, training, and firing of subcontracted personnel are not the responsibility of the producer, but rather of the subcontractors' companies. Occasionally, as mentioned, the producer or the producer's company might, as an individual entity, assume the tasks of some of these positions. For example, the producer's company will in all likelihood be the one administering contracts for suppliers and paying them. Likewise, the producer might be very accomplished at technical direction and might assume the task of coordinating all technical setup and operation, as well as calling the show. Otherwise, all team members will be subcontractors to the producer.

Most event producers have a database of reliable and creative subcontractors in all of the resource areas in Figure 5.1. These resources are the very ones that are described in detail in *Special Event Production: The Resources*. Although the producer may decide on a competitive bid for some of the areas, it is not unusual for a choice to be made based on a company's or an individual's competency in a certain aspect of that specialty. For example, a producer may know three excellent audio companies and audio engineers, but because the event will be having a show with the Beach Boys as a headline act, the producer may decide to go with one of the audio companies that has previously mixed for the Beach Boys or has had expertise with a similar group. Another example may be in décor design. A client may want to have lavish florals as part of the décor design so the producer may decide to go with a designer who has won awards for floral design instead of another who specializes in movie set decoration. Other choices may be made based on the producer's knowledge of subcontractors' pricing and nothing more.

Reporting to each subcontractor will be that company's own employees or more suppliers subcontracted by them (e.g. independent technicians to operate and set up equipment). These employees and subcontractors may not be the same persons who initially are in contact with the producer when the event RFP comes in. As with many companies, the initial contact person may be a reliable industry colleague that is known to the producer and with

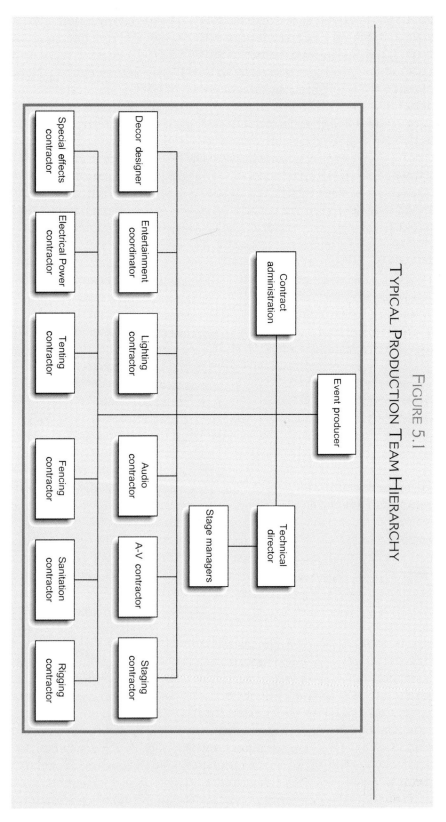

FIGURE 5.1

TYPICAL PRODUCTION TEAM HIERARCHY

whom the producer has a good relationship. The initial bid is created typically with this contractor representative – possibly someone in sales or marketing – and once a contract is awarded, the contractor representative may hand off the project to the operational side of the company, so the producer must deal with a number of different persons from a single supplier throughout the course of organizing and executing the event. This is mentioned for two reasons. The first is that the eventual onsite contractor representative may not have or understand in detail the vision originally conceived and must have it explained, and second, the two contractor representatives' personalities may be entirely different, meaning that the management style of the producer may have to change.

If volunteers are to be a part of the production team, they normally are the responsibility of the event manager and must be given very strict guidelines as to what their tasks are and what their schedule is. It is not recommended that volunteers be a part of this team due to the fact that most of the tasks within the production team require specialized training. In addition, the risk associated with these tasks can be high and the liability of a producer taking on this responsibility is not warranted for the potential small amount of time or expense that might be saved by using volunteers. Extensive personal experience forms the basis for these comments.

5.2 WORKING WITH THE TEAM: CONCEPT AND PROPOSAL PHASE

The production of a special event requires both inspirational leadership and skillful management. This means that the producer must be both a leader who creates the vision for the event (with client feedback, of course), and a manager who achieves the vision with the help of a team of professionals. The challenge is that the producer's leadership or management style must change at different points in the event's organization in order to do this.

Although numerous authors and experts have tried to define leadership, management, and their respective styles, there is still some confusion about the exact difference between a leader and a manager. In the interest of minimizing the confusion factor, let us simply refer to the three most commonly accepted styles of leadership/management as we review how the producer works with the team in each event phase. These are: *laissez-faire style*, a more or less hands-off approach in which the leader/manager depends on the self-motivation of his team to accomplish tasks; *democratic style*, a consultative approach in which the leader/manager allows the team to decide how the tasks will be accomplished; and *autocratic style*, an authoritarian approach in which the leader/manager unilaterally makes most of the decisions about how the tasks will be accomplished. Interestingly enough, these three styles correspond almost exactly to the type of leadership that is required in the concept and proposal phase, coordination phase, and execution phase of the event, respectively.

The concept and proposal phase is all about ideas and how the many creative minds of the chosen team of experts can arrive at one clear vision for the event. During this phase, the producer initiates contact with team members by asking them for creative and budgetary input for their part of the event, based usually on an initial concept that the producer and client have discussed. For example, the producer may call upon a designer to develop a plan for décor, a number of different performing groups to develop their segment of an entertainment program, a lighting company to light the proposed décor and the proposed entertainment, an A-V company to provide exciting visuals for a multimedia component, a staging company to design a custom stage, and so on. This process may or may not require meetings of the entire team, but it almost certainly requires a meeting of key suppliers at and with the event venue to discuss how the event will work. During these meetings and any preliminary discussions with team members, the producer probably uses a laissez-faire approach to leadership as it avoids stifling creative input. The entire goal of the producer during this phase is to develop and write a timely, creative, and attractive proposal using the relatively unrestricted inputs of the production team.

5.3   WORKING WITH THE TEAM: COORDINATION PHASE

The coordination phase begins with the awarding of a contract to the producer. At this point, the leadership/management style of the producer probably changes to democratic. This phase demands that all team members deliver on their promises and coordinate their inputs with each other, which means the producer may need to acknowledge the will of the group in the interests of achieving a common vision. Often, this results in meetings between the team and the producer. If the event is a large one and the team comparably large, time can be wasted unless the meetings are run efficiently. In this section, we will review what it takes to run such a meeting and then review the general tasks that the producer must oversee as part of this phase.

5.3.1   Running Efficient Meetings

Good, effective meetings with clear results do not just happen on the spur of the moment. They are planned. This involves work before, during, and after the meeting. What follows are some of the most important points to consider to get the best results.

5.3.1.1 *Getting Ready*

Getting ready for a meeting begins early, at least several days if not 1 or 2 weeks. The organizer must:

- Reserve the meeting venue if necessary.
- Set the date, time, and location of the meeting in advance and distribute the information to all team members.
- Set, write, and distribute the agenda and a meeting reminder within 1 week of the meeting. If this is done any sooner, the majority of people will forget the meeting.
- Inform all attendees with action items that they will be required to prepare a status report before the meeting (e.g. 2 or 3 days).
- If possible, distribute copies of the status reports to all attendees at the meeting, or ideally, 1 or 2 days prior to the meeting.
- Assign a secretary.

5.3.1.2 *Preparing the Meeting Location*

Again, arriving early is critical. The organizer must:

- Ensure sufficient tables and chairs are arranged in a correct and comfortable setup.
- Ensure that lighting is adequate.
- Ensure pens/pencils and paper are available for each attendee.
- Ensure refreshments are available in the form of coffee, water, or juice. Occasionally, muffins or cookies help.
- Ensure room temperature is comfortable and not too cold or too hot.

It is amazing what effect creature comforts have on the success of a meeting. People have long memories and if their memories are positive (e.g. 'I really enjoyed those muffins at the last meeting.'), they will be a lot more inclined to be cooperative than if their memories are negative (e.g. 'All I wanted to do was leave the last meeting because the room was so cold.').

5.3.1.3 *Conducting the Meeting*

Although far from an exhaustive list, the following tips are essential to running an effective meeting:

- Deal with the most important agenda items first. Too often, the items requiring key decisions are left until the end of a meeting when everyone is tired and ready to leave. Key items should be discussed when people are the most energized. For example, leave a decision about green room amenities to the end but put a key discussion about multimedia content at the beginning.
- Follow *Robert's Rules of Order* for more efficiency. US Army Major Henry Martyn Robert first wrote this now world-famous book in 1876 after presiding over a church meeting and discovering that delegates

...as of the country did not agree about proper proce-
...ne the best and most widely used guide in existence to
...meetings, yet amazingly, few people who chair meetings
...basis are aware of many of the key rules. The tenth edition,
...0, is the only officially accepted version (Robert et al., 2000).
...cer should have a copy.

...nits for each agenda item. This forces attendees to be aware
...e allowed.

...cussion to one statement per attendee until all others who want to,
ha... ...d a say. This, in more detail, is one of the essential points of Robert's
Rules of Order. It is the best way to stop a meeting from getting out of hand.

- Have attendees address all discussion and questions through the chair-
  person to reduce the possibility of heated arguments and of personality
  conflicts interfering with the conduct of the meeting. This is also a key
  Robert's rule.
- Sum up each agenda item, clearly establish any action required, name
  the person responsible for the action, set a target date for the action to
  be completed, vote on the decision if necessary, and record the results.

5.3.1.4 *Following Up after the Meeting*

Success from a meeting only happens when attendees are reminded of
their responsibilities to act on action items. Therefore, an organizer must:

- Type up meeting minutes that include as a minimum: a list of all attendees; action items including the person(s) responsible for them and their
  target completion dates; and all decisions made.
- Distribute the minutes as soon as possible, ideally within 1 week of the
  meeting.
- Set reminders to check on action items on a regular basis and at least 1 week
  before each one is due.

In event production, there is no room for error, and meetings are often full
of minute details pertaining to the production. By efficiently conducting
meetings and recording their results, the possibility for error is significantly
reduced. Recorded meeting minutes and decisions can also help in providing specifics should any contractual disputes arise at a later date either with
suppliers or with clients.

5.3.2 The Producer's Tasks during the Coordination Phase

Assuming that most of the production team will be subcontractors, a
producer's typical general task list during this phase includes the following:

- Conceptualize and finalize all event details with respect to the resources
  to be used and under the responsibility of the producer, namely décor,

entertainment, lighting, audio, visual presentation technology, staging, and other technical areas (e.g. tenting, special effects, waste management, electrical power, rigging, and fencing). Conduct meetings as required to achieve this objective.

- Call all suppliers of these services to confirm the names of actual personnel who will be working on the event. At the same time, reconfirm with them all contract details or write up contracts as required, and review all current scheduling. Ensure that the entire team has as much information as possible about the event: who it is for, the background of the client, and how they, the suppliers, all fit into the overall goals of the event.

- Ensure all event stakeholders (including the venue, suppliers, and other people involved who may not be subcontracted by the producer such as caterers or an A-V company) have the same event details the producer has (e.g. the correct date, location, and setup schedule).

- Delegate as much as possible, even to suppliers/subcontractors. Along with delegating the responsibility for certain tasks should be given the requisite authority to make necessary decisions. For example, the responsibility for designing the décor for an event can be delegated to the designer; however, the designer should not be second-guessed by the producer or client if the designer will be spending a lot of time to create the design. The designer needs to have the authority to change the design within certain guidelines on his or her own if required rather than continually having to seek approval for small changes from the producer or client.

- Let everyone, including non-production team persons (e.g. venue event manager or catering manager), know what the production team reporting hierarchy is for the event, including where the producer, the suppliers, the team, and the client all fit in.

- Ensure that the team knows the expected standard of dress and whether they must wear badges or other clothing identifying them as part of the team or will be able to wear their own company attire. At the same time, ensure that the event team will have safety wear as required by Workers' Compensation Board (WCB) or in accordance with venue standards.

- Review all risk management concerns. This must be a team effort and may include a review of relevant operational procedures, design standards, and safety regulations and standards for everything from fire to temporary structures and machinery, to ensure compliance. Non-compliance instances should be noted and signed off by the appropriate authority whether the client, venue, or other organization before proceeding with the execution of the event.

5.4 WORKING WITH THE TEAM: EXECUTION PHASE

Once onsite, the producer's whole job is devoted to directing the production team in setting up, executing, and striking the event. It is 100 percent human resource management. The producer must know the team, what they are capable of, and what they must accomplish. In this phase, the producer's leadership style probably switches to a more autocratic one, due to the urgent nature of the tasks to be performed and also due to the fact that the entire production team should, by this time, know exactly what their tasks are and the time they have to complete them.

Unfortunately, when a significant number of skilled workers of widely diverse backgrounds and personalities interact closely in a tightly scheduled, stressful situation driven by profit, there are bound to be conflicts. Certainly special events as an industry has friendly, gregarious people in abundance. It also has a seemingly disproportionate share of power trippers, egomaniacs, and irrational 'wing nuts.' Usually most production team members, if well chosen and well briefed about the event, will cooperate amongst themselves and with external stakeholders (e.g. venue staff) for the common good. When they do not or when an unstable personality has a problem, conflicts inevitably arise. It is in the resolution of these conflicts that the event producer learns life's lessons, difficult though they may be. We will spend some time on the topic of conflict resolution at the beginning of this section because it is extremely important to correctly handle these situations as soon as they occur. We will then move on to review the remaining tasks that must be supervised by a producer in this phase.

5.4.1 Conflict Resolution

Although theory abounds on conflict resolution, it does not always work during a real-life event setup or execution due to the necessity for an urgent solution. Our discussion, therefore, must start with a recommendation to event producers to 'pick their battles.' The conflicts that arise while the production team is onsite usually involve two or more team members (one could be the producer), a team member and a non-team member (e.g. typically venue staff), or a team member and the client. How these conflicts are resolved will depend to a large extent on the producer's priorities. Let us see how this may happen by considering some of these priorities:

- Maintaining company and personal reputation. Perhaps the producer and the producer's company have a reputation for fair dealing, or for being hard-nosed, or for being ethical above all else. How the producer wants to be seen in the industry may very well affect the conflict resolution outcome and deliberations.
- Preserving the integrity of the event. Perhaps the producer is so committed to the contract and to the vision of the event that he/she will do anything to preserve it and to make it happen regardless of the effect that decision may have on relationships or reputation.
- Preserving relationships. Regardless of the outcome of the event and the reputation of the producer's company, conflict resolution decisions may be influenced by a producer who values relationships over other options.

For example, if there is a conflict between the producer and a catering manager in a venue, the producer may opt to agree with the catering manager because the preservation of that relationship is worth more than keeping a client or team member happy. Perhaps the catering manager sends the producer's company $100,000 worth of business every year and the client for the present event is one time only and difficult to deal with. It would not be hard for most producers to opt for a decision that favors preserving the relationship with the venue over satisfying the client. Ethically wrong? Maybe, depending on the circumstances. Smart business? Definitely. A little humble pie eaten with business survival in mind is not necessarily bad – or stupid.

Most producers will, without knowing it, have a priority list similar to the one above, at the back of their minds during any event setup and execution, and will react in a manner that reflects that list in a conflict situation.

PRODUCTION WAR STORY:
DRIVEN TO TEARS

Everyone has a client who likes to micro-manage. One such client of mine – a regular and fairly lucrative one – had been present during an entire day of décor setup for a large theme event for their national sales staff. I had delegated the authority for setup to one of my long-time designers who was accustomed to lengthy and complex setups, but who had not worked with this particular client before. By the time I arrived onsite to supervise the event itself, I was confronted by a very distressed designer who claimed that the client had driven her to tears with incessant requests for minor changes to the décor. This had put her behind schedule and there was a good chance that the setup would not be complete on time. She had neglected to call me prior to my arrival thinking that she could handle the situation but it had proven too much.

I needed to resolve this conflict fast. Fortunately, it was not an all-out personality clash, but rather a continuing annoyance. I approached both parties separately to try to resolve the problem. My first concern was to try to calm my designer who still had a considerable amount of work to accomplish. I basically told her that she should only communicate with me now that I was onsite and not directly with the client any longer. Likewise, I politely asked the client to try to minimize changes from now on as we were on a very tight schedule. I reassured her that once all the décor was in place the venue would look spectacular. Since we had a good relationship, she agreed to my request. The event turned out well and the client was very pleased.

What were the conflict resolution principles in play here? First, I purposely kept both parties separated in order not to trigger any arguments. Second, I tried to keep both parties calm and focused on completing the event setup rather than focusing on their disagreements, part of which the designer interpreted as an insult to her creative ability.

Courtesy: Doug Matthews

5.4.1.1 *Comparison of Approaches in Conflict Resolution*

Having said that, conflict experts are in agreement that the best resolution is one that arrives at a 'win–win' situation, in other words as might be expected, a compromise. However, it is not as easy as it seems and involves moving to an *interest-based approach* from a *positional approach*. It means moving toward a position that, in the case of event production, probably focuses on doing what is required to achieve the vision and goals of the event. It means getting to the bottom of what is really making the two sides angry. Is it the way that someone reacted to a statement or the way that a person ordered another to do a task? It might be a simple reaction to a poor attitude or a personality clash that needs to be moved to a broader focus. Table 5.1 outlines the two approaches (Justice Institute of BC, 1991a).

TABLE 5.1
WIN/LOSE AND WIN/WIN COMPARISON

Win/Lose (Positional Approach)		Win/Win (Interest-Based Approach)
Attitude of me versus you or us versus them.	Attitude	Us versus the problem or the issue.
Take on the issues personally. Get self-righteous or feel like a failure.	Issues	The issues are just that – issues, and you don't take them personally.
Narrow focus on the conflict, particularly what you will say or do next.	Focus	Focus on the larger picture and how this conflict impacts short and long term.
Get really stuck on your own viewpoint. Your solution/position is obviously right.	Flexibility and openness	Openness to other points of view; open to be influenced by another's point of view.
Manipulate the other to your point of view. Hide your feelings. Add pressure to the situation. Try to get them to feel bad.	Sincerity	Be honest with what is going on for you. Communicate openly and authentically.
Get angry and cut off contact with the other person if they don't see things your way.	Contact	Keep the lines of communication open.
Assumes that someone will come out the winner and someone the loser.	Outcome	Look for outcomes which will be mutually satisfying.

Courtesy: Justice Institute of BC (1991a)

5.4.1.2 *The Language of Resolution*

From a practical standpoint, as the person in the middle of a conflict situation and ultimately the person responsible for resolving the conflict, a producer can defuse the situation by using both body and spoken language. Here are some tips that may help defuse a situation.

5.4.1.2.1 Body Language

Body language is a very large part of how we communicate. In a conflict, it is necessary to demonstrate that one is interested, concerned, and listening attentively. The following are suggestions offered by the Justice Institute of BC's Centre for Conflict Resolution to do just that (Justice Institute of BC, 1991b):

- Square your shoulders with the person. Face them directly rather than pointing energy in another direction. If they are very upset, you will want to attend to them obliquely (i.e. from a 30° to 45° angle).
- Concentrate fully on the person you're trying to understand. Avoid interruptions and habits which imply boredom (e.g. playing with pencil, fingernail, looking elsewhere). (Definitely do not answer a cell phone – author).
- Open your posture toward the person. Arms and legs should be uncrossed, hands open, and in sight.
- Lean forward a bit if that is comfortable, but avoid crowding the other's 'personal space.' If they move back, lean back a bit until your distance feels comfortable.
- Eye contact is important, but tricky. Be aware that in many cultures and subcultures, direct eye contact is a sign of disrespect, defiance, or challenge. Offer eye contact, but don't demand it.
- Relax. Try to incorporate these body messages into your personal style. Don't use them mechanically, but use them as an expression of your concern and interest.

5.4.1.2.2 Spoken Language

Assertive spoken communication is important in event production. Bower and Bower (1976) identify several steps for doing this including three that can be used in conflict situations: describing, expressing, and specifying (Table 5.2).

As a final note to this discussion, Rutherford-Silvers (2004) makes some good points about separating from the situation. She recommends: 'postponing discussion to a different time and place if possible; handling the situation in private; and/or referring to the applicable policies, procedures, and provisions of contractual, collective, or waiver agreements.' Using these suggestions in themselves may be all that is needed to defuse the situation.

5.4.2 The Producer's Tasks during the Execution Phase

The general task list of the producer in this phase with respect to working with the production team includes the following:

- Ensure the entire team is aware of the goals of the event, what must be set up, where each component fits in, the schedule for setup and strike, the floor or site plan, and the event running order. This is best done by

TABLE 5.2
ASSERTIVE COMMUNICATION

Do's	Don'ts
Describing	
Described the other person's behavior objectively	Describe your emotional reaction to it
Use concrete terms	Use abstract or vague terms
Describe a specific time and place	Generalize for 'all time'
Describe the action, not the motive	Guess at the other person's motives or goals
Expressing	
Express your feelings	Deny or hide your feelings
Express them calmly	Unleash emotional outbursts
State feelings as positively as possible and relate them to your needs	State feelings in an attacking or demeaning way
Stick to the problem behavior or situation	Attack the person's character or personality
Specifying	
Explicitly ask for what you want	Merely imply that you want something
Make reasonable requests	Ask for too large a change
Request one or two changes at a time	Ask for too many changes
Specify what concrete action needs to stop and what needs to be performed	Ask for vague or general behavior or outcomes
Focus on both of you meeting your needs	Try to win at the expense of the other
Specify what you are willing to change	Expect that only the other person is to change

Courtesy: Bower and Bower (1976)

holding a short meeting at the beginning of the setup with all key team members (e.g. onsite contractor representatives).

- Plan for crew meal and coffee breaks and try to fit them around other tasks that are best done without that particular component of your team in order to minimize downtime. In this regard, try to provide basic amenities such as coffee, water, soft drinks, sandwiches, cookies, and such onsite.
- Maintain continuous liaison with the various members of the production team and venue staff to minimize conflicting tasks.
- Ensure compliance with appropriate state/provincial or federal occupational health and safety (OHS) regulations (see Section 5.5).
- Ensure the team has appropriate attire, including identifying clothing and appropriate safety gear (e.g. steel-toed boots, hard hats if rigging, etc.) according to regulations.
- Ensure personnel operating specialty equipment such as genie lifts or electrical hookup, are properly qualified according to regulations.
- Continuously monitor working conditions and watch for safety hazards such as too much noise, wet or cold weather, slippery surfaces, fire or

electrical hazards, and give breaks or shelter as needed according to regulations. Ensure that first aid is easily accessible. Ideally, at least one onsite production team member should be qualified in industrial first aid.

- Allow sufficient time to brief the production team well before each major segment of the event (e.g. a briefing before tech setup, a briefing before rehearsals and sound checks, a briefing before the event, and a briefing before strike).
- Have emergency contact information for all key suppliers who are not onsite, as well as contact information for key team members onsite.

These suggestions are not intended to be exhaustive or all-inclusive and many producers have their own way of working with their team onsite. This is only a recommended starting point.

5.5   HEALTH AND SAFETY ISSUES

As with all chapters of these books where the risk of injury to workers or event attendees or the risk of damage to property are concerns, we discuss the appropriate standards or regulations that apply to the particular subject. In the case of the production team, the potential risks are associated primarily with injury to workers.

The United States and Canada are slightly different in their individual approaches to employee safety. In the USA, there is a core federal statute which is binding nationally. The Occupational Safety and Health Administration (OSHA, www.osha.gov), a US federal agency, administers the Occupational Safety and Health Act, and the associated standards, *29 CFR Part 1910, Occupational Safety and Health Standards*. These standards go into considerable detail in most of the areas in which production team members work (e.g. electrical safety, personal protective equipment, fire safety, working on scaffolding and ladders, etc.). Section 18 of the Occupational Safety and Health Act of 1970 also encourages states to develop and operate their own job safety and health programs that must be at least as stringent as the federal standards. Not all states have these programs and not all are identical. The best guidelines for worker safety for special events are ultimately the OSH standards, and producers should obtain and follow these as a minimum.

In the Canadian system, separate occupational health and safety (OHS – note different word order from the US) statutes have been enacted in individual provinces. The basic OHS statute in each jurisdiction is supported by regulations or other subsidiary legislation. As well, Part II of the *Canada Labour Code* and the *Canada Occupational Health and Safety Regulations*, apply to federal workers, venues, and jurisdictions. Both the provincial and federal regulations are typically very detailed in the areas in which event production team members work. Worksafe BC (1997) provides a good overview of the different regulations.

Of interest in the majority of these regulations are the rights of workers to the following:

- *Right to know*: This means they have the right to know the regulations, which in turn means that a copy of the regulations must be available in the workplace. They also have the right to be informed about harmful substances.
- *Right to participate*: This requires that in certain industries and companies of specific sizes, workers have the right to participate in safety committees and also that in certain industries, there must be monthly safety meetings.
- *Refusal of unsafe work*: Workers may refuse to do work they consider unsafe and shall not be disciplined for it.
- *Protection from discrimination*: This is obvious.
- *Right to protective reassignment*: This means a worker who refuses to work in unsafe conditions may be temporarily assigned to other work with no disciplinary action against that worker.

In summary, in all jurisdictions, it is recommended that event producers understand and follow all the OHS standards and regulations that pertain to them. They should keep a copy available at their workplace and at event sites. It is also a good idea if at all possible, to have at least one team member who is certified in industrial first aid onsite at all times. For further reference and reading, Van Beek (2000) provides an overview of personnel health and safety in the UK, much of which is applicable to North America.

PRODUCTION CHALLENGES

1. You have been asked to provide the stage entertainment, including a multimedia component, and decorations, for an incentive dinner at a high-end hotel. Suggest what subcontractors you may need on your team and what areas are unlikely to be your responsibility.
2. As the entertainment producer for a large outdoor world music festival with 20 international acts, all with individual managers, you are chairing a production meeting to finalize the show running order, individual act technical needs, and all setups and sound check requirements at the venue, a large public park near the ocean with two stages for the entertainment. Suggest which members of the production team and which non-members should be at the meeting. Recommend an efficient agenda for the meeting.
3. Describe in detail at least six key items of information that must be conveyed to production team members during the coordination phase.
4. You have a serious conflict with the venue catering manager during the setup for an event in his hotel. He claims that one of your trusted employees (an excellent female producer) has been very rude to him personally and has demanded that the 'housemen' in the hotel set up a larger stage than was

Continued

originally expected in a floor plan sent to the hotel 2 weeks earlier. You tell him that there is a newer floor plan that was sent last week. Unfortunately, his secretary did not give it to him. Suggest how to resolve this conflict, including body and verbal language you would use and what your personal priorities would be in this situation. The event is for a good client and the catering manager also refers a lot of business to your company.

5. What steps can you take to ensure the production team is both happy and safe onsite during an event setup and execution?

REFERENCES

Allen, J., O'Toole, W., Harris, R. and McDonnell, I. (2005). *Festival and Special Event Management*, Third Edition. Milton: John Wiley & Sons Australia, Ltd.

Bower, S.A. and Bower, G.H. (1976). *Asserting Yourself: A Practical Guide for Positive Action*. MA: Addison-Wesley.

Goldblatt, J. (2002). *Special Events: Twenty-First Century Global Event Management*. New York: John Wiley & Sons, Inc.

Justice Institute of BC. (1991a). *Conflict Resolution: Dealing with Interpersonal Conflict*. Vancouver: Justice Institute of BC, Centre for Conflict Resolution Training.

Justice Institute of BC. (1991b). *Dealing with Anger*. Vancouver: Justice Institute of BC, Centre for Conflict Resolution Training.

Robert III, H.M., Evans, W.J. and Honemann, D.H. (November 14, 2000). *Robert's Rules of Order* (Newly Revised, Tenth Edition). Cambridge: Perseus Books.

Rutherford-Silvers, J. (2004). *Professional Event Coordination*. Hoboken: John Wiley & Sons, Inc.

Van Beek, M. (2000). *A Practical Guide to Health and Safety in the Entertainment Industry*. Cambridge: Entertainment Technology Press Ltd.

Van Der Wagen, L. and Carlos, B.R. (2005). *Event Management for Tourism, Cultural, Business, and Sporting Events*. Upper Saddle River, New Jersey: Pearson Education, Inc.

Worksafe BC. (March 3, 1997). *Comparison of Occupational Health and Safety Statutes: A Briefing*. Worksafe BC. Retrieved July 14, 2006, from http://www.worksafebc.com/regulation_and_policy/archived_information/royal_commission_briefing_papers.

CONTRACT MANAGEMENT

Where would the world be without contracts? One would like to think it would be less litigious but who is going to be the first one to test the theory? Unfortunately, nobody in the special events industry will, so producers must continue to write down everything they plan to do and even make plans for things they do not want to do. This is what forms the basis of contracts and an event producer must be knowledgeable in this area or at least know the basics and where to go to get help. This chapter is a combination of personal experience and knowledge from industry experts Sheryl Daly of the BC Touring Council (Daly, 2001) and Terry Quick of ENTCO International (Quick, 2004). Contract law is a complex topic, and the chapter is not intended to be a substitute for legal advice. It is recommended that producers seek competent advice before drawing up any form contracts for their business.

Contracting during the event organization process begins during the Coordination Phase. There are two main types of contracts involving producers: those between the producer and the client, and those between the producer and suppliers. We will examine these by defining what a contract is, considering what should be included in a contract, specifying how to correctly issue and sign contracts, examining what happens when a contract is broken, and finally, determining the courses of action available to resolve disputes. We end the chapter with some sample producer/client and producer/supplier contracts from actual event companies that exemplify the variety of presentations available.

6.1   DEFINITION OF A CONTRACT

A contract is a bilateral agreement. In other words, it is between two or more persons or parties. It explains an obligation in which each party mutually acquires a right to what is promised by the other. It is a tool that outlines the details of an agreement. Most importantly, it is legally binding. A contract can also be called a letter or memorandum of agreement, a letter of confirmation, and a letter of intent.

A contract should always be in writing and should:

- use clear words and uncluttered language,
- represent and protect mutual interests,
- spell out the details of the agreement,
- withstand scrutiny in the legal sense.

Why must it be in writing? The answer is simple. A verbal or oral contract is too confusing and is hard to enforce if there is a dispute. It is far too easy for the two sides to have different recollections of what each promised to the other.

6.1.1   Elements of a Contract

The key elements of a binding contract are as follows:

- *Competent parties*: Each side must have the capacity to enter. For example, minors cannot enter into a contract without parental consent and anyone under the influence of alcohol or drugs or deemed mentally incompetent at the time of signing is not competent.
- *Consideration*: If one party is to be held to the contract, there must be something given in exchange, normally money (or possibly property or rights).
- *Meeting of the minds*: This means 'mutual assent.' Both sides must be clear about the details, rights, and obligations of the contract.

6.2 WHAT SHOULD BE INCLUDED IN A CONTRACT

There are two main parts to contracts: Terms and Conditions, and Clauses, with each one having a specific purpose.

6.2.1 Terms and Conditions

These are what can be considered the variable parts of a contract, those myriad details pertaining to a specific event. In contract law, they are considered to be essential to the contract, whereas non-essential ones are called *warranties* (Smyth and Soberman, 1976; p. 292). Terms and conditions normally comprise several specific types of information.

6.2.1.1 Contact Information

Contact information applies to both client and supplier contracts, and should include:

- The legal name of the client and producer organizations and in the case of suppliers and artists, their stage name or company or individual names.
- The name of the contact person(s) who has signing authority.
- The mailing address of both parties.
- The physical address of both parties if different from the mailing address.
- The phone and fax numbers of both parties.
- The e-mail address of both parties.

6.2.1.2 Event Details

The event details form the heart of the contract, whether it is a client or a supplier contract. They provide a summary of all the points that have been agreed upon by both parties, including:

- *Venue details*: This refers to the time and location of the event, and lists the event venue name, a specific room name if applicable, address, phone number, contact person, date, start and end times of the event, start/setup/strike times for suppliers and artists, technical and rehearsal times, and the length of performance if there is to be an entertainment show.
- *Specifics of service(s) or product(s) to be provided*: This section covers the services or products in detail and is most likely the section from which most disputes will arise. Care should be taken to ensure everything is an accurate reflection of initial conversations and written messages or letters between parties, including a list of all components to be

provided (e.g. a detailed list of lighting or audio equipment, a list of décor items and where and how they will be used, the names, types and lengths of performances, etc.) and the number of persons involved if applicable (e.g. number of performers in an act for a supplier/artist contract). If there is a strict schedule to be followed, it should also be included.

- *Specifics of additional services to be provided*: In most cases, there will be additional requirements by either the client in the case of client/producer contracts or by the producer in the case of producer/supplier contracts. For example, the client may be asked by the producer to provide the audio system, or a changing room, or food and beverages for staff. In the case of extras the producer may have to provide for suppliers, the supplier would have to ensure the same details were included in the producer/supplier contract (e.g. the need for a quick-change area behind the stage).

- *Additional insured*: Many policies for commercial and general liability (CGL) insurance now require producers to obtain copies of client and supplier policies that name the producer as an 'additional insured.' This may be included as a condition or on a rider, or it may even be a clause in these contracts. For example, for some events I produced, I used the simple wording 'A copy of client CGL insurance policy in the amount of no less than $2,000,000 naming producer as additional insured must be provided to producer no later than ... (specific date),' in contract riders with clients; however legal advice is recommended for final wording and placement. See Chapter 7 for further discussion.

- *Compliance with regulations and standards*: As discussed extensively in Chapter 7 and throughout *Special Event Production: The Resources*, compliance with safety and design regulations and standards should be part of all supplier contracts. As an example, a contract with a lighting supplier for an event in the United States might include a condition that resembles the following:

'Supplier shall comply with the following regulations and standards as a minimum.

- 29 CFR Part 1910, Occupational Safety and Health Standards for personnel safety
- National Electrical Code for all electrical installations
- National Fire Code for fire safety
- Underwriters Laboratories certification for all equipment
- ANSI E1.2-2006: Entertainment Technology – Design, Manufacture and Use of Aluminum Trusses and Towers, for all trussing used for lighting. Additionally, supplier shall make available all calculations for truss loading if and when required by producer.'

Again, legal advice is recommended for correct wording and placement.

6.2.1.3 *Financial Information*

Financial details must be extremely clear in order to avoid any potential for non-payment. Typical information includes:

- The compensation amount agreed upon by the parties for the services/products to be provided. If it is a contract that spans two or more countries, then the currency of payment should be clearly stated. It is also a wise idea to include the method and date for calculating the currency exchange rate.
- Taxes as applicable. Most countries and jurisdictions have at least one tax on the services and products of special events. These must be spelled out in detail, so there are no last-minute surprises, particularly for clients. Another reason for stating the taxes to be paid is that for some contracts spanning international boundaries, taxes may be refundable from the host government upon proof of payment for certain services and products. When one is dealing with the potentially large sums for events, this may be a significant amount for event organizers.
- Deposit amounts and deadlines. Common practice amongst most event production companies now seems to be a deposit of 50–75 percent of the total contract value upon contract signing, with the remainder due on or before the actual event date. For some extended contracts with ongoing expenses, the two parties may prefer a series of progress payments rather than a single initial deposit and final payment.

6.2.1.4 *Rider Information*

A contract rider is a special provision for services that forms an attachment to an original contract and is considered part of the contract. For special events, contract riders can take two forms. One is as an attachment to a producer/client contract, and the other is as an attachment to a producer/supplier contract.

6.2.1.4.1 Riders to Producer/Client Contracts

Most production companies have form contracts of one or two pages, usually spelling out the terms and conditions of the event and the company's boilerplate clauses. Unless the event is very simple, these pages invariably are too short and a rider detailing all the services to be provided must be added as an attachment. A separate signature line for both parties, date line for both parties, and rider title referring to the file number, date, and names of the contracting parties should also be present on the rider. This assumes that the contract for event production is issued by the production company.

6.2.1.4.2 Riders to Producer/Supplier Contracts

Producer/supplier contracts can take two forms: one being a contract issued by the producer that spells out the services or products to be provided from the point of view of the producer, and the other a contract issued by the supplier of the service or product. In the former, a rider will be similar to that in a producer/client contract. However, in the latter, especially in the case of celebrity talent or other specialized suppliers, the rider can include many additional requirements to the main contract and in some cases, the cost of the rider may approach the cost of the basic contracted services. It may include such things as transportation and accommodation requirements (e.g. first class return airfare for a certain number of persons from the performer's home, first class non-smoking hotel rooms, local limousine transportation, and similar items), food and meal requirements, green room (changing room) requirements, and technical specifics (e.g. stage plot, audio and lighting requirements, and backline equipment such as extra instruments and amplifiers). In fact, some celebrity contract riders can be up to six pages or more in length. The rider will come with the supplier contract and should in turn be passed on to, or be made part of, the producer/client contract so that no details are missed. Sonder (2004) goes into considerable detail about performer contracts.

6.2.2 Clauses

These are what may be referred to as the 'boiler plate' or fixed part of the contract. Although definitions of the word 'clauses' vary, they may also be used to further define, and expand on, some of the contract 'conditions' and hence may be placed under a heading in contracts called 'terms and conditions.' They generally do not vary from one event to the next and may include such items as:

- *Cancellation policy*: This details how much of the total value of the contract, usually as a percentage, is payable to the producer or to the supplier in the case of a cancellation by the client or producer, respectively. In other words, the client in either case does the canceling. Most event companies nowadays seem to enforce a policy that entitles them to full payment if the event is cancelled within 14 days of the event date, with a sliding scale of decreasing penalties going back from that date.
- *Termination policy*: This indicates what will happen if either party fails to perform any or all of its respective obligations. This may include the amounts payable to the parties and the amount of time and method required to indicate termination (e.g. must give 30 days notice in writing).
- *Force majeure*: This removes liability from one or more of the parties due to unavoidable circumstances preventing them from performing their obligations, such as an Act of God (e.g. snowstorm), strikes, natural disasters, or failures of third parties. Sometimes it may allow for substitutions to be made.
- *Indemnity and limitation of liability*: To indemnify a party means to protect or secure them against harm or loss. To limit liability means limiting

a party's exposure to liability for their actions. In the case of events, this type of clause may show up in a contract issued by any of the parties. It is of serious concern at this time because of the cost of liability insurance and the fact that many high-risk events are difficult and costly to insure, and none of the parties wants to be liable for possible injury or damage. In some jurisdictions, these clauses have proven hard to enforce. Many clients will not sign a contract from a producer with this type of clause in it and it will be negotiated out. It is advisable to seek legal advice before drawing up or signing a contract with an indemnity or limitation of liability clause.

- *Legal jurisdiction*: This names the province/state and municipality in which the law governing the contract resides, and where legal cases are to be heard and dealt with. It is usually the jurisdiction of the contract issuer.

- *Arbitration*: This provides for arbitration or *alternate dispute resolution* (ADR) as the preferred method for solving disputes. See Section 6.5.1.

- *Intellectual property*: Particularly in the case of producer/artist contracts, this outlines any restrictions on the recording of performances and specifies the owner of the property.

- *Performing organizations and unions*: This type of clause indicates that the contract is subject to any regulations of performing or trade unions. For example, a jazz band may be subject to the musician's union requirements for a minimum 10-min break after performing background music for a maximum of 90 min.

- *Rights of assignment*: This prevents either party from selling their interest to a third party without mutual consent.

- *Independent contractor status*: This clause specifies that the contractor is an independent contractor. It would typically be placed in a producer/supplier contract when the producer does not want to be liable for paying all supplier income taxes, wage source deductions, and Workers' Compensation Board (WCB) fees.

- *Special clauses*: Often, producers or event managers will have unique boilerplate clauses of their own for producer/client contracts based on the nature of their business. Some that have proven useful include:
  - A clause that states that electrical hookup fees, staging, and copyright license fees are normally payable by the client.
  - A clause that states that all props or equipment, unless otherwise stated in the terms of the contract, are considered rentals and any loss or damage may be billed to the client at replacement cost. This helps to cover losses of attractive props such as table arrangements.
  - A weather clause. Bernie Gaps of Absolutely Fabulous Events and Productions, Inc. in California has a rain call clause that requires clients to make an indoor/outdoor decision by noon on an event day or be liable for all contract costs (Bernie Gaps, personal communication, February 2006).

- Although the commencement of delivery of actual services constitutes the fulfillment of a contract in law even if the contract has not been signed, it is not a bad idea to specify this in a separate contract clause, to the effect that, 'commencement of this event and physical delivery of this contract constitute verification of an oral agreement and bind all parties to the terms contained herein.'

Sometimes it is preferable to have fewer strict clauses and be more flexible in the specific conditions for each event. Simplicity often works the best (i.e. it assumes honesty to start, rather than emphasizing a fear of litigation), but that is a decision to be made between a producer and lawyer.

6.3   ISSUING AND SIGNING CONTRACTS

Although issuing and signing contracts are straightforward procedures, there are some fine points of the law worth mentioning. These points apply to all types of contracts, no matter who the issuer is.

6.3.1   Issuing Contracts

Many production companies issue dozens, even hundreds, of contracts annually. Standardizing this process makes it easier to track the contracts and whether they have been signed and/or changed. Here are some considerations:

- A deadline date to receive the contract back should always be included within the contract. This is normally accompanied by an initial deposit if the contract is a producer/client one.
- At least two signed copies should be sent to the receiving party along with any riders. This applies for mailed copies. If faxed or e-mailed contracts are used, the receiver is responsible for keeping a copy. The safest method is to mail the contracts.
- If both parties (e.g. producer and supplier) want to issue their own contracts, this creates what lawyers call the 'battle of the forms.' There should be no contradictory clauses or statements in either contract. If there are, an attempt should be made for both parties to agree on whose interpretation is correct and put it in writing and/or change the offending contract and initial the change. Note that legally, any changes must be initialed by both parties to the contract for the changes to be valid. This sometimes necessitates sending the contracts back and forth several times.
- According to the 'mailbox rule,' a signed contract that is mailed is effective the moment it is deposited in a mailbox. Faxed and e-mailed contracts are generally acceptable but to be on the safe side, a mailed hard copy is best.

- A hard copy of any signed contract should be kept on file as insurance against computer crashes, theft, and data loss.
- All items on a contract are negotiable before and until the contract is signed by both parties.
- If there are any changes to a signed contract, it is always best to re-issue a revised contract that includes the revision date. If this is impossible, the receiving party should authorize changes in writing either by e-mail or fax.
- If possible, it is best to use some sort of electronic contract in order to save time. The task of issuing many contracts often with repeat suppliers, clients, and venues is made easier by using a relational database program such as Microsoft Access or one of the excellent event planning software suites available on the market. Basically, such a program enables the incorporation of many individual databases (e.g. clients, suppliers, and venues) and the creation of forms and reports (e.g. contracts) that integrate all of them. With some customization, they can be made to create all the types of contracts needed for any event by entering the data only once.

6.3.2 Signing Contracts

Again, standardization of procedures and forms is the best way to ensure contracts are complete:

- All event details and names should be checked for accuracy.
- All signatures should be dated. This applies to both parties.
- Both parties should ensure that the other party has signing authority. It is best to have the same person who signs the contract also be responsible for signing checks to minimize invoicing complications.
- If a producer is signing a supplier's contract rather than the producer's, all details should be double checked to ensure that they agree with the services/products for which the supplier is being contracted. If not, then necessary changes should be made in ink and initialed. Both parties should initial any such changes to the contract to be valid.

PRODUCTION WAR STORY:
THE HANDSHAKE CONTRACT

It was the Friday before a large themed event that was to take place on the following Monday night at a conference center ballroom, and we noticed that the client had neither signed the contract sent weeks before nor paid a deposit, although communications had been continuing up to that point with both parties

Continued

6.4   BREAKING A CONTRACT

A broken contract is one of those situations that a producer, or supplier, dreads; however, there will be instances when it will happen, especially in the events industry where contracts are very short term and there are many of them. We will examine what constitutes a breach and how to remedy it.

6.4.1 When Does a Breach Occur

Usually, the contracting parties will know when one of them breaks the contract, but for reference outlined below are the legal definitions with some simple examples:

- When one party fails to stick to their part of the agreement (e.g. a client does not pay a producer the required deposit on time, thus also making it impossible for the producer to pay a deposit to a celebrity who subsequently cancels his performance).
- When one party makes it impossible for the other to perform (e.g. a client guarantees that a venue will be available for 5 h for setup after

their afternoon meeting, but ends up going overtime and only allows 2 h for setup; the supplier has to completely drape the room in black curtains but cannot do so in the given time).

- When a party to the contract does something against the intent of the contract (e.g. a reputable comedy magician who was supposed to deliver a family show instead adds his own color in the form of 'blue' material, thus forcing mothers to cover their children's ears).
- When a party absolutely refuses to perform the contract (e.g. a producer's very experienced but somewhat irrational audio engineer states that he will not run a show unless the producer retracts comments about his mother wearing army boots).

6.4.2 What Can Be Done

For the event producer, a contract breach can spell potential disaster, especially if it is close to or possibly at an event. Although they may not avert disaster, there are some temporary remedies. These are written from a producer's point of view to make them easier to understand:

- Be firm about the contract terms and details, but remain willing to communicate.
- Remind the offending party of the agreement but be as calm as possible and try to work out differences in a rational manner.
- Consider alternative solutions that may solve the problem in order to buy time until the event is over.
- Try to get a third neutral party involved to assist.
- If the breach occurs at a non-critical time in relation to the execution of the event or if the differences between the parties are such that the event can still proceed at least under a slightly modified agreement, then after the event ensure that all differences and specifics are immediately conveyed in writing between the offending parties.

6.5   RESOLVING DISPUTES

After everything has been tried when a contract breach occurs, and all details of differences have been recorded, there are several methods available to settle disputes.

6.5.1 Alternate Dispute Resolution

ADR is cheaper and more expeditious than litigation. It allows the parties to sit down together, sometimes with a qualified and trained third party, to come to an agreement. It includes negotiation, mediation, conciliation, and arbitration in increasing order of complexity, and decreasing amount of decision-making control by the parties. Event producers should seriously consider ADR as a contract clause.

6.5.1.1 Negotiation

This is the simplest form of ADR and gives the disputing parties the most control over the outcome. It is the conferring of the two parties with each other, without the assistance of a neutral party, with the purpose of arriving at a settlement (Justice Institute of BC, 1991; p. 97). Occasionally, a neutral third party may be brought in to simply keep the parties talking and to record proceedings.

6.5.1.2 Mediation

Mediation brings in a neutral third party intervener (mediator) to facilitate the process but not to impose a solution (Justice Institute of BC, 1991; p. 96). The parties select the mediator and once selected, the mediator arranges the mediation process. The mediator makes no decisions, but acts as a facilitator only to assist the parties to understand the dispute, to provide structured discussion, and to help the parties reach a dispute settlement agreement. If the parties cannot reach a settlement agreement, they are free to pursue other options. The parties generally decide in advance how they will contribute to the cost of the mediation. Mediation is a very important form of ADR, particularly if the parties wish to preserve their relationship (Verge, 2000). It is more structured than negotiation.

6.5.1.3 Conciliation

Conciliation also uses a neutral third party to act as a go-between and to re-establish the relationship. In conciliation, more control is vested in the conciliator, who is usually seen as an authority figure responsible for determining the best solution for the parties. The conciliator, not the parties, often develops and proposes the terms of settlement. The parties come to the conciliator seeking guidance and the parties make decisions about proposals made by the conciliator (Sgubini, 2006). The parties must decide in advance whether they will be bound by the conciliator's recommendations for settlement. The parties generally share equally in the cost of the conciliation (Verge, 2000).

6.5.1.4 Arbitration

In arbitration, the opposing parties choose a neutral third party (arbitrator) or a panel of arbitrators to listen to each disputant and to make a decision that is binding on them. Costs of the arbitration are disposed of as part of the settlement unless the parties have agreed otherwise beforehand. Arbitration removes all decision-making authority from the two parties. Because of this, there is less likelihood of the prior relationship being maintained after the process.

6.5.2   Small Claims Court

In most jurisdictions, these are typically used to recover disputed amounts that are under a specified value. They are quite simple to work in and an individual company owner or event producer can easily go through the process without a lawyer, although some professional help is always wise. There are some cautions, however. First, the process can be very lengthy and can take over a year just to get to court, mainly because of the backlog of court cases. Second, even if one wins in court, there is no guarantee that payment will be forthcoming from the offending party, and the hardest part often comes after the court judgment in trying to collect on the judgment. This can get into the costly use of bailiffs to recover property to sell to provide the debt payment.

6.5.3   Litigation

This assumes that the disputed amount is over the maximum value for small claims court, which can be different amongst jurisdictions. It is to be avoided at all costs, particularly for small businesses unless the amount at stake is very high, as it can sap a lot of energy and cash. If it happens, expert legal advice and probably very deep pockets will be required.

The best way to settle breaches of contract is between the two parties directly with each one being willing to see the other's point of view. A little humility never hurt anyone and in the case of an event producer looking to establish a reputation, it just may help to save that reputation. That being said, if the breach involves only the lack of payment of the contract amount or part of it and all other services have been delivered as required, then the best defense is a continued, polite attack on accounts receivable, either personal or through a collection agency. See Chapter 3 for more details.

6.6   SAMPLE CONTRACTS AND RIDERS

At the end of this chapter are appendices with several sample contracts, riders, and forms. These samples should provide producers with ample model templates for their own contracts. However, it is strongly recommended that legal advice be sought within producers' own jurisdictions before using any of these forms.

- Appendix A: This is a Simple Client Contract that contains a minimum number of clauses, and even those that have been included are very simple. Specific details of each event are normally completed either on the contract itself or as a rider if space is insufficient on the main page of the contract.
- Appendix B: This is a Medium Complex Client Contract, the main body of which contains all the clauses, and the details of every event are specified on a rider. This type of contract more strictly binds the client.
- Appendix C: Courtesy of Marc Wright at www.simply-communicate. com in the United Kingdom, this is a complete, complex producer/client contract plus a sample budget form, a payment schedule form, a production schedule form, and a project change notice (useful for documenting changes to contracted services).
- Appendix D: This is a sample rider to a producer/client equipment rental contract for equipment that will be used by individual members of the client's group. Typical examples of this type of equipment include any physical activity equipment such as dunk tanks, simulators, or carnival games and rides.
- Appendix E: This is a sample waiver form that each individual participant using the rented equipment of Appendix D would have to sign. It may be attached to a producer/client contract and referred to as a 'Schedule' as it is in this instance.
- Appendix F: This is a basic producer/supplier contract with easy-to-read clauses.
- Appendix G: This is a sample rider to a supplier contract that outlines some general requirements for suppliers.
- Appendices H and I: They are alternatives to the producer/supplier contract and its rider, respectively.

PRODUCTION CHALLENGES

1. You have been asked by a mother to produce an expensive bar mitzvah for her son. Being unfamiliar with contract law, she is surprised when you send her a written contract. What would you say to her to explain why a written contract is needed?
2. You are an event producer based in Sydney, Australia and will be producing a large incentive event in Thailand for a client from Shanghai, China. You have reached an agreement on what you will provide through weeks of dialog with the operations manager in Shanghai and are ready to send a contract when you learn that the head office of the company is located in Beijing and your deposit and final payment will be coming from there. How do you determine the correct client information to put on the contract, and in what currency will the contracted amount be?

Continued

PRODUCTION CHALLENGES (CONTD.)

3. Your production company has strict dress and conduct rules for suppliers and performers. What is a good contractual method to use to ensure that they abide by these rules?

4. You have just signed and sent a contract to a client for a $50,000 event that is less than a week away, after spending much time and effort creating a mind-blowing multimedia show. Your client has so far verbally agreed to everything but suddenly calls to say the event is cancelled. If your company policy requires that a 100 percent fee be paid for cancellations of less than 7 days, would you charge a cancellation fee and why or why not? If you would, how much would it be?

5. After trying for 6 months to be paid the remaining $5000 of a $20,000 invoice for a highly successful event, you have decided to take stronger action than e-mails and letters to recover the amount. Explain the possible courses of action you can take.

REFERENCES

Daly, S. (April 2001). Contracts Pertaining to the Performing Arts. Paper presented at *Pacific Contact 2001*, Burnaby, BC, Canada, sponsored by the BC Touring Council for the Performing Arts.

Justice Institute of BC (1991). *Negotiation Skills*. Vancouver: Justice Institute of BC.

Quick, T. (2004). Understanding Contracts. *Hot Tips for Events That Sizzle*. Vancouver: Total Events and Meeting Network, pp. 87–93.

Sgubini, A. (2006). Arbitration, mediation and conciliation: differences and similarities from an International and Italian business perspective. Retrieved March 10, 2006, from http://www.mediate.com/articles/sgubiniA2.cfm.

Smyth, J.E. and Soberman, D.A. (1976). *The Law and Business Administration in Canada, Third Edition*. Scarborough: Prentice-Hall of Canada, Ltd.

Sonder, M. (2004). *Event Entertainment and Production*. Hoboken: John Wiley & Sons, Inc.

Verge, D.C. (2000). Arbitration mediation. Retrieved March 10, 2007, from http://www.goodbyecourts.com/index.html.

Simple Producer/Client Contract

ABC EVENT COMPANY LTD.

MEMORANDUM OF AGREEMENT

Production No: 02120507   Producer: Arthur Fancypants

THIS AGREEMENT made and entered into on this date, April 15, 2007 by and between

(Organization):   XYZ Insurance Co.

by (Contact):   Joan Getalife
hereinafter called the CLIENT, and
ABC Event Company Ltd., as Producer.

The Producer agrees to present the following:

7:00–9:00 p.m. – Background music by the Musical Marvels jazz ensemble

9:00–10:00 p.m. – Stage show by the Fabulous Friars comedy troupe

All audio and lighting to be included. Setup and sound check at 5:00 p.m.

At Best Sleep Hotel   On December 5, 2007
5490 West Honeysuckle St., Vancouver, BC   Time of Show(s): 7:00 p.m.
In Pinnacle Ballroom   Length of Show: 1 h

For this program, I/We the undersigned agree to pay
ABC Event Company Ltd. the sum of:

$10,000.00 plus $0.00 PST plus $700.00 GST = $10,700.00
(GST Reg.#Rl23904997)

Advance due with return of signed Agreement Memo: $7500.00

---

1. Payment: 75 percent of contract value due with return of signed Agreement Memo within 14 days of receipt. Remainder due 14 DAYS PRIOR TO EVENT. Producer reserves right to withhold services if a signed Agreement Memo and payments are not received in accordance with this schedule. Terms on unpaid additional amounts: 2 percent per month after 7 days.

2. Commencement of this event and physical delivery of this contract constitute verification of an oral agreement and bind all parties to the terms contained herein.

3. Cancellation Policy: Greater than 60 days prior to event, no penalty; 59–30 days prior to event, 25 percent of contracted amount; 29–15 days prior to event, 50 percent of contracted amount; 14 days or less prior to event, 100 percent of contracted amount.

4. It is agreed that in case of emergency or act of God preventing act(s) or supplier(s) scheduled from appearing, suitable substitutions may be made, subject to Client approval.

5. This binding agreement between parties hereto shall be governed by all rules and regulations of unions involved and is subject to the return of signed contracts by act(s)/supplier(s). Client shall be notified within 14 days of the date of this contract of any act/supplier's non-acceptance.

6. It is understood that any props or equipment utilized for the above event shall be considered as rentals and any loss or damage caused by the Client's guests may be billed at replacement cost by the Producer. Costs of staging, electrical power hookup, facilities and copyright license fees are not included in above prices unless otherwise specified.

7. This binding agreement between parties hereto shall be governed by the laws of the Province of British Columbia, Canada and any action initiated to enforce the terms of this contract by or against the Producer or by or against act(s)/supplier(s), will have its sole and exclusive forum in the City of Vancouver, British Columbia, Canada.

ACCEPTED BY CLIENT _____

DATE: _____

ABC EVENT COMPANY LTD. _____

ABC Event Company Ltd.
1234 Main St. Vancouver, BC, Canada V4R 5T7
Phone: 123-567-8901; Fax: 123-456-7890;
E-mail: info@abceventcompany.com

Appendix B

Complex Producer/Client Contract

ABC EVENT COMPANY LTD.

SERVICES AGREEMENT

This agreement for services is between ABC Event Company Ltd. and the Client indicated below. This agreement is effective on the date last signed below.

1. **Services:** ABC Event Company Ltd. will perform the services noted on Exhibit A attached ('Services') for the Event and on the date(s) and location indicated thereon. Client's responsibilities in connection with the Services are also outlined on Exhibit A. Client acknowledges that ABC Event Company Ltd. will commence providing the Services upon execution hereof by both parties.

2. **Compensation:** As compensation for the Services, Client will pay ABC Event Company Ltd. the compensation indicated on Exhibit A ('Compensation'). Compensation does [not] include the costs associated with all entertainment, subcontracted services, equipment rentals, and the like to be provided and/or coordinated by ABC Event Company Ltd. Such costs, if not included in the Compensation, shall be paid directly by Client when due.

3. **Contact Persons:** The Contact Persons for the Services for ABC Event Company Ltd. and for the Client are listed on Exhibit A. ABC Event Company Ltd. may assign any one or more of its representatives to perform the Services.

4. **Proprietary Contacts:** Client understands that ABC Event Company Ltd. is in the business of event planning and coordination and as such, its contacts, suppliers, contractors, entertainers, and the like ('Proprietary Contacts') are considered by ABC Event Company Ltd. as proprietary and a valuable business asset. Client agrees that for a 2-year period after the date hereof Client will not directly or indirectly contact, except through ABC Event Company Ltd., any of the Proprietary Contacts. If Client should breach this provision, as liquidated damages therefore, Client shall promptly pay ABC Event Company Ltd. its then current commission for the type of service provided to the Client by or through the Proprietary Contact.

5. **Limitation of Liability:** Client understands that all of the Proprietary Contacts are independent contractors to ABC Event Company Ltd. ABC Event Company Ltd. will make reasonable efforts to secure quality Proprietary Contacts for the Event but cannot guarantee the quality of performance and/or services of such contractors and will not be

liable for such contractors' acts, errors and/or omissions including their failure to provide the required services. Further, if ABC Event Company Ltd. is providing any third party products as part of the Services, ABC EVENT COMPANY LTD. MAKES NO REPRESENTATIONS OR WARRANTIES OF ANY KIND, EXPRESS OR IMPLIED, INCLUDING BUT NOT LIMITED TO THE WARRANTIES OF MERCHANTABILITY AND FITNESS FOR A PARTICULAR PUR-POSE, WITH REGARD TO THOSE PRODUCTS. In any event, ABC Event Company Ltd.'s liability for any and all claims shall be limited to the amount of Compensation actually earned by ABC Event Company Ltd. from the item giving rise to the claim and under no circumstances shall ABC Event Company Ltd. be liable for indirect or consequential damages, including lost profits.

6. **Bad Weather, Unforeseen Events:** ABC Event Company Ltd. shall not be responsible for events beyond its reasonable control which negatively affect the Event or the Services, including but not limited to rain, snow, fire, flood, earthquake, lightning or other acts of God; acts of civil or military authority; wars; riots; strikes; and sabotage. In all such cases, the Client shall remain responsible for the Compensation payable to ABC Event Company Ltd.

7. **Insurance:** Client will maintain general liability insurance for the Event in the amount of at least $1,000,000 per occurrence naming ABC Event Company Ltd. as an additional insured. If requested, Client will promptly deliver a Certificate of Insurance indicating the above to ABC Event Company Ltd.

8. **Termination:** Either party may terminate this Agreement at any time upon 30 days written notice to the other. In the event of such early ter-mination, ABC Event Company Ltd. shall be entitled to the Compensation for the Services performed through the effective date of termination, including but not limited to compensation for time spent, contractors engaged, deposits made, and the like.

The parties have executed this Agreement as a document under seal to be construed in accordance with the laws of the State of Louisiana, USA.

ABC EVENT COMPANY LTD.   CLIENT

x _____   x _____

Arthur Fancypants, President   Joan Getalife

DATE: _____   DATE: _____

ABC Event Company Ltd.
1234 Main St., New Orleans, LA 76543, USA
Phone: 123-567-8901; Fax: 123-456-7890;
E-mail: info@abceventcompany.com

ABC EVENT COMPANY LTD.

EXHIBIT A

CLIENT:

EVENT:

DATE(S):

LOCATION:

DESCRIPTION OF SERVICES
PROVIDED BY ABC EVENT COMPANY LTD.:

DESCRIPTION OF CLIENT
RESPONSIBILITIES:

COMPENSATION AND TERMS
OF PAYMENT:

CONTACT PERSONS:

ABC EVENT COMPANY LTD: Arthur Fancypants: 123-567-8901

CLIENT: Joan Getalife: 123-765-4321

ABC Event Company Ltd.
1234 Main St., New Orleans, LA 76543, USA
Phone: 123-567-8901; Fax: 123-456-7890;
E-mail: info@abceventcompany.com

Appendix C

Complete Producer/Client Contract with Budget, Schedule, and Change Forms (Courtesy Marc Wright, www.simply-communicate.com)

CONTRACT

1. This agreement is between (**The Production Company**) and (**The Client**).
2. (**The Production Company**) is commissioned by (**The Client**) to produce (**Project Name**) at (**Location**) on (**Date**).
3. The budget for the contract is (**amount in numerals, excluding taxes**), full details of which are contained in Schedule 1, found on page 2 of this contract.
4. The Terms and Conditions of trading are set out in Schedule 2, which is included with this contract on page 4.
5. The Payment Terms of the contract are set out in Schedule 3, which is detailed on page 6. Purchase orders must be issued by (**The Client**) for each payment stage, and these stages are as follows:
   - 30 percent on commissioning – in order to secure the availability of the above personnel and to cover pre-production expenses;
   - 40 percent of staging and equipment costs – to be paid by the eve of the event;
   - balance – to be paid within 30 days of the event's completion.
6. Any budget revisions will be agreed between (**The Production Company**) and (**The Client**) using a PCN (Project Change Notice) prior to any additional investment being undertaken. (An example of a PCN is included with this contract as Appendix 1.)
7. The Outline Production Schedule, detailed in Schedule 4, is found on page 7 of this contract.

Signed for and on behalf of:

(**The Production Company**)	(**The Client**)
Date:	Date:
Name:	Name:
Position:	Position:

Schedule 1: Budget

Name of Event:

No.	Item	Billing	Billing Total
1	**Production Fees**		
	(a) Pre- and Post-production		
	(b) On-Site Time		
	Subtotal		
2	**Software**		
	(a) Generation of Speaker Support Graphics for Main Event		
	(b) Editing of Conference Material		
	Subtotal		
3	**Technical Equipment** All equipment is based upon a 2-day hire		
	(a) Set		
	(b) Sound		
	(c) Lighting		
	(d) Video equipment		
	(e) Cameras		
	(f) Recording equipment		
	(g) Graphics equipment		
	(h) Transport		
	(i) PC equipment for Breakouts		
	Subtotal		
4	**On-Site Crewing**		
	(a) On-Site Crew		
	Subtotal		
5	**Site Survey**		
	(a) Production Team site survey		
	Subtotal		

No.	Item	Billing	Billing Total

6   On-Site Travel and Subsistence
   (a)   Production Team
        Subsistence
        Travel
   (b)   Crew
        Subsistence
        Travel

       Subtotal

7   Insurance
   (a)   Producers' indemnity insurance
   (b)   Crew insurance
   (c)   Event insurance

       Subtotal

8   Management Fee

       Subtotal

       Grand Total

Exclusions:

Tax

Couriers

Copies of edited videos

Delivery of videos worldwide

Please note that costs do not include tax (e.g. GST, VAT, sales taxes, etc.)

Schedule 2: Terms and Conditions

Charges: Costs, charges, and expenses, as shall be agreed for the supply of any goods and services, will be exclusive of tax unless otherwise stated. The Production Company reserves the right to make additional charges in respect of extra costs, charges, and expenses incurred, caused or arising out of changes and additions ordered by The Client, after the acceptance of The Production Company's estimate, proposal, and schedule. Such additions will only be chargeable once a budget amendment has been agreed to and signed by The Client.

Confidentiality: The Production Company assures The Client of total confidentiality and security on the content of all presentations, conferences, programs, speeches, or productions. Any reproduction from tapes in whole or part will only be with The Client's permission. The Production Company shall not divulge or communicate to any person, persons, or company any of the trade secrets, secret or confidential material, operations, processes, or dealings concerning the organization, business, finance transactions, or affairs of The Client, which may come to its knowledge during the production of the event.

Client Material: The Production Company will take reasonable care of any Client's property held by it but will do so at The Client's risk, and The Production Company will not be liable for any loss or damage however caused. The insurance of such property will be the responsibility of The Client.

Liabilities: The Production Company shall not be liable for any failure or delay in the supply of its services caused by any acts of force majeure or any dispute, fire, accident, civil commotion, government action, or any other cause beyond its control; and The Production Company will not be liable for any loss, damage, or expense suffered by The Client or any third party arising directly or indirectly from any of the matters referred to in this condition. The Production Company shall not be liable for any consequential loss incurred by The Client howsoever arising and the liability (if any) on any other account shall be limited to the amount of The Production Company's charges to The Client in respect of the matter in question. For the avoidance of doubt, the default or failure of any subcontractors or suppliers engaged by The Production Company will be taken to be acts within the control of The Production Company for the purposes of this condition.

Indemnity: The Client shall indemnify The Production Company against all or any costs, claims, damages, demands, and expenses that may be incurred by or made against The Production Company by any third party by reason of negligence on the part of The Client.

Cancellation: In the event of the cancellation of a project after the contract is agreed, The Production Company will charge for all work undertaken plus a 15 percent fee up to 60 days before the event. Thereafter, a charge of 50 percent of the contract total up to 30 days before the event, 80 percent up to 15 days before the event, and 100 percent of the contract total within 2 weeks of the event start date. In the event of delays or postponements not caused by The Production Company and/or its subcontractors, any costs incurred will be passed on to The Client.

Waiver: The waiver or non-enforcement by The Production Company of any breach or non-observance of these conditions shall not prevent the subsequent enforcement of these conditions in full and shall not be deemed a waiver of any subsequent breach.

Jurisdiction: These conditions shall be governed and construed according to United States Law and the parties irrevocably submit to the non-exclusive jurisdiction of United States Courts.

Project Change Notification: Should The Client require further services or amendments outside the agreed project investment, or should materials supplied by The Production Company reduce significantly, a PCN will be issued to The Client for approval before the appropriate action is taken (see Appendix 1).

Production Schedule: A Production Schedule is provided as part of this Contract, which outlines deadlines for tasks to be completed by The Production Company and The Client. Any deadlines that are not adhered to by The Client may result in an increase in their investment.

Schedule 3: Payment Terms

Payment Stage	Total	Issue Date	Payment Terms	Total
Deposit Payment	30%		Immediately	(30% of Projected Total)
Second Payment	40%		30 Days from Issue Date	(40% of Projected Total)
Balance Payment	30% (including any PCN calculations)		30 Days from Issue Date	(Balance)

Schedule 4: Outline Production Schedule

Week No.	Date	Activity	Action
10			
9			
8			
7			
6			
5			
4			
3			
2			
1			

Appendix 1: Project Change Notice

(Client)   PCN Date:

(Client Address)   PCN Number:

(Project Name and No.)

As agreed, please find detailed below the budget revisions for this project. We would be grateful if you could sign and return this agreement to (**The Production Company**) at your earliest convenience.

Current Running Total For Project		$
Details (Insert details of any items to be added)	**+$ (Amount)**	
(Insert details of any items to be removed)	**−$ (Amount)**	
PCN Total		$ Total of Detail
Revised Running Total For Project		$

Please note that costs do not include tax (e.g. GST, VAT, sales taxes, etc.)

Signed for and on behalf of:

(**The Production Company**)   (**The Client**)

Date: Date:

Name: Name:

Position: Position:

Appendix D

Rider to Equipment Rental Contract

ABC EVENT COMPANY LTD.

CONTRACT RIDER FOR EQUIPMENT RENTAL

1. Title to the Equipment shall remain with Lessor at all times. The only right to the Equipment granted to the Lessee is the right to retain and use the Equipment during the Term upon and subject to the terms of this contract.

2. The Lessee shall ensure that the Equipment is returned to the Lessor at the expiration of the Term. If the Lessee fails to do so, then in addition to any other damages the Lessor may suffer as a result of the Lessee's breach of this contract for which the Lessee shall be liable, the Lessee shall also pay to the Lessor for each 24-h period or part thereof after expiry of the Term and prior to the return of the Equipment to the Lessor over holding rent at the agreed rates.

3. The Lessee will use the Equipment only at the address on this Rental Contract.

4. The Lessee will use and operate the Equipment in a prudent and careful manner and in accordance with all instructions supplied with the Equipment by the Lessor, printed on the Equipment, or given verbally or in writing by the owners or employees of ABC Event Company Ltd. The Lessee will not alter the Equipment in any fashion and will take reasonable care to safeguard it from damage, theft, unreasonable wear and tear, and other loss. The Lessee shall ensure that the Equipment is returned to the Lessor in the same condition as it was in at the time of delivery to the Lessee under this contract.

5. The Lessee uses the Equipment at its own risk. The Lessor shall have no liability to the Lessee or any third party for any loss, damage, injury, or death caused by the Equipment or use thereof during the Term and thereafter, prior to acceptance of its return by the Lessor. The Lessee shall indemnify and save the Lessor harmless from and against any and all claims, demands, liabilities, losses, costs, damages, and expenses that may be suffered or incurred by the Lessor arising from any damage to or loss of property, or injury to or death of any person arising from the use, operation, storage, or transportation of the Equipment at any time after its delivery to the Lessee and prior to acceptance of its return by the Lessor

6. In the event that the Lessee breaches any term of this contract, the Lessor may at any time thereafter terminate this contract, with or

without notice to the Lessee. Whether or not it has terminated this contract, the Lessor may, in the event of default by the Lessee, demand immediate return of the Equipment and shall be entitled to repossess the same by any method permitted by law. In so doing, the Lessor, its employees, and agents may use reasonable force to gain entry to any premises of the Lessee where the Equipment may be located without liability for damage caused or for trespass or any other liability whatsoever. The Lessee shall be liable for all costs, expenses, and damages of the Lessor associated with the Lessee's default, including the costs of enforcement and repossession. No termination of this contract as a result of the Lessee's default shall relieve the Lessee from any of its obligations to the Lessor, including the obligation relating to the return of the Equipment, payment of rent and indemnification of the Lessor, nor shall the Lessor's election to terminate this contract or to repossess the Equipment preclude the Lessor from exercising any other remedies available to it at law for the Lessee's breach of contract including its right to claim and recover damages for breach of contract.

7.   This contract shall be governed by the laws of the province/state of British Columbia.

8.   This contract may not and shall not be assigned by the Lessee without the prior written consent of the Lessor.

By: _____

    ABC Event Company Ltd. (Lessor)

By: _____

    Lessee

ABC Event Company Ltd.
1234 Main St. Vancouver, BC, Canada V4R 5T7
Phone: 123-567-8901; Fax: 123-456-7890;
E-mail: info@abceventcompany.com

Participant Waiver for Equipment Rental Contract

ABC EVENT COMPANY LTD.

SCHEDULE A

PARTICIPANT'S DECLARATION, WAIVER, AND INDEMNITY AGREEMENT

WHEREAS:

A.   ABC Event Company Ltd. owns a 'Dunk Tank' (the 'Tank'), being a tank filled with water above which a chair is suspended. A volunteer sits in the chair and is dropped into the water when someone hits a target on the tank with a thrown ball;

B.   The Tank is being used for fund raising or other purposes by _____ (the 'Operator');

C.   The undersigned (the 'Participant') has agreed to sit in the chair and be dunked in the Tank;

D.   ABC Event Company Ltd. and the Operator have agreed to permit the Participant to operate the Tank, but only on the terms and conditions set out herein:

TERMS AND CONDITIONS

By signing this Agreement, the Participant declares and agrees:

1.   That I have sought and obtained all information and instructions necessary for me to fully understand, use, and operate the Tank safely in the manner for which it was designed.

2.   That I am aware of all the risks associated with the use and operation of the Tank including, without limitation, potential property damage, injury, or death which could result from perils such as drowning or anxiety.

3.   That I:
  a)   am in good physical and mental health;
  b)   have provided satisfactory written proof that I am older than 19 years of age;

c) am not under the influence of any alcohol or drug;

d) will not use the Tank in any manner that is illegal, unlawful, or may cause damage to the Tank or any other public or private property, or injure or endanger any person's life.

PARTICIPANT'S LIABILITY AND INDEMNITY

4. That I will be fully liable for and hereby agree to indemnify and hold ABC Event Company Ltd. and the Operator and their respective officers, directors, employees, representatives, and affiliates harmless from and against all losses, costs (including without limitation costs of insurance deductibles or increased insurance premiums resulting from or associated with any loss or claim by ABC Event Company Ltd. on any insurance maintained by ABC Event Company Ltd.), damages, expenses, fines, liabilities, lawsuits, judgments, property damage, injury, or death arising out of or in any way related to the Tank.

WAIVER OF ALL CLAIMS

5. That I elect to use the Tank at my own risk and absolutely and irrevocably release ABC Event Company Ltd. from all claims, including without limitation any claim against the ABC Event Company Ltd. based in contract or negligence for any losses, costs, damages, expenses, fines, liabilities, property damage, injury, or death whatsoever occurring or arising.

6. That I acknowledge that neither ABC Event Company Ltd. nor the Operator has made any representations or warranties to me regarding the Tank, and have not agreed to train, instruct, or educate me on the safe operation of tanks, or evaluate my knowledge or abilities.

7. That I have read and understood all of the terms of this Agreement and, in consideration for ABC Event Company Ltd. and the Operator permitting me to use the Tank, I agree on behalf of myself and my personal representatives and assigns to be bound by each and every term of this Agreement.

IN WITNESS WHEREOF the Participant has signed and delivered this Agreement this _____ day of_____, 20___.

_____   _____
Signature of Witness   Signature of Participant

Name:_____   Name:_____

ABC Event Company Ltd.
1234 Main St., New Orleans, LA 76543, USA
Phone: 123-567-8901 Fax: 123-456-7890
E-mail: info@abceventcompany.com

Producer/Supplier Contract

ABC EVENT COMPANY LTD.

STANDARD FORM CONTRACT

The Undersigned engages the Artist(s)/Supplier(s) named hereinafter for the engagement/work described below, subject to all of the provisions contained herein or attached to this contract, which conditions are hereby a part of the agreement:

Name of Act/Supplier: The Best Party Band   **Contact Person:** James Smith

Address: 12345 - 57A Avenue, Vancouver,   **Phone:** 345-987-5432
BC, V7F 2L4

Fax: 345-987-3210

Production No: 07120701   **Client:** Honest Jake's
Insurance Co.

Performance Date: December 7, 2007   **Show Time:** 9:00 p.m.

Type of Event: Christmas Party

Performance Location: Rest Easy Hotel   **Room:** Ballroom

Address: 49th Street, Vancouver,
BC V5R 5U6

Report to: Barry Jones   **1/2 HOUR BEFORE SHOWTIME/
START OF EVENT**

FEE: $3800.00 + Tax: $266.00 = $4066.00

Details of Performance/Work:

The Best Party Band, 7-piece band to play for dancing, 9:00 p.m.–1:00 a.m. Fee includes all sound and lights. Setup and sound check time TBA. A greenroom has been requested.

1. It is understood that the artist(s)/supplier(s) execute(s) this contract as an independent contractor(s) and is/are not an employee(s) of ABC Event Company Ltd. As such, artist(s)/supplier(s) understand(s) that it is his/her/their responsibility to submit all CPP, WCB, and income tax payments as required by the Governments of British Columbia and Canada.

2. Artist(s)/supplier(s) must contact ABC Event Company Ltd. prior to commencing work/the engagement for any change of instructions.

3. Any overtime must be authorized by Client, and any problems or disputes must be reported to ABC Event Company Ltd. within 24 h following engagement/completion of work.

4. Artist(s)/supplier(s) is/are responsible for their own equipment, appropriate costumes/attire, and control of performance/work, as well as all matters of public safety. This includes holding liability and equipment insurance.

5. Artist(s)/supplier(s) shall not consume food or drink in performing area unless authorized by Client.

6. All contracts are subject to receipt of signed Memorandum of Agreement by Producer from Client. In case of emergency or act of God preventing artist(s)/supplier(s) from appearing/commencing work, suitable substitution may be made.

7. ABC Event Company Ltd. cancellation policy is: greater than 60 days prior to event, no payment; 59–30 days prior to event, 25 percent of contracted amount; 29–15 days prior to event, 50 percent of contracted amount; 14 days or less prior to event, 100 percent of contracted amount. However, if Client fails to pay and a settlement cannot be reached, ABC Event Company Ltd. will endeavor to negotiate a fair settlement with artist/supplier when possible.

8. It is understood that all future engagements/work resulting from above performance/work (e.g. request made directly to artist/supplier by Client or by one of Client's guests) up to 18 months following the date of this engagement/work shall be contracted by ABC Event Company Ltd.

In Witness whereof, we have signed this Contract on the day and year written below.

Name of Act/Supplier: _____

By: _____

Date: _____

ABC Event Company Ltd., Producer

By: _____

Date: _____

PLEASE SIGN AND RETURN ONE COPY WITHIN 14 DAYS TO:

ABC Event Company Ltd.
1234 Main St., Vancouver, BC, Canada V4R 5T7
Phone: 123-567-8901; Fax: 123-456-7890;
E-mail: info@abceventcompany.com

Appendix G

Rider to a Producer/Supplier Contract

ABC EVENT COMPANY LTD.

In order to present the most professional image possible and to maintain good working relationships with our clients and venue staffs, we ask for your cooperation in adhering to the following guidelines:

1. Once you have signed a contract with ABC Event Company Ltd. you are considered to be working *for* ABC Event Company Ltd., and no other company, whether it is your own or someone else's. In such capacity, you will be expected to conduct yourself professionally and with courtesy at all times. When first contacting clients or venue staff, please identify yourself by name and the fact that you are representing ABC Event Company Ltd. If, for any reason, disputes arise over any matter, ABC Event Company Ltd. must be notified as soon as possible if no company representative is on site.

2. Prior to any load-in of equipment or decor and prior to any setup of equipment or décor at a venue, the crew supervisor will report to the Banquet Captain in charge or to the appropriate venue manager to ascertain:
    *   The correct location to park vehicles for unloading and how long the vehicle may remain there.
    *   The correct route to take to load-in equipment.
    *   Any scheduling problems.
    *   Any special requirements (e.g. request for no noise, etc.).

3. The same procedure as in (2) shall be followed for equipment strike at the end of an event.

4. The **minimum** dress for **all** technical personnel (e.g. decorators, technicians, and laborers) shall be clean T-shirt and work pants (same for males or females). Whenever possible, all personnel shall wear a clean ABC Event Company Ltd. T-shirt (available at no charge at the company office). Technicians (e.g. audio and lighting) on duty at events shall wear shirts, ties, sports jacket and slacks as a minimum. Performers shall **always** wear appropriate stage attire (except when a costume is called for). Blue jeans and scruffy clothes are not acceptable.

5. All technical staff, decorators, and performers shall re-check the details of their contracts with ABC Event Company Ltd. at least 48 h prior to an event.

6. For those required to meet a schedule (e.g. setup of decor), a re-check of contract details is vital, and any deadlines that are not met **may**

immediately following the engagement for billing and payment purposes. Any additional time will be prorated and billed to the client by ABC Event Company Ltd.

PLEASE NOTE: In signing this form, I agree that I am being engaged as an independent contractor. I am aware that ABC Event Company Ltd. issues 1099's for this purpose. I have read and agreed to the additional terms and conditions on the next page. (Please initial) _____

Make Check Payable to: _____

Social Security #: _____   Federal ID#: _____

Are you incorporated?   YES: _____   NO: _____

_____   _____
Artist Signature   ABC Event Company Ltd., Producer, Signature

Please sign the contract and return it to ABC Event Company Ltd. Please see Additional Terms and Conditions on the reverse of this contract. Retain a copy for your records.

ABC Event Company Ltd.
1234 Main St., New Orleans, LA 76543, USA
Phone: 123-567-8901; Fax: 123-456-7890;
E-mail: info@abceventcompany.com

Alternate Rider to a Producer/Performer Contract

ABC EVENT COMPANY LTD.

ADDITIONAL TERMS AND CONDITIONS

1. Do not discuss fees with Client.
2. Payment will be made through the ABC Event Company Ltd. office on the first and fifteenth of each month. If you play on the first, you will be paid on the fifteenth of the month. If you play on the fifteenth, you will be paid on the first of the next month. Do not try to negotiate overtime rates with the Client. It is your responsibility to report any overtime played to your respective producer immediately following the engagement.
3. Unless invited, we ask that you do not drink on the job. Many clients complain that the musicians take advantage of the buffet lines and open bars at their expense.
4. Be on time: Give yourself plenty of time in order to start the engagement promptly!
5. Look your best. Costumes or tuxedo attire are requested unless otherwise stated in this agreement.
6. Only ABC Event Company Ltd. cards are to be handed out at ABC Event Company Ltd. events. To do otherwise will seriously jeopardize your credibility and future work potential through this office.
7. This contract is not subject to cancellation without written agreement of both parties and notification delivered in writing to ABC Event Company Ltd.
8. Performer(s) agree to refer any and all offers of future engagements resulting from the above engagement to ABC Event Company Ltd.
9. It is expressly agreed that ABC Event Company Ltd. acts herein as Producer, and is not responsible for any act of commission or omission on the part of either Client or Performer.
10. Be sure to insert your social security number or federal employment ID numbers. Failure to do so may cause a delay in payment for a completed engagement.
11. This contract cannot be assigned or transferred without the prior written consent of the Producer.

ABC Event Company Ltd.
1234 Main St., New Orleans, LA 76543, USA
Phone: 123-567-8901; Fax: 123-456-7890;
E-mail: info@abceventcompany.com

RISK MANAGEMENT

Everybody knows Murphy's Law:

'If anything can go wrong, it will.'

But wait. How about O'Toole's Commentary on Murphy's Law?

'Murphy was an optimist.'

What is risk management if not the endless pursuit of the refutation of Murphy's Law and its many corollaries? (See Bloch (2003) for more on Murphy's Law.) Perhaps nobody on the event management team knows about Murphy's Law more than the producer, who must start considering risk during the Coordination Phase of event organization. It is within the responsibility areas of the producer that risk in its most lethal forms becomes reality. The producer must understand how Murphy's Law can affect an event and how these effects can be minimized.

My opening statement is not intended to denigrate the countless books, papers, and studies on risk management that have preceded the writing of this book. In fact, my intention is quite the contrary; however, my approach to risk management for event producers is a non-traditional one compared to other authors and experts in the more general field of event management. This will become apparent as we proceed through the chapter. We will examine production risk in light of current theory and compare it to the reality of working at a live event, we will then look at compliance with standards, and finish with a discussion of insurance. By the end, a clear picture will emerge of how event producers might want to rethink their role in risk management.

7.1   THEORY VERSUS REALITY

Readers will notice by now that most chapters of this book contain a war story that relates a production problem to the topic of the chapter, all of which demonstrate that Murphy is alive and well. For this chapter, I am going to begin with the war story, an incident that happened to me personally late in my career as an event producer.

My company was contracted to produce an original entertainment show for an international convention that integrated cirque-type acts with traditional west coast native performers. This involved dancers, musicians, a magician, fire performers, and aerial silk artists. The performers were to act out a simple story told in segments between dinner courses, with the finale being the aerial silk performance at the end of dinner.

In preparing for the show, we had jumped through many hoops in order to obtain the appropriate insurance for the fire performances. We had also drawn the event layout completely on computer-aided design and drafting (CADD) leaving sufficient safe distances between performers and the audience as well as safety areas below the aerial performers. All the necessary fire safety equipment was nearby, the proper technical equipment and personnel were in place, and security personnel were standing by.

The performances went off without a hitch and the client was very pleased. After congratulating everyone for a job well done, I proceeded backstage to thank the performers. While I was there, one of my assistants ran back to inform me that someone was trying to climb the two silks left hanging by the aerial artists. I rushed back out to the event space to find two guests making their way up the silks (each about 25 ft high) while a security official tried to get them down. Since there was only one official and the silks were about 30 ft apart, the official only managed to dissuade one of the perpetrators. By the time I and the official arrived at the second silk, the guest was about

20 ft up and hanging upside down. The performer responsible soon arrived and together we managed to convince the guest to come down safely, but not before I had visions of endless rounds of litigation by a quadriplegic in a wheelchair, designed to divest me of all my retirement funds, not to mention the assets of my client's company.

What happened? In terms of the plain facts, this guest was one of the several who had a bit too much to drink and had bet each other during dinner that one could climb to the top of a silk before being caught. In terms of risk management, we had assumed that the room would immediately clear after the finale performance because it was the end of the event. To remove the silks right after the performance would have spoiled the effectiveness of the performance and would have made it seem as if we were striking the event too soon while guests were still present (i.e. it would have required a Genie lift to untie the silks from the ceiling rigging). Until that moment, we were unaware that the bars were staying open and many guests had no intention of leaving immediately.

The 20/20 hindsight by risk management experts would lead to some obvious actions that could have alleviated this risk: add another security person or stage manager to watch over the silks; improve communication between producer and client about the bars remaining open; close the bars, turn the lights up, and ask everyone to clear the room; or remove the silks immediately after the performance. Yes, they all would have been viable options. Was I an incompetent producer for not having thought of what could happen? Perhaps. Would other producers have anticipated the consequences? Maybe. Did my production team follow good risk management protocol? I and my team plus the venue and my client thought we did. Unfortunately, in event production, there is only one chance to get it right and no rehearsals under event conditions. My team was convinced we had assessed all the risks and had done everything correctly, from having fire guards with extinguishers (we thought fire was going to be the biggest problem), to leaving a large safety area around the silks, to having security personnel present. This story really illustrates that event production is inherently unpredictable to some degree and that risk management is an educated attempt to predict human nature, which of course is not possible with 100 percent effectiveness.

7.1.1 Theory

Could this story have turned out differently if we had more closely followed risk management theory? Let us take a look. Current event risk management theory – to which I subscribe – as clearly explained by numerous experts, including IRMI (2006), Allen et al. (2005; pp. 346–370), Rutherford-Silvers (2004; pp. 51–60), and Van Der Wagen and Carlos (2005; pp. 99–112), breaks the risk management process down into three generally accepted phases, while others such as O'Toole (2004) add other phases, notably monitoring. For review purposes, the basic process consists of the following phases.

7.1.1.1 Identification of Risks

During this phase, data are gathered from past experience and various sources and potential risks are considered by the entire event team. It is worth noting that there are companies that conduct this type of research for special events (as subcontractors to event production companies) and follow it up with the completion of risk assessment documentation as well as the creation of emergency response plans.

7.1.1.2 Assessment and Evaluation of Risks

During this phase the risks are evaluated with respect to the likelihood of their occurring and the severity of the consequences, and risk assessment forms are completed documenting the results. RGIB (2006) provides an excellent risk management checklist form, although it is geared more for overall event management and lacks the detail needed for event production.

7.1.1.3 Management of Risks

During this phase, risk controls are put into effect through avoidance, reduction, retention, and transfer techniques. Tarlow (2002) spends most of his extensive book on this topic, examining the most critical risks to attendee well-being from a sociological point of view, including the necessary – and now familiar – components of event risk management such as: proper crowd management techniques; documentation in the form of adequate liability and property insurance; event permits and licenses (e.g. for alcohol); participant waivers where necessary; provision of adequate security personnel; and screening of employees. The references given should be read for further enlightenment on this topic. As well, refer to Chapter 6 for sample contracts with appropriate clauses, a sample indemnity rider, and a sample waiver form.

7.1.1.4 Monitoring of Risks

While the previous three phases take place before the event, monitoring risks takes place during the event. One of the tasks of all event production team members is to continuously monitor their responsibility areas for potential risks as the event unfolds. The success of risk monitoring is often a direct result of how good a producer is at anticipating potential problems before they arise, as we discussed in Chapter 1.

In my real-life example, we did identify and assess what we considered to be the most critical risks and we managed them according to the industry-accepted norms in that we obtained the necessary extra liability insurance to cover the risks of fire and aerial performances, and we ensured that fire risks were minimized as were security risks. We just did not anticipate the actions of intoxicated audience members. For that matter, if those same members had decided to get into a brawl with each other or with the wait staff rather than climb the performers' silks, could the brawl have been stopped before any injuries were incurred? Probably no more so than with the incident that actually happened. Was the single nearby security person sufficient to handle the situation – or even a brawl situation? No. Should there have been more security personnel? Yes, based on the outcome of this event but not based on the countless similar events that I had produced and the venue had hosted (statistics that played into the original evaluation of risks and the number of assigned security personnel). The logical conclusion to this is that even though risk management theory is conscientiously applied to an event, there may still be the potential for Murphy's Law to make an appearance.

Having said that, I am not advocating throwing one's arms in the air and leaving risk outcomes to chance. I believe in probabilities, and the lower they are for risk, the better. Producers must still do their due diligence in the application of risk management theory to their components of the event, namely in the areas of entertainment, décor, audio, lighting, visual presentation technology, special effects, staging, tenting, electrical power, rigging, and other temporary structures. They must still identify and evaluate the risks involved in these areas and document the results of this assessment on paper for any and all events. They must still manage these identified risks by doing the same sorts of things we did for the event described, notably obtain special insurance, and set up proper fire and security protocols. Not only will this assist them with obtaining the proper insurance if needed, it will also go a long way to making the event actually safer by lowering risk probabilities. In spite of Murphy's Law, risk management does pay off!

7.1.2 Reality

That, however, is not the end of the story. Before going any further, we need to examine the reality of the event production environment and compare it to the above recommended theoretical approach to risk management. As a retired event producer with no vested interest in the ramifications of what I am about to say, I can in good conscience 'tell it like it is.' Here, then, is the reality of event production.

Most event producers are the owners of small businesses and the production contracts on which they work are for relatively small events, such as corporate dinners, award shows, fundraising galas, and others. They are key members of a usually small event team that is faced with short lead times to prepare for the event, rather than the year or more lead times for public events with large event teams, such as festivals, parades, or sports. In short, they must concentrate on work that is directly related to making a profit, and to be blunt, gathering and evaluating risk data is not a task at the top of their priority list. In short, unless required by contract or by law, it is not done to the extent that risk management theory demands. For the war story described, I did not complete a risk assessment form; I did not have time, and it was not required in order for me to execute the event. I did the minimum work necessary to obtain the insurance for the event, pure and simple.

The responsibility areas of the producer are arguably the most hazardous of any in the event, as the chapters in *Special Event Production: The Resources* demonstrate. Not only that, but competition and client demands regularly force producers to push the boundaries of safety in these already risky areas by creating new ways of presenting entertainment and new ways of allowing guests to participate in activities. This is not done at every event, but it is certainly done at enough events that it is of concern, and it is of concern to the insurance industry, already skittish because of regular event disasters around the globe.

There is also an underlying current of 'ego versus safety' within much of the technical community. According to Rick Smith of Riggit Services in Vancouver, Canada, seasoned technicians in fields such as rigging, lighting, audio, staging, and such are sometimes too ready to accept client demands because they like the challenge of creating something new in spite of the risks involved and standards that might otherwise dictate that it should not be done. In other words, they refuse to say no to a client when safety might be compromised (Rick Smith, Personal Communication, September 7, 2006).

We are thus left with an impasse between risk management theory and the realities of event production, the quest for profit, and human nature. How can this impasse be broken? There are two answers. The first is education, which means that event managers and event producers have to understand in much more detail what comprises event production and what the risks are within the areas of event production, so they can at least ask the right questions and demand the right answers of suppliers. That is one of the primary purposes of these books. The second answer lies in compliance.

7.2   COMPLIANCE

By definition, compliance is the act of conforming to a specification, standard, or law that has been clearly defined. In the case of event production and its relevant areas, these fall into four broad categories.

7.2.1   General Standards for Workplace Safety

These are published by the Occupational Safety and Health Administration (OSHA) in the US and the various provincial Workers' Compensation Boards (WCBs) in Canada. They detail safe practices that must be followed by employers and contractors for personnel safety.

7.2.2   General Standards for the Safe Design and Use of Equipment

These are typically sets of detailed standards drawn up by industry organizations called standards development organizations (SDOs). The products to which these standards apply are thus certified by these organizations and often carry labels attesting to this fact. In both Canada and the United States, the certification procedures of these SDOs must be approved by a national accreditation body. In the US, this body is the American National Standards Institute (ANSI) and in Canada it is the Standards Council of Canada (SCC). ANSI and SCC also both participate in the development of international standards through other international standards organizations and sometimes take North American standards to these bodies for adoption as international standards. Examples of other such organizations are the International Organization for Standardization (ISO) and the International Electrotechnical Commission (IEC).

The content of standards from SDOs may relate to products, processes, services, systems, or personnel. For example, in Canada, the Canadian Standards Association (CSA) is responsible for coordinating the development of the Canadian Electrical Code, and in the US, the National Fire Protection Association (NFPA) has the same responsibility for drawing up the National Electrical Code. Both these organizations (CSA and NFPA) are SDOs within their respective countries. Similarly, other standards in such event production areas as rigging, audio, lighting, and staging are drawn up by relevant organizations and given numbers and names, some of which may end up as ANSI standards or come with the name of the SDO that created them.

7.2.3 General Guidelines for the Operation and/or Use of Equipment

These are typically drawn up by advocacy or user groups (also called *nontraditional standards development bodies*) who feel it necessary to adopt guidelines or standards where none exist. These groups are not accredited by either of the national organizations (i.e. ANSI or SCC).

7.2.4 Regulations

These are standards that have been legislated into law. They are enforceable by the related federal, state/provincial, or municipal governing bodies that implement them. It should be emphasized that every jurisdiction is different. Some standards may have been turned into law in some municipalities or states/provinces, while other jurisdictions may take a completely different approach. Producers should familiarize themselves with all relevant municipal and state/provincial regulations in the jurisdiction in which they work. A typical example might be the treatment of fireworks and pyrotechnics in different states or provinces.

It is important to understand that compliance with standards or guidelines is voluntary. Compliance with regulations is a legal requirement. For example, most jurisdictions (e.g. states/provinces) have adopted personnel safety standards (e.g. those published by OSHA or WCB) as regulations. However, compliance with standards and guidelines can also become mandatory by having them adopted by venues, clients, or producers and by having compliance turned into a contractual obligation. This is now the case with many venues that have adopted occupational safety standards for all workers – whether employees or outside contractors (i.e. event production companies and their subcontractors) – as well as other standards like the National Electrical Code and the National Fire Code.

According to Bill Naughton, Jr., President of Event Flooring Professionals in Sanford, Florida, USA, astute clients who are vulnerable to public scrutiny, such as the Professional Golfers' Association (PGA) Tour, already make compliance with the International Building Code, the National Fire Code, Americans with Disabilities Act (ADA) requirements, and local state and municipal regulations a contractual obligation. Naughton states that he must often make numerous site visits and detailed engineering analyses in order to design compliant installations of such equipment as flooring, bleachers, or scaffolding, and to obtain the necessary sign-offs by certified structural engineers and local authorities (William D. Naughton, Jr., Personal Communication, August 23, 2006). The result is not only a safer event, but also protection from litigation and a much higher level of professionalism.

As the special events industry matures, this sophisticated level of professionalism must follow. No longer should it be acceptable to pay lip service to risk management theory. Compliance with existing standards mixed with the educated adoption of new standards where safety and risk dictate must be the norm. Contractual obligations to comply with existing standards should be considered for all subcontractor contracts that come under the responsibility of the event producer (see Section 6.2.1.2 for an example). The benefit to this methodology is that risk is also transferred and the onus is placed squarely on the shoulders of the specialists to comply with equipment safety, use, and design standards. Likewise, producers should be contractually obligated by clients and venues – and be prepared – to complete risk assessments that list not only the perceived risks unique to a particular event, but also the references to contractual compliance with standards by production subcontractors. Apart from some additional paperwork, this new direction should alleviate many of the concerns of the insurance industry as well as raising the level of professionalism, reducing risk, and separating the serious practitioners from those who are incompetent.

To this end, I have adopted this new direction to production risk management throughout *Special Event Production: The Process* and *Special Event Production: The Resources* of these books by including in each chapter where necessary, a discussion of the applicable existing standards as they are known at the time of writing. The standards reviewed are primarily for North America (USA and Canada) but where none are available or known, reference is made to standards from other countries that may be worth considering. Because new standards are adopted and old ones are updated on a regular basis, producers and their suppliers should always check for the most current versions and for other applicable standards and regulations in their area of expertise.

As previously mentioned, there is and should always be a requirement to document production risk assessment for all events. Indeed, many of the references at the end of this chapter contain some form of checklists for common risks at events, including some within event production responsibility areas. However, it has to be completely understood that to follow only a simplified checklist for all areas of event production as a singular form of risk management is patently inadequate and professionally irresponsible given the complex nature of the equipment and the many hours of expertise that have been devoted to establishing well-conceived standards by nationally and internationally recognized organizations. In almost every case, the standards referenced in the chapters of these books are significantly more detailed than any list that even an experienced producer is able to devise. For some less risk-prone areas of event management (e.g. volunteer management, financial accounting, marketing, and such) simplified checklists may suffice, but not in event production.

I strongly advocate that event producers spend the time and money to become familiar with as many of the key standards as possible. At first glance, the plethora of standards from numerous organizations may make this seem like a daunting and pointless task. However, only one serious injury and lawsuit caused by negligence can make it seem like a much easier route. Reading accounts of the many accidents that occur annually around the world in event production (e.g. collapsed trussing, crowd crushes, people falling off stages and out of bleachers, fireworks injuries, tent disasters, and such) should convince producers to adopt this new direction as an indication of their level of professionalism. Most production suppliers should have a good grasp of the standards within their areas and can point producers to the most relevant ones, which are invariably the ones that need to be referenced in contracts. For example, in the area of electrical safety, producers should have copies of *NFPA 70 (the National Electrical Code)* and *NFPA 70E (Electrical Safety in the Workplace, 2004 Edition)* in the US, and the *Canadian Electrical Code Parts I and II* in Canada. In the area of production personnel safety, producers should have copies of *29 CFR Part 1910, Occupational Safety and Health Standards* in the US, and the relevant provincial WCB standards in Canada. The important standards in other areas can easily be found with those referenced in these books as a starting point. Again, Section 6.2.1.2 contains an example of how standards may be referenced in a producer/supplier contract.

7.3   INSURANCE

There are two irrefutable facts about insurance and special event production. First, commercial general liability (CGL) insurance is absolutely necessary in order to work in special event production. Second, the ability to obtain this insurance is directly related to the perceived risk in conducting the event production business. It is this second fact that presents a constant challenge to event production companies. In this section we will examine why this is so and how this challenge may be ameliorated. For purposes of this discussion, we will only be concerned with CGL insurance, the most important and relevant one for the event producer. Information on other types of event-related insurance that are the responsibility of the event manager, such as event cancellation insurance, can be found elsewhere (e.g. Rutherford-Silvers, 2004).

7.3.1 The Realities of Insurance and its Relationship to Event Production

CGL insurance is defined as insurance providing broad coverage for claims made against an individual or company arising from bodily injury or property damage sustained by others for which the company may be liable in law or contract. Part of the challenge of obtaining such insurance for event production companies stems from a lack of information and understanding by all parties involved in the decision.

In order to obtain CGL insurance, a company must submit an insurance application to a broker which is passed to an insurance company to check against *underwriting guidelines*. As mentioned by Glenn (2000), 'Underwriting is the process of determining which applications the insurance company should accept, and for those who are accepted, in which program they belong. The process of risk selection (as underwriting is also known) has two faces, one that is presented to regulators and applicants, and a second that is used by underwriters. ... The outward face is one of numbers, statistics, and objectivity. The inward face is that of narratives, character, and subjective judgment. The rhetoric of insurance exclusion – numbers, objectivity, and statistics – form what I call "the myth of the actuary," a powerful rhetorical situation in which decisions appear to be based on objectively determined criteria when they are also largely based on subjective ones.' He goes on to say, 'Underwriters use a set of guidelines produced by the company, and the standards may differ from firm to firm, allowing the "insurability" of a given individual (or company–author) to shift depending on the company with which the application is placed.' In other words, if the insurer sees the applicant as a high risk because of not only the business the applicant – or the applicant's company – is in but also because of other subjective characteristics (e.g. personal, racial, financial, demographic, etc.) the application may be denied.

Insurance remains a cyclical industry. There have been nine insurance cycles since 1950 that lasted from 4 to 7 years (CTC, 2003). When profits are high, the market is 'soft' and insurers underwrite more risky companies; when the market is affected by such events as 9/11, the Rhode Island nightclub fire, and numerous other disasters, natural and otherwise, the market is 'hard' (due to decreased insurance industry profits). In such a market, underwriting guidelines tighten up, often resulting in companies either not being able to obtain CGL insurance, having certain activities such as fire or pyrotechnics performances excluded from a policy, or having insurance premiums rise exorbitantly.

There are no underwriting guidelines specifically for special event production companies. In many cases, insurers revert for reference to what they perceive to be the closest type of business to what producers do, which may be based either on their own experience or on the application from the producer. It could end up being a consultant in one case and a fireworks company, construction company, or entertainment agency in another, all with widely varying levels of perceived risk; there is no consistency of application across the insurance industry. Hence, some producers can obtain insurance and some cannot, even though they may be in exactly the same business. Because the underwriting guidelines are insufficient, when the industry is in a 'hard market,' insurers have no interest in special event production as they perceive it as overly risky. In other words, to paraphrase CTC (2003), 'the "special events industry" must provide underwriting information and convince insurers with organized facts, numbers, and historical data regarding the real insurability of the risks and hazards of their industry.' (Ironically, insurance industry clients sometimes demand that producers create the most leading edge, risky events for their incentive groups, and this from the very industry that denies event producers CGL insurance!)

7.3.2   Bringing Event Production to Insurers

Until clear underwriting guidelines are written for the special events industry, there may always be a gap in understanding between insurers and event producers. In the meantime, however, there are certainly steps that can be taken to improve the situation. One is for industry initiatives and another is for individual production companies to know how to apply for CGL insurance.

7.3.2.1   Industry Initiatives

In 2003, the Canadian Tourism Commission (CTC) conducted a study of insurance and the outdoor tourism sector in Canada, a sector that closely resembles the special events industry in company size, operation, and inherent risk (CTC, 2003). They, too, were suffering from often unobtainable or costly CGL insurance due to perceived risk. Some of their recommendations are worthy of note due to the similarity of the two industries, and included: the creation of nationally or internationally sponsored insurance initiatives; the introduction of an industry group insurance program; the establishment of national or international risk management standards; and the training of industry company owners in the preparation of risk management plans and insurance portfolios. While some similar steps are underway in the special events industry, the underlying point is that continuing dialog is necessary if the perception of the special events industry is to be changed in the eyes of the insurance industry.

7.3.2.2 *Individual Production Companies*

In the meantime, individual production companies can still be proactive in increasing their chances of obtaining reasonably priced CGL insurance. Fitzgerald (2003) states, 'Developing a positive underwriting profile is one of your most effective tools for a successful insurance renewal. ... It must be comprehensive, accurate, and delivered well in advance of your insurance renewal.' For producers, this means understanding and acting upon two key points.

7.3.2.2.1 Risk Management Policy

Event production companies should have in place a good risk management policy. All insurers agree that in today's world this is essential. Without a plan that clearly outlines a working risk management policy, event producers are going to have a very difficult time obtaining insurance. This plan should address such items as:

- Event risk assessment checklists. These we have discussed and there are many examples in the literature, all of which can be modified to suit individual companies.
- An obvious policy for compliance with safety standards. Again, this is discussed at length throughout these books and such compliance should be treated as a method of contractually transferring risk to suppliers.
- Other methods of transferring risk. Lawyers stress the need to transfer risk in several ways. The first is through 'hold harmless agreements' that effectively take the risk from the producer and transfer it to either a supplier or a client, depending on the situation, in essence making either the supplier or client responsible for any injury or damage that may occur as a result of working on or participating in the event. For example, if a producer is contracting for a number of physical games for guests to play, the guests and/or the overall client should be contractually bounded by a hold harmless agreement or participant waiver forms. See Sections 6.2.2 and 6.6 for examples.
- The second way is to insist on 'additional named insured' clauses in contracts with all event stakeholders, including clients, suppliers, and venues. The fact is that they will probably also insist on the same thing from producers, so basically all parties name each other as 'additional insureds' in all contracts, in effect lessening the payment of claims by any individual insurer. This 'additional insured' courtesy means that the entity specified (either the client, supplier, venue, or producer) will be defended by their or the producer's policy if brought into a suit that relates to the operations being insured. See Sections 6.2.1.2 and 6.6 for examples.

A final way that some producers are now considering is the use of risk management consultants who basically manage the risk policy of the production company, thereby helping to demonstrate a solid commitment to risk management. Whether having this as the sole method of transferring risk is grounds for release from liabilities is really a question for lawyers.

For all contractual forms of risk transfer, wording is critical and a knowledgeable lawyer in this field – and in the producer's jurisdiction – should be consulted to draft the appropriate contract clauses for the producer.

7.3.2.2.2   Completing Insurance Applications

Applications are the guiding documents for insurers. They must be completed thoroughly and accurately. Insurers want to feel confident that a producer is not high risk and to do this, they need detailed information about the company and its employees. Fitzgerald (2003) provides a good checklist of what companies should be prepared to provide as part of their insurance application:

- Completed insurance questionnaires and application forms
- Claims experience for the previous 5 years
- Brochures and advertizing literature
- Description of all business activities
- Client profiles
- Maintenance procedures
- Automobile listings
- Schedule of values for buildings, contents, equipment, and stock
- Business interruption value worksheets
- Engineering inspections
- Background profiles of all professional staff
- Membership in professional associations
- Risk management mission statement
- Health and safety mission statement
- Safety standards, procedures, and programs
- Insurance and risk management manuals
- Loss prevention manuals
- Environmental standards, procedures, and programs
- Hazardous materials handling manuals
- Crisis response plans, resources, and training
- Business recovery plans
- Emergency medical plans and equipment
- Copies of signage, waivers, contracts, and agreements showing the transfer of risk to another party.

Once this information has been gathered, potential brokers can be approached. As stated by Van't Haaf (2005), a 6-week lead time is not too soon to begin the process. This allows the broker sufficient time to fully canvas the marketplace for suitable insurers. As part of the application, it is strongly advised that attempts be made to obtain a package that covers all events produced on an annual basis, especially if the events produced are consistently similar. Many insurers also make the application process an annual requirement, so being prepared can save considerable time.

PRODUCTION CHALLENGES

1. You have been asked to create a checklist for personnel safety during event setup. Consider a complicated setup with flown lighting, full audio system, staging, and room décor that will take approximately 12 h in total. Using your present knowledge, create a list. After doing so, look up the occupational health and safety standards for your jurisdiction and check the list against them. Discuss how many critical items you missed on your original checklist.
2. Review the chapters in *Special Event Production: The Resources* if you have it, and list what you consider to be the most important standards in each area that could be considered for compliance in supplier contracts.
3. In a 'hard market' for insurers, describe some of the ways in which event production companies and the special events industry in general may become more proactive in order to make it easier for production companies to obtain CGL insurance.

REFERENCES

Allen, J., O'Toole, W., Harris, R. and McDonnell, I. (2005). *Festival and Special Event Management*, Third Edition. Milton: John Wiley & Sons Australia, Ltd.

Bloch, A. (2003). *Murphy's Law: The 26th Anniversary Edition*. New York: Perigree Trade.

Canadian Tourism Commission (CTC). (August 28, 2003). *Insurance Issues and Alternatives in the Outdoor Tourism Sector in Canada*. Retrieved September 18, 2006, from http://www.canadatourism.com/ctx/files/publication/data/en_ca/product_development/insurance_issues_and_alternatives_in_the_outdoor_tourism_sector_in_canada/Insurance%20Issues%20Report%20-%20Eng.pdf.

Fitzgerald, P. (2003). *Risk Management Guide for Tourism Operators*. Canadian Tourism Commission. Retrieved September 28, 2006, from http://ftp.canadatourism.com/ctxUploads/en_publications/RMG.pdf.

Glenn, B.J. (2000). The Shifting Rhetoric of Insurance Denial. *Law and Society Review, 34(3)*, 779–808. Retrieved September 18, 2006, from Questia database: http://www.questia.com/PM.qst?a=o&d=76943555.

IRMI (2006). *Practical Risk Management: The Handbook for Risk and Financial Professionals*. Dallas, TX: International Risk Management Institute, Inc.

O'Toole, W.J. (May 2004). Special Event Risk from a Project Management Perspective. Retrieved September 14, 2006, from http://www.personal.usyd.edu.au/~wotoole/conferen/isesrisk.htm.

Rural & General Insurance Broking Pty Ltd. (RGIB). (2006). Checklist for Event Management. *Risk Management Checklists*. Retrieved September 28, 2006, from http://www.ruralandgeneral.com.au/PDF/checklists/eventmanagement-insurance-checklist.pdf.

Rutherford-Silvers, J. (2004). *Professional Event Coordination*. Hoboken: John Wiley & Sons, Inc.

Tarlow, P.E. (2002). *Event Risk Management and Safety*. New York: John Wiley & Sons, Inc.

Van Der Wagen, L. and Carlos, B.R. (2005). *Event Management for Tourism, Cultural, Business, and Sporting Events*. Upper Saddle River, New Jersey: Pearson Education, Inc.

Van't Haaf, C. (2005). Planners Ponder Insurance Puzzle. *Meeting Places: A Guide to the Meeting and Event Planning Industry in British Columbia*. Vancouver, BC: Business in Vancouver Special Publications.

PRODUCTION MANAGEMENT

Production management, also occasionally called technical direction, is the task of integrating all the technical – and many non-technical – event elements. This can include staging, audio and A-V, lighting, décor, entertainment, stage management, scheduling, rehearsals, and scripting. It may also involve some of the other logistical event requirements such as coordinating electrical and rigging, waste management, fencing, and the setup of temporary structures. Usually, it is one of the jobs of the event producer, but for large, complex events, a separate Technical Director (TD) is often hired. Production management is essentially a two-part process: the first part occurring during the Coordination Phase and consisting of venue liaison and the creation of production schedules and CADD (computer-aided design and drafting) drawings; the second part occurring during the Execution Phase and consisting of technical setup and event direction or *show calling*. We will examine all these tasks in the logical order of their occurrence.

8.1   DURING THE EVENT COORDINATION PHASE

In this phase, all the details of the site or venue are established and preliminary plans generated for the event layout and execution. Included in the tasks are site inspection and liaison with the event venue, the creation of CADD drawings of the venue with all event elements incorporated, the writing of an event production schedule and running order, and possibly the writing of a show script.

8.1.1   Site Inspection and Venue Liaison

Note that throughout this section we will be using the terms 'site' to refer to an outdoor location and 'venue' to refer to an indoor location. To accurately produce an event, a thorough familiarity with the venue or site is required. Gaining this familiarity usually begins as early as the Concept and Proposal Phase of the event when an initial site inspection may take place. Once the event is confirmed, however, there are typically one or more extended visits in which all specific details about the venue or site must be determined and appropriate plans made, usually in conjunction with other key technical resource suppliers. There are three aspects of sites and venues that will be discussed: understanding site and venue management, determining venue capacity, and establishing logistical limitations.

8.1.1.1   *Understanding Site and Venue Management*

Although sites and venues can be varied, their individual methods of internal operation and management are surprisingly similar. In order to produce a successful event, a producer should understand the management hierarchies of these sites and venues. The first point to bear in mind is that when in any venue or on any outdoor site, the event producer is a guest and not an employee or even a contractor of that venue. Certainly the event producer is usually a contractor of the client who is also a client of that venue or site, but that does not automatically allow the producer to demand whatever he or she wants of the venue. Common sense should always prevail and can only serve to maintain good relations if the producer adopts an attitude of being the 'perfect guest.'

Understanding internal management hierarchies is the key to working with a venue. Because a producer is constantly interacting with venue staff members, it is necessary to know who does what and who reports to whom. Venues typically fall into one of three categories: hotels, convention centers, and other locations. In hotels – and for purposes of our discussion we are referring only to larger hotels with meeting space – producers usually work directly with either the *catering director* or the *convention*, or *conference*, *services manager*. The catering director is normally the person responsible for the event if a food and beverage (F&B) function is planned, such as a meal or reception. The convention services manager is often the person responsible if no meal or F&B function is planned and/or if the group is a large one. In convention hotels, the responsibilities of these senior managers may be delegated to subordinate managers (e.g. one of the several *catering managers*), and it is then this individual who is the venue's main point of contact for the producer. It is this person who should always be approached first for any services required from the venue such as electrical power hookup, staging, or green rooms, and this person who needs to be kept updated of all production plans and schedules.

In the case of convention centers, the key senior staff members are either the catering director or one of several *event coordinators*, again depending on whether an F&B function is planned. One difference between a hotel and a convention center is that often catering services are subcontracted in a convention center, so that both a catering manager (subordinate to the catering director) from this subcontracted company and an event coordinator from the venue are dual contact points for the event producer and the producer must keep both in the loop for all event production plans. For example, the catering manager may be the point of contact for requesting staging, but the event coordinator may be the point of contact for security and green room assignments. Each convention center may operate with slightly different responsibility areas.

A similar situation as in convention centers exists in arenas, stadiums, and sometimes theaters, although occasionally key technical staff may belong to IATSE (The International Association of Theatrical Stage Employees), making it a *union house*. The terms of the union's working relationship with the venue frequently require that union personnel perform certain technical tasks such as installing and operating audio or lighting systems. Unions do, however, often allow non-union personnel – and companies – to operate their own equipment but with the addition of a union person shadowing the non-union technician. Of course, producers, or most likely event managers, must pay for the additional union labor at union rates which are often higher than the technical supplier's rates. Production schedules are also subject to union working regulations, including clearly defined break periods. Before producing any event in a union house, producers are strongly urged to obtain and understand all pertinent regulations and to ensure that all parties agree about who will pay the extra costs resulting from following the union regulations.

Other locations (e.g. private clubs, parks and public spaces, restaurants, attractions, etc.) all operate differently. Most indoor venues do, however, either have a general manager or catering manager and it is one of these individuals who is usually the main contact for producers. Some attractions employ their own event coordinators who are the producer's contacts. Public outdoor sites such as parks or streets require contact through the governing body. In some jurisdictions, this body may be a Parks Board (e.g. city, state/provincial, or federal) or a City Special Events Department. Private outdoor venues may require contact with the property owner and the appropriate city, state/provincial, or federal governing authority.

8.1.1.2 Determining Indoor Venue Capacity

During initial venue inspection (i.e. in the Concept and Proposal Phase) it will be necessary to determine the capacity of the venue for the desired event. This requires particularly critical communication between the producer and the venue contact, especially if unusual room setups are involved. By this is meant something other than the standard classroom or dining setup. We will first consider how to determine the capacity for standard setups.

8.1.1.2.1 Capacity with Standard Setups

Harris (2000) specifies guidelines that can be used to accurately calculate the area required for certain events, as below with additional sizing recommendations from Mr. Bruno Patassini, long-time Catering Manager with the Westin Bayshore Resort and Marina in Vancouver, BC, Canada (Bruno Patassini, Personal Communication, May 2003):

- *Standup reception*: 9–10 ft^2 (0.84–0.93 m^2) per person.
- *Theater seating (less than 60 people)*: 12–13 ft^2 (1.1–1.2 m^2) per person. This allows at least 24 in. (61 cm) of space between rows, which is the most comfortable.
- *Theater seating (60–300 people)*: 11–12 ft^2 (1.0–1.2 m^2) per person.
- *Theater seating (more than 300 people)*: 10–11 ft^2 (0.93–1.0 m^2) per person.
- *Schoolroom general*: 17–22 ft^2 (1.6–2.9 m^2) per person. This allows for rectangular tables that are 6 or 8 ft (1.8 or 2.4 m) long and 18 in. (46 cm) wide, with 2 ft (0.61 m) per person and 3.5 ft (0.91 m) between tables as a minimum for optimum comfort.
- *Banquet seating (60 in. or 152 cm diameter rounds)*: 13.5 ft^2 (1.25 m^2) per person for optimum comfort for eight persons at the table. Patassini recommends a 12-ft (3.6 m) center-to-center separation for maximum comfort and safety.
- *Banquet seating (66 in. or 168 cm diameter rounds)*: 13.5 ft^2 (1.25 m^2) per person for optimum comfort for nine persons at the table. Patassini recommends a 12.5-ft (3.75 m) center-to-center separation for maximum comfort and safety.
- *Banquet seating (72 in. or 183 cm diameter rounds)*: 13.5 ft^2 (1.25 m^2) per person for optimum comfort for 10 persons at the table. Patassini

recommends a 13-ft (3.9 m) center-to-center separation for maximum comfort and safety.

Note that these numbers do not allow for any staging or other elements such as décor in the venue. The area occupied by these extra event elements must be taken into consideration if an accurate estimate of capacity is to be determined. For ease of illustration, let us assume that an event will have a stage against the long wall of a rectangular room. The calculation for capacity is therefore given by the following formula:

$$\text{Capacity} = \frac{\text{Useable area}}{\text{Area per person}}$$
$$= \frac{(\text{Room length} \times \text{Room depth}) - (\text{Room length} \times \text{Stage depth})}{\text{Area per person}}$$

Likewise, the area used by any other décor elements or hard impediments must be taken into account and deducted from the total useable area. This method of course assumes that the area behind the stage or other impediment is unusable area. See Figure 8.1 for a graphical representation of this

FIGURE 8.1

DETERMINATION OF THE USEABLE AREA OF AN INDOOR VENUE

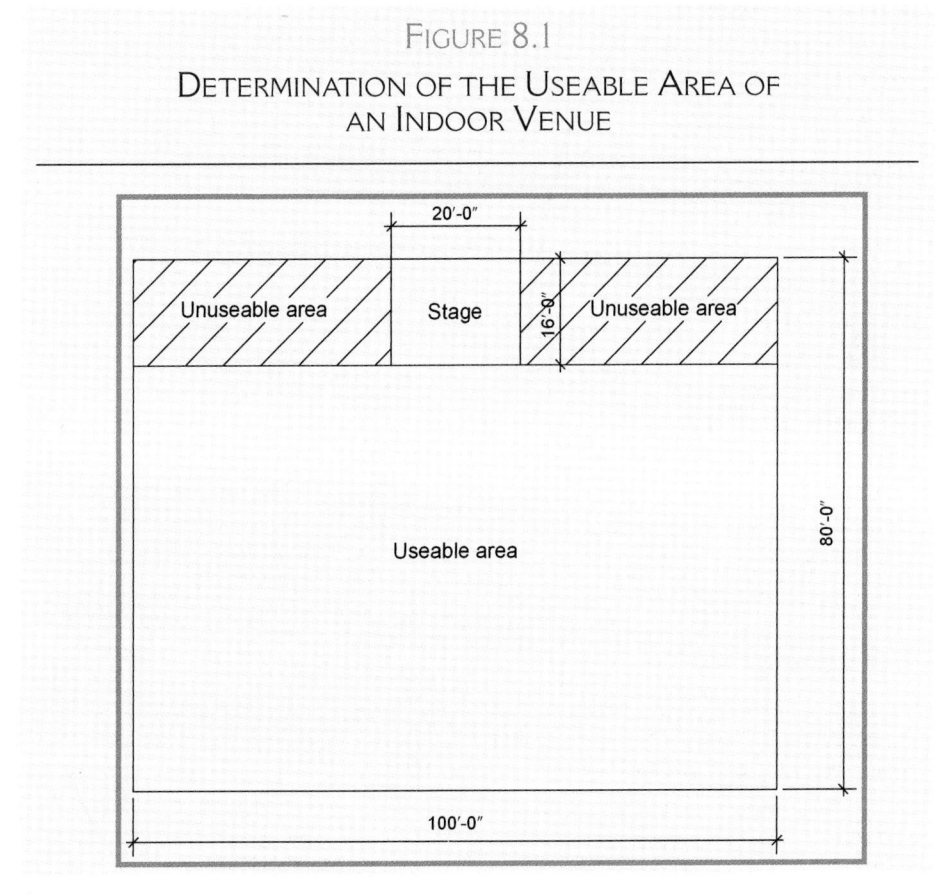

Courtesy: Doug Matthews

methodology. In this case, using imperial units, the room length is 100 ft, room depth 80 ft, stage width 20 ft, and stage depth 16 ft.

In this example, the total room area is 8000 ft^2 (i.e. 100 ft × 80 ft) but the useable area is only 6400 ft^2 (i.e. 8000–1600 ft^2) where 1600 ft^2 represents the unusable area occupied by the stage and the area behind the front of the stage that runs the length of the room. Assuming that this event is to be a dinner, then the room capacity in this example would be 592 persons (i.e. 8000 ft^2/13.5 ft^2 per person) if there were no stage, and 474 persons (i.e. 6400 ft^2/13.5 ft^2 per person) if the stage were to be used in the location drawn.

8.1.1.2.2 Capacity with Non-Standard Setups

For dining setups, the distribution of tables throughout the event space is beginning to be explored much more creatively than ever in the past. This can involve not only the round dining tables mentioned above, but also the creative arrangements of rectangular tables (e.g. each typically 2.5 ft wide × 6 or 8 ft long; 0.75 m × 1.8 or 2.4 m), and now even octagonal tables with connecting bridges that permit wild and random arrangements (Figure 8.2). No matter what the layout, however, there are still some important guidelines for spacing. Optimum table layout design within the event space should allow for a minimum of 2 ft (0.6 m) between chairs at any two adjacent tables to enable the safe passage of wait staff. Furthermore, tables should be

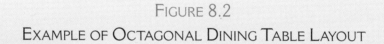

FIGURE 8.2

EXAMPLE OF OCTAGONAL DINING TABLE LAYOUT

Courtesy: Event Solutions Magazine, MH Concepts, and Visual WOW

optimally placed no closer to walls than 2 ft (0.6 m). This permits safe foot traffic and meal service and is useful in planning room layouts, most often done now on CADD drawings. Indeed, the use of CADD is the only way to accurately determine capacity with creative arrangements.

For all setups, whether standard or non-standard, place settings should optimally be 24 in. wide × 18 in. deep (60 cm × 45 cm) for comfort, although with the typical 2.5 ft (0.75 m) wide rectangular tables, this usually ends up being 15 in. (37.8 cm) deep.

For outdoor sites, the estimated capacity is not as accurately determined and is more a result of careful analysis of security capabilities, safety concerns, site accessibility, box office throughput, and demand (if a public ticketed event).

8.1.1.3 *Establishing Logistical Limitations*

Whether the event is at an outdoor site or indoor venue, the producer must become intimately familiar with the location and all its limitations in order to prepare for additional support or to change the production accordingly. Indoor venues and outdoor sites each have their own set of concerns.

8.1.1.3.1 Indoor Venues

Some of the key points to be determined both during initial site inspection and during the Coordination Phase are:

- Where is power located, what options are available, what is the cost for tie-in, how will it be tied in, and who will do it? Usually lighting and audio prefer power tie-in near or behind the main stage.
- Is adequate staging available and can it be set up in a timely manner? Is there a cost for staging as well and is the surface appropriate for the show? Is it steady? Are there safety rails? Is a wheelchair ramp necessary and if so, is one available from the venue or must one be constructed or brought in?
- What are the exact dimensions of the room? Where are entrance doors and exits? Where will catering be coming from? Where will bars and other venue-provided services (e.g. buffets) be located?
- Where is the best location for the technical riser?
- Is there a remote house lighting control available?
- Where are the hanging points located in the ceiling and what is their load capacity?
- Are there any specific restrictions about installation of equipment or décor such as no nails in walls?
- What will the venue be doing during event setup? There can be no clashes between technical personnel and venue staff, such as setting up tables at the same time as lighting is being flown. Neither can there be conflicting events in other rooms.
- What time is room access?
- Is there easy freight elevator and loading dock access and how long does it take to move from the loading dock to the event location? Will all

equipment and props fit into the freight elevator or will they have to be brought in via an alternate route and perhaps even at an alternate time? Can all equipment be moved safely through access hallways and doors?

- Are ladders or automated lifts (e.g. Genie lifts) available for use to help with rigging in the ceiling? Must a venue qualified operator be used?
- Are there green rooms readily available with all necessary amenities for technical personnel and performers?
- Is there an area or spare room set aside for technical equipment container (otherwise known as *dead cases*) storage?
- What time is strike and will there be any clashes when loading out?
- Where are emergency exits located and where are fire extinguishers located?
- What, if any, are the specific venue safety regulations that pertain to any of the responsibility areas of event production?

Following this site visit and as part of the subsequent preparatory event paperwork, the producer must communicate back to the venue or site exactly what technical assistance will be required from them. This can be done in any number of ways such as by e-mail, fax, or phone call, but the main thing is to have a request on paper. My own company used to create an 'Event Requirements' form that would be printed out from our database program that outlined all these basic needs, including such items as staging and the required size, audio needs (e.g. house audio and the number and type of microphones if the event were simple), house lighting and power tie-in needs, changing room (i.e. green room) sizes and additional support (e.g. coat racks, mirrors, refreshments, etc.), and any other special requests. This form would also be copied to the client who invariably had the responsibility of paying for some of these requirements (e.g. refreshments, staging, house power tie-in, etc.), but of course we would have obtained the client's approval before sending the form to the venue. See Appendix A for an example of this form (Courtesy Pacific Show Productions, www.pacificshow.ca – Copyright 2006).

PRODUCTION WAR STORY: A FEW DETAILS MISSING IN THAT LAST COMMUNICATION

For the grand opening of an upscale department store, we were contracted to do the lighting for a fashion show to be held on the fourth floor. It went downhill from there. The show was fine, but the "getting there and back" was the real battle.

Normally we would have been allowed to use the loading docks to move our truss, rigging, and lighting in and out, but the Loss Prevention Department nixed this idea as they were concerned about tying up the elevators with all the inventory/furnishings moving in and out as the store readied itself for the big day.

Continued

8.1.1.3.2 Outdoor Sites

Outdoor sites present an entirely different set of concerns for producers, some requiring extensive and ongoing monitoring. Some of the key ones are:

- What is the optimum layout of the site for the most benefit to attendees and the least impact on surrounding neighbors? This includes optimization for foot and possible vehicular traffic.
- Where will each and every temporary structure be located? How will necessary power be run to them if needed?
- What is the potential acoustic impact on neighbors and must event parameters be changed to minimize the impact?
- Where will entrances and exits be located and how many of each will there be?
- How accessible is the site for technical equipment load-in and also for emergency vehicles (e.g. fire, police, and ambulance)? Where can technical vehicles be parked?
- What is the ground surface and is there anything required to protect it from damage?
- Is security fencing required and how much?
- Are there any dangerous areas or areas that cannot be used because of hidden infrastructure (e.g. water mains, telephone lines, sewage, electrical)?
- Where exactly are water and electrical power located, if any? Can either be tapped into for use at the event? Is portable power required?
- What is the best location for portable toilets?

- What is the best central location for waste and refuse accumulation?
- Is there any available site lighting and is it adequate or must additional be brought in?

Armed with the answers to these questions, the producer can now proceed to drawing a site or venue plan to scale and to producing a preliminary production schedule.

8.1.2   Site/Venue Layout and CADD

As the technical complexity of events increases, so does the demand for exact sizing and placement of all elements in the event space. The only way that this can be achieved is through the use of CADD software. There are several excellent CADD programs on the market today, the most well-known, industry-specific programs being Vectorworks and Vivien. Both of these programs are capable of two-dimensional drawings and vivid three-dimensional renderings of the entire event space, incorporating actual lighting and surface textures. As well, many less complex – but quite usable – two-dimensional programs are included with some of the event planning software available on the market. The benefits to using this type of program are many. First, it enables all elements to be drawn to exact scale with no room for error, so that spacing within a venue – or outdoors – is easily and accurately determined. Second, it enables changes to be made quickly and accurately to match any changes in event plans. For example, table templates can be loaded quickly in order to illustrate the effect of adding or deleting tables, all with correctly pre-determined spacing. Third, with only a one-time input or creation of a basic venue or site plan, future events can easily be planned within the same venue or at the same site. Fourth, it gives both clients and suppliers alike better visualization of the event concept if a three-dimensional rendering is used. In fact, the top programs allow an actual fly or walk-through of the event space as a movie.

Of course, to create the initial plan in two dimensions as a top view, accurate measurements must be taken of either the venue or site. Most hotels and convention centers now have CADD drawings of their meeting spaces which they will willingly share with producers. In some cases, they may only have old scale draftings of the spaces but these are easy to convert to actual drawings with the CADD software. When no drawings exist, particularly in the case of outdoor sites, accurate measurements can be obtained in several ways. The first is through the use of aerial photographs, which give a broad overview but accuracy depends on scale and camera resolution. The second is through the use of *laser distance measuring devices*, which can measure very accurately to within about ¼–¹⁄₁₆ in. (0.6–0.16) at distances up to 100 ft (30 m) at the lower quality end, to accuracies of around 0.06 in. (0.15 cm) at 650 ft (195 m) at the upper quality end. The ranges of these devices are somewhat limited and depend on quality and manufacturer. Their benefit is ease and speed of use. Finally, a *surveyor's measuring wheel* can also be helpful for taking quick and accurate measurements in any venue at any distance. It is a manual device that accurately records a running distance as one walks with it rolling on the ground.

Figures 8.3–8.5 are examples of CADD capabilities. Figure 8.3 illustrates a two-dimensional outline of a real outdoor event site based on an aerial photograph. In this case, the main event boundaries have been drawn in red over the aerial photo, and the more detailed internal components have been drawn in blue and sized at the actual site with a measuring wheel. For the final event site plan, the bottom layer (the photo) is removed. Figure 8.4 is

FIGURE 8.3

TWO-DIMENSIONAL CADD DRAWING OF
THE BOUNDARIES OF AN OUTDOOR EVENT BASED ON
AN AERIAL PHOTOGRAPH

First Night
Preliminary Site Boundaries

Site Boundaries

Indy Boundaries

FIGURE 8.4

THREE-DIMENSIONAL RENDERING OF THE VOLVO 2005
LAUNCH PARTY

Courtesy: Vivien Design by Chad Yeary, Portal Design Services, www.viviendesign.com

a three-dimensional rendering example of an indoor event, the Volvo 2005 Launch Party, showing the effects of lighting and surface textures, and Figure 8.5 is a photograph of the actual Volvo event, showing how close to reality CADD can be. Many more examples of two- and three-dimensional CADD can be found in *Special Event Production: The Resources*.

A venue layout should be created as soon as possible once the basic details of the event are known. It can then be used as a planning tool for all participants including the venue itself, so that there is no room for error in setting up all the elements.

8.1.3 Production Schedules, Running Orders, and Scripts

The last crucial task for the producer in the Coordination Phase is to commit all production plans to paper in the form of a detailed event schedule

FIGURE 8.5

ACTUAL PHOTO OF THE 2005 VOLVO LAUNCH PARTY

Courtesy: Vivien Design by Chad Yeary, Portal Design Services, www.viviendesign.com

that includes setup and strike details, plus a more specific show running order for the event itself. This outlines all the specific cues for actions during the event, from the president coming to the stage to give a speech, to video and audio cues, to the exact entrances and exits of performers. This document becomes the 'Bible' for the producer or TD. It is from this document that the show is run or *called*, and all technical personnel (e.g. audio engineer, lighting director, A-V director, stage managers) must be in possession of a copy. Often, the running order is combined with a Master of Ceremonies script that permits all technical personnel to see and understand exactly what is happening onstage and at the event as it unfolds in real time.

Appendix B illustrates a production schedule for an actual awards show. Individual producers have their own preferences for the layout of this document, with some incorporating three or more columns to permit separate headings for the person responsible for each action. In this particular case, the person or company responsible for each action item has been included in the Details column (specific names have been substituted with general terms for this illustration, but were used in the real schedule). Appendix C illustrates a single page of a 43-page combined script/running order for the same awards show event as in Appendix B. In this case, separate columns have been incorporated for the individual responsibility areas and the actual spoken script has been written in italics in the third column which also includes cues for key participants. Although some producers are gifted at writing scripts, more often than not a separate speech writer may need to be hired to create extended scripts for complex shows. These critical documents would be distributed to all technical suppliers, to the client, to the venue, to the event manager, and to any other personnel who would need to be kept informed of the progress of the event.

For more complex, large public or private events, project management software is sometimes useful as a supplement to the production schedule as it allows for conflicts in scheduling, offering options to get around them, besides making it easier to track the multiplicity of tasks required of a large team. Microsoft Project is an example of such a sophisticated program. Rutherford-Silvers (2004; pp. 44–47), Allen et al. (2005; p. 301), and Van Der Wagen and Carlos (2005; pp. 121–123) discuss this type of program in more detail.

If an event is particularly complex, many producers compile the schedules, running orders, and scripts into a larger *production book* that also includes client and supplier contracts, budgets, CADD drawings, licenses and permits, contact lists, and other useful and essential information. This book can then be brought onsite for handy reference during setup and event execution. Rutherford-Silvers (2004; pp. 406–408) also goes into more detail about this book. Included in the book may be further details concerning the show itself (the *showbook*), as recommended by Robertson (2006).

8.2   DURING THE EVENT EXECUTION PHASE

The Coordination Phase turns into the Execution Phase when setup of the event begins. This can vary from a few hours before the event to weeks before in the case of large public events or festivals. Once execution begins, there are three components to it that a TD must supervise: event setup, running the event and show, and event strike.

8.2.1   Supervising Event Setup

Somebody has to know the master plan for the event and generally the only person who can put all the technical pieces together is the producer or TD. It is this person or a delegated representative who must be present at all times during setup. It is also this person whom all suppliers will call upon to resolve problems, be they technical or personal. The primary tasks of the TD during setup include:

- Ensuring the event schedule is followed with respect to setup timing.
- Ensuring all equipment and access are provided by the site or venue according to pre-agreed plans between the producer and venue or site (e.g. staging and power in place at the correct time, freight elevator and loading dock access available at the correct time, etc.).
- Resolving any scheduling conflicts among suppliers and site or venue staff.
- Ensuring all equipment meets contractual requirements, including necessary compliance with safety and design regulations and standards.
- Monitoring the safety of the setup and of crew members.
- Assessing potential risks that may arise during the event as a result of equipment setup.
- Maintaining continuous liaison with the client and venue or site staff to ensure that they are aware of progress and that no changes to the setup are required.

The technical direction job can be physically demanding and mentally draining because it usually requires considerable standing and walking around on hard floors for long periods of time. It also requires that the occasional emergency be dealt with expeditiously and sometimes such emergencies need small supplies to solve. Therefore, TDs should be prepared with an onsite tool kit that includes both personal and technical components. Van Keken (2005) lists some suggested items among the following:

- *Communication.* The ability to communicate with any and all suppliers and colleagues throughout the setup is paramount. Essential items include:
  - Radios and chargers
  - Cell phones with additional batteries
  - PDAs
  - Contact list that includes client, venue, staff, and suppliers.
- *Administrative.* Most of these items make the job a bit easier:
  - Copy of all supplier and client contracts in order to confirm deliverables
  - If the TD is also the producer, then payment for all suppliers in the form of signed checks
  - Plain paper
  - Company ID badge and/or identifiable clothing (if permitted by client)
  - Production schedule, running order, script, and floor or site plan, all with extra copies
  - Various supplies (e.g. colored marker pens, extra pens and pencils, stapler, calculator, envelopes).
- *Technical.* Some minor supplies help in emergency situations in case they are not available elsewhere or from the appropriate suppliers:
  - Small flashlight
  - Pocket knife with various accessories such as scissors and screwdriver

- Rolls of duct tape in various colors (particularly the venue carpet color for emergency taping of miscellaneous cords, although suppliers should have this already)
- Rolls of narrow fluorescent tape to mark stage and stair edges and backstage pathways, and to spike key equipment and performer positions onstage
- Surveyor's measuring wheel to take accurate and fast measurements of large distances
- 50 ft measuring tape for doing the same in smaller confined spaces.

- *Personal.* These help to overcome fatigue and make the experience more enjoyable:
  - Toiletries, including shaving kit and after shave for men or essential cosmetics for women, plus deodorant and breath freshener or gum
  - First aid kit
  - Water and granola bars or energy food (e.g. fruit, energy bars)
  - Sunscreen, hat, and jacket if the event is outdoors
  - Change of clothes and comfortable shoes.

8.2.2 Running the Event

From the time doors or gates open, it is the job of the Production Manager or TD to ensure that the event running order is followed to the letter and that the event proceeds according to plan. From here on in this section, we will refer to the event as 'the show.' Correctly directing technical personnel and stage managers is the key to getting it right. Having knowledgeable staff, using the right communication equipment, and understanding what is involved in 'calling the show' are essential to success.

8.2.2.1 *Staffing the Show*

Most shows incorporating lighting, audio, A-V, and entertainment also have a requirement to provide subcontracted technical staff from all these areas to run the show, especially if there are many awards, presentations, speeches, or entertainment segments. The TD should have voice communication with all the players, including followspot operators, audio engineer, lighting director, A-V director (especially if complex equipment such as multiple PowerPoint presentations, video wall, teleconferencing, or videotape changes will be involved), and stage managers.

All technical personnel should be fully conversant with the entire show and be familiar with the total running order. All should be prepared ahead of time to make the appropriate changes when the time comes in the show. Examples include microphone changes and re-sets onstage, special lighting cues for performers, CD/DVD/tape changes, video wall cues, switching equipment (e.g. video wall to PowerPoint to straight video) cues, performer cues, and followspot cues.

All personnel should be extremely familiar with the equipment under their control. This means that they should be able to analyze and fix any problem very quickly. Not only that, but with today's complex equipment, they should be able to program it for maximum effect. A good example is intelligent lighting such as Vari-lites that can be programmed to follow moving people ahead of time if the path will not waver much (e.g. walking up to a stage). This can be an easy way to eliminate a followspot and operator but programming does take time.

It is always wise to schedule a complete rehearsal or at minimum a full talk-through of the event with all technical personnel before the event begins. In this way, everyone knows exactly what to expect and has an opportunity to bring up any potential problem areas. Shows also run much more smoothly when everyone literally is on the same page and this means they should all have a copy of a complete script or at a minimum, a complete and detailed show running order. It is the producer's responsibility to generate these documents.

Stage management is an essential component of a complex show as stage managers can save much time, effort, and stress. In theater, a stage manager is like the TD and is responsible for calling the show. In special events, stage managers have slightly different responsibilities and are primarily used to:

- alert speakers ahead of time and prepare them by bringing them to the stage holding area;
- physically assist with stage changeovers;
- take performers to and from green rooms;
- cue performers, speakers, and others who will be using the stage;
- keep the show flowing.

They should always be in voice contact with the TD either by intercom or radio.

8.2.2.2   Communications (Comm) Equipment and Protocol

TDs usually communicate using either two-way radios with multiple channels (if walls or distance preclude using intercom) or intercom, most notably equipment made by Clear-Com, also with multiple channels. Radios generally come with the option of a headset and microphone to allow privacy. Clear-Com units come with headset microphones (Figure 8.6) and can be either wired to a fixed station, or completely wireless with a belt pack and antenna. The current industry standard seems to be Clear-Com. The equipment has a press-to-talk function or a continuous talk, hands-free function.

In addition, there is other equipment that has only a one-way talk function called IFB ('in-ear fold-back' or 'in-ear monitor'). This is used by broadcasters and increasingly by informed Production Managers and TDs to communicate with people onstage such as MCs, hosts, and musicians. It consists of a small earpiece with a wire and a receiver pack that must be affixed to the person on a belt or dress on their back out of sight of the audience. It is

FIGURE 8.6
CLEAR-COM HEADSET UNITS

Courtesy: Clear-Com, www.clearcom.com

an extremely useful item if sudden changes must be made (e.g. shorten or lengthen a presentation, change something due to a mistaken technical cue, etc.), and the TD does not want to make the mistake or change obvious to the audience. This is the same equipment used for in-ear monitors for musicians (see Chapters 1 and 3 of *Special Event Production: The Resources* for further discussion).

There are two other considerations before launching into calling a show that should be mentioned: assigning communication channels and understanding communication protocol.

8.2.2.2.1 Communication Channel Assignment

On Clear-Com there are multiple channels at the main control station (see Figure 8.7) and the TD (or show caller) needs to decide which technical personnel must talk to each other throughout the show. If the TD sits at this control position, which he or she usually does, it means that for many cues, there will be a necessary switching of channels so that the correct technical personnel will hear the cue. Mainly to minimize the amount of switching, my personal choice is to have one main channel that incorporates the individuals responsible for the most important parts of the show (e.g. TD, stage managers, and audio or TD, stage managers and video wall, etc.). Depending on the show, sometimes lighting for example, has a couple of followspots and lots of separate cues. They might be better off on their own channel so as not to interrupt the other calls, especially if they are intimately familiar with the show and really need no formal cues for each major stage change. Likewise, sometimes an orchestra leader may not want to be disturbed except for specific cues relating to him, in which case he needs a separate channel as well.

FIGURE 8.7

EXAMPLE OF A MAIN CLEAR-COM STATION
(PLPRO MS-440)

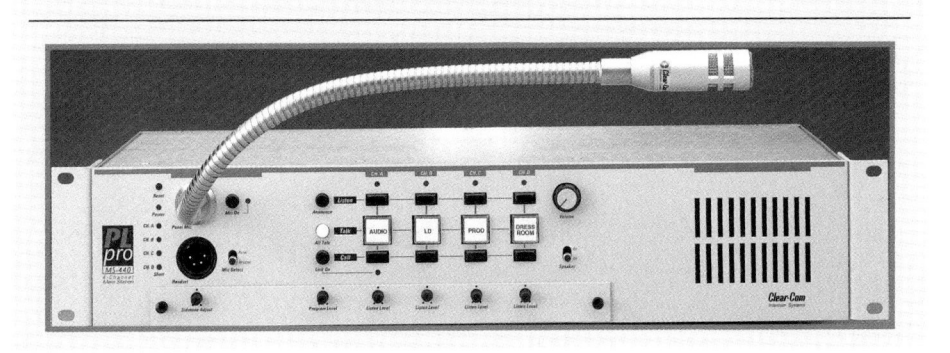

Courtesy: Clear-Com, www.clearcom.com

8.2.2.2.2 Communication Protocol

Although radios and intercom equipment are relatively uncomplicated to use, there is certain protocol for using them correctly which serves to make communications more understandable. For either radios or intercom, there is no magic to it. There is a button that must be pressed to talk. General polite protocol means that one says only what is required in a minimum number of words. The finger is then removed and the green 'on' light checked to ensure it is out. Not doing so can result in an open microphone on one comm set that sends all ambient noise throughout the entire system, making understanding very difficult in a noisy event venue.

To get someone's attention is also simple and obvious (e.g. 'Dave calling Susan,' or 'Susan from Dave'). To acknowledge someone calling, again simplicity works the best (e.g. 'Go for Susan'). To acknowledge an instruction, simple code can be used (e.g. '10-4') or just a statement of 'understood.'

Other things to keep in mind include keeping idle chatter to a minimum, not coughing into a live microphone, keeping the volume loud enough to hear but not too loud for others, and letting others know when one is going 'off comm.'

In the world of communications, there are also codes and an alphabet that have developed to make understanding easier:

- *Radio code numbers*: Although for the majority of events most TDs work on, security radio codes as used by police will not be necessary. Sometimes it is useful to have them and it is definitely a bonus if the event is a large public one. Table 8.1 lists the more important code numbers that may be encountered or useful for an event. The phrases 'lost child' or 'cash' should never be used over the radio during a public event for obvious reasons.

TABLE 8.1

RADIO CODE NUMBERS

Code Number	Meaning
One	Major incident
Two	Reportable incident
Three	Coordination meeting
Four	Lost Child
Five	VIP/Cash Escort
10-4	Acknowledgement
10-7	Out of service (i.e. off comm)
10-8	Back in service (i.e. back on comm)
10-9	Say again
10-20	State your location
10-21	Call by telephone
10-26	Detaining suspect
10-30	Improper use of radio
10-50	Transmission is good
10-52	Ambulance needed
10-100	Bomb/major threat

Courtesy: Doug Matthews

TABLE 8.2

RADIO CODE ALPHABET

A	Alpha	N	November
B	Bravo	O	Oscar
C	Charlie	P	Papa
D	Delta	Q	Quebec
E	Echo	R	Romeo
F	Foxtrot	S	Sierra
G	Golf	T	Tango
H	Hotel	U	Uniform
I	India	V	Victor
J	Juliet	W	Whiskey
K	Kilo	X	X-Ray
L	Lima	Y	Yankee
M	Mike	Z	Zulu

Courtesy: Doug Matthews

- *Radio code alphabet*: As with the number codes, usually most of us will not need them. However, they can be very useful if transmission is problematic or to avoid misunderstanding similar sounding alphabet letters (e.g. b, c, d, g, p, t, etc.). Table 8.2 lists the radio code alphabet.

8.2.2.3   *Calling the Show*

A producer works hard to create and bring together all of the elements of an event. However, some producers are either not confident enough to bring the actual show together on cue, or may be spread too thinly with the added responsibility. In these cases, the producer may hire either a TD as described above who can also call the show or a separate show caller. Show callers are usually people who have worked in theater and called cues in theatrical extravaganzas as stage managers (in the theatrical definition). They are seasoned and experienced in interpreting a producer's requirement for the crew to make sure everything happens at the right time and with maximum theatrical impact, where appropriate. If a show caller is hired to run only the show, that person is coming in to the event 'cold' with no knowledge about it whatsoever and must therefore be brought up to speed very quickly. We will assume this scenario for the following explanations, much of which has been provided by Venables (2006), and courtesy www.simply-communicate.com. For purposes of easy explanation, the show caller's job will be divided into two main segments, pre-show and show.

8.2.2.3.1 Pre-Show

Before the actual job of calling the show begins, a certain amount of preparation is required. If time permits, a separate briefing for the show caller is helpful and avoids any last minute panic onsite. The show caller then needs some time to prepare for the show by reviewing the material provided. This is typically followed by a rehearsal, particularly if the show is complex:

A show caller will need the following information which will usually be provided either by the Producer or TD:

- Names of all crew members on intercom.
- Any announcements needed (e.g. asking the audience to turn off cell phones or any health and safety announcements).
- Running order.
- Scripts (including entrance and exit points).
- Printouts of PowerPoint slides (for checking if correct ones are projected).
- Video play list showing each video's duration time.
- Music play list showing each track's duration time.
- Production schedule showing crew call times, any rehearsals, and all show times (to be reviewed throughout the day with the producer).
- Presets (i.e. required pre-placements of persons, props, or other items at specific points in the program).
- Creative interpretation of the running order.
- Background of any speakers or other useful information.

Typically, there are some procedures that a show caller will use to prepare the script and himself/herself for the show. Much of it is personal preference, but the following are general guidelines:

- A show caller will need pencil and/or marker pens, rubber bands, ruler, stopwatch (with big numbers and preferably no beeping noise), watch (synchronized with the producer's), water, mints, plain paper.

- If you are the show caller, have the script/running order on a right-hand page and your writing on the left-hand page. Write alongside where the cue in the script needs to happen (on the left-hand page) and use a ruler to draw a horizontal line (in pencil) to link into the cue point. At the point where the cue happens, draw a short vertical line up from the horizontal line to mark this cue point.
- Plan timings for when you are going to do certain things.
- Ensure all technical crew members are on headsets.
- Make an announcement for crew to turn cell phones and pagers off.
- Put in all presets to check they are all in place.
- Put in cues for yourself for announcements (e.g. to announce '10 min until doors open').
- To minimize the amount of words or space used on a page when you are writing in information, you can use abbreviations for key elements to be used, such as 'A' or 'SND' for audio/sound, 'L' or 'LX' for lighting, 'V' or 'VT' for video, and 'VW' video wall.
- Try out cues by speaking out loud, never in your head or you won't get a sense of the timing.

A technical run-through of the script is a must if there are numerous technical cues and a long program, such as an extended awards show. The show caller can once again make it easier to run the show by considering the following during rehearsal:

- Create your space. For most show callers or TDs, this is usually at the technical console position, next to the producer. Position yourself so your free ear is next to the producer, when you are on headsets. Again, everyone has a preference. I personally prefer to call a complex show from the rear of the venue from a central communication station that is connected to all the technical people involved, and from where I can see the whole picture. Other times, if the show involves a lot of entertainment that might be entering and leaving from different parts of the venue, I work better calling the show using wireless comm that gives me the flexibility to move around and change the way the show flows if I see it needs it, or to talk directly to an entertainer or presenter. See Figure 8.8 for a typical TD or show caller position.
- Talk to the crew casually before the technical rehearsal to determine: Have they got all their software? Do they know their running order? Is there anything you need to know (e.g. how a piece of technology works and what you need to cue)?
- Agree to cue numbers if the crew wants to use those. (LX usually does; others probably don't but it's worth asking.)
- Tell the crew what sort of cues you are going to give them.
- Always get crew to acknowledge standbys.
- Be firm but fair, listen for their feedback or suggestions but remember you are in control.

- Take it steady and do one cue sequence at a time. Get it right, and then move on.

- Make sure you have re-written your cues before you try a cue or sequence again; take your time and make sure you really understand what the producer wants and how to achieve it.

- Start your stopwatch for videos, just in case the video engineer forgets to count you down. Also make a note of a sequence 30 s before the end so you can start the standbys to come out of the video.

Finally, and most critically, speakers and entertainment need time to rehearse. They must understand how long they are allowed onstage because impromptu, unrehearsed speeches and entertainment acts that are longer than promised can wreak havoc with a show and cause it to go much longer than planned. A full or partial speaker and entertainment rehearsal can help to avoid this, by having the show caller consider the following:

- Be alert so you can respond to changes, update your cues, put people on standby, etc.

- Keep communicating with the crew so they know what is going on and what to prepare for.

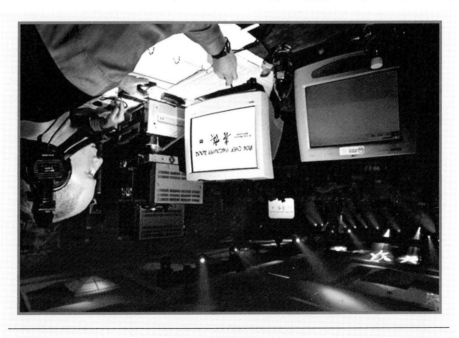

Courtesy: Darren Dreger, BC Event Management, www.bceventmanagement.com

FIGURE 8.8
TD CALLING A SHOW

- Try out any changes the producer may have made after the technical rehearsal.
- Time all speakers with a stopwatch as they will ask how long they were and it will help you plan timings for the actual show.
- If possible, remind the producer to ask the speakers for their last few words leading into a video to help with the cueing.
- Ensure all speakers tell you where they will be located in the audience for the 30 min preceding their time onstage in order that stage managers can find them easily.
- For entertainment, ensure they know how long they are allowed onstage, where and what equipment must be pre-placed onstage and removed after their act, and at what point in the program (exact time) they are to be ready in their green rooms.
- Ensure all speakers and entertainers understand how they will enter and exit the stage.
- Work out a standardized method of removing speakers or entertainers from the stage if they go over their allotted time – and ensure they all know what the signal is. This could be the subtle playing of a musical tune on CD or by an onstage orchestra, the flashing of a light from the technical console, the frantic waving of an offstage stage manager in the wings, or if all else fails, turning off the microphone.

8.2.2.3.2 The Show

Do exactly what is in the script and what has been rehearsed but watch and listen to what is going on onstage and all around you constantly; don't relax. The secret is to get a flow established:

- Be consistent. If you always say it in the same order, then people will get used to it (e.g. SND, LX, VT, etc.).
- In general terms, three to four words is about a second when spoken out loud.
- Cue process one: standby. Remind crew what they are standing by for in general terms at the beginning (e.g. a speaker changeover, the name of the video, etc.). Then put everyone on standby together, saying what each is to do as you go (if you have time), particularly if video or music is to be used (use specific names to be absolutely sure). Standbys are usually given around 5–10 s before a go, subject to how many people you have to standby and how long you have between cues. You should also allow time for people to acknowledge their standby and a bit of space before the cue.
- Cue process two: go. Allow time to state the item to be cued first, then say 'go' (never the other way around or they will all go and that may not be the creative direction).
- Performers, presenters, and other individuals who know they must appear onstage during an event program (i.e. are not award winners) should be

escorted to the backstage or holding area so they are standing by at that location a minimum of 10 min prior to their appearance onstage. This means that the show caller – and especially the stage managers – will have to gauge the time it takes to travel with these individuals (or groups for that matter) from their green room or other location to backstage and be ready to go at the correct time. This is not necessarily as easy as it seems, since the green room may be on another building level, there may be large crowds or long convoluted hallways to navigate, and some groups may take time to assemble themselves. It is always better to err on the side of arriving backstage earlier rather than later.

- If there haven't been cues for a while, then let everyone know there are 2 min to go before the next cue so they wake up, set up a CD or VT, or prepare accordingly.
- React to changes that may occur once in show mode (e.g. a speaker is faster or slower than you thought) and immediately adjust your running order as needed.

In the example below, the Production Manager or TD is 'Doug,' who is 'calling the show,' the Stage Manager (SM) is 'John,' LX is Lighting, and the Video Director is VD.

TD: 'Doug for John.'
SM: 'Go for John.'
TD: 'Standby with Mr. Smith at stage right and put him at stage right lectern after this speaker finishes.'
SM: '10-4.'
TD: 'Standby lighting with new wash for Mr. Smith.'
LX: 'Standing by.'
TD: 'John, Mr. Smith onstage. Go.'
SM: 'Mr. Smith is onstage.'
TD: 'Lighting, change to a blue wash for Mr. Smith. Go.'
LX: 'Blue wash is on Mr. Smith.'
TD: 'Standby video with the next clip after Mr. Smith. It's the clip for the new sales program.'
VD: 'Standing by with video clip of new program.'
TD: 'Video clip of new program. Go.'

And so on, as per the show running order and script. To reiterate, there is a standard sequence for giving verbal cues:

- 'Standby Sound Cue 19' (The word 'Standby' first).
- 'Sound Cue 19 Go' (The word 'Go' last).

Repeat this same order for the next series of presenters or stage segment and try to keep it going throughout the event. The key is to anticipate and know exactly what must be done at least four or five steps ahead of where you are in the show running order or script. Give everyone lots of time to get to their assigned positions and complete their tasks. Check off each item on the running order or script as it finishes. Try to keep calm and not get flustered if things go wrong. Think logically. Keep in mind that, like an airplane taking off and landing, the first and last 10 min of the show are the most critical and they are the times when something is most likely to go wrong. If you are new to the game, start on a really simple show and work your way up from there.

8.2.2.3.3   Post-Show

Only the final finesse remains:

- Thank all crew.
- When are crew needed again? Find out before you let them off headsets or agree to a short break and gather them in a given location for a briefing.
- Debrief with all crew if you are doing the same thing again and you want to change something or do another technical rehearsal.
- If it's the end of the show, then ask them to bring all software, tapes, and CDs or DVDs to you or say you will collect them.
- Hand your script and running order to the producer and thank him/her.
- Have a large drink! You have earned it.

A well-rehearsed and technically seamless show is the goal that producers want. Working with a professional to call the show is one of the best ways to achieve this.

8.2.3   Supervising Event Strike

The strike of all technical equipment and décor is the final task of the Production Manager or TD. By the time this happens, it is not unusual for the TD to have been onsite for 16 or more hours. This necessitates that the TD delegate another person to supervise the strike of equipment that often can take up to 8 or more hours if the event is large. The TD must ensure that the delegated person understands what must be done and in what order so that conflicts among contractors rushing to exit on freight elevators and from loading docks is avoided. When crew members are tired, there is also more potential for injury and damage to equipment and property, so the supervisor must be vigilant to avoid this. Proper safety procedures must be followed as much for the strike as for the event setup. In my personal experience, more damage and conflicts have occurred during the strike than at any other time. Professionalism dictates that the event is not complete until the venue or site has been returned to its original state in an orderly and controlled manner.

PRODUCTION CHALLENGES

1. Describe the persons most likely to be your main contacts if you produce events in a hotel, a convention center, a football stadium, a shopping mall, a city park, an aquarium, an aircraft hangar, and a mountain chalet.

2. You have been asked to provide décor, entertainment, and all technical support for a 3-h standup indoor reception for 300 persons. The room provided is 150 ft long and 80 ft deep. You need a stage on one of the long walls that is 20 ft deep and 24 ft wide, plus there will be rear-projection A-V screens and drapes running from the end walls to the downstage corners of the stage. A standup buffet occupying an area of 16 ft long and 10 ft deep will be placed along each of the end walls in the center. Can all 300 persons be safely and comfortably accommodated?

3. You will be providing all production for a summer folk festival for 20,000 persons in a city park, with performances running from noon to 10:00 p.m. on a single main stage. Your contact is a member of the Parks Board. List as many questions as you can think of that you must ask this person to determine what you need to know in order to produce this festival.

4. You are to produce an awards show in a convention center ballroom. Lights are to be flown, as are the mid/high audio speakers, from a single truss in front of the stage. The stage is to be custom-built by a contractor. There will be two ground-supported A-V screens and runoff drapes on either side of the stage. There will be dining tables with linens and tables centers provided by your designer, as well as chair covers. There will be a short entertainment program and there will be two keynote speakers speaking from a lectern using PowerPoint during dinner. Setup goes from 6:00 a.m. to 5:00 p.m. and the doors to the event open at 6:00 p.m. Write a complete production schedule for the event incorporating all necessary activities.

5. Describe how a TD assigned the responsibility of calling the awards show in Question 4 would prepare for the task.

REFERENCES

Allen, J., O'Toole, W., Harris, R. and McDonnell, I. (2005). *Festival and Special Event Management*, Third Edition. Milton: John Wiley & Sons Australia, Ltd.

Harris, B.W. (December, 2000). Function Room Setup. In S. Krug, C. Chatfield-Taylor and M.C. Collins (Eds.), *The Convention Industry Council Manual: A Working Guide for Effective Meetings and Conventions*, Seventh Edition. McLean: Convention Industry Council, pp. 191–192.

Robertson, F. (2006). *Showbooks*. Retrieved August 17, 2006, from http://www.simply-communicate.com.

Rutherford-Silvers, J. (2004). *Professional Event Coordination*. Hoboken: John Wiley & Sons, Inc.

Van Der Wagen, L. and Carlos, B.R. (2005). *Event Management for Tourism, Cultural, Business, and Sporting Events*. Upper Saddle River, NJ: Pearson Education, Inc.

Van Keken, M. (June, 2005). On Site Survival Tool Box: List of Supplies and Tools You Can't Do Without. In S. Wyatt (Ed.), *The Event Plan: Everything You Need to Know to Plan a Successful Event*. Vancouver: Canadian Event Perspective Magazine.

Venables, N. (2006). *Showcalling*. Retrieved August 11, 2006, from http://www.simply-communicate.com.

ABC EVENT COMPANY LTD.

EVENT REQUIREMENTS

Memo to: Contact at venue or site

Venue Name: Name of venue or site   **Room Name:** Room in venue

Client/Sponsor: Name of client or event manager

Name of Event: Title of event   **Event Date:** Date

Schedule: Schedule of event and show (e.g. such as an event schedule or show running order that can be attached)

Suppliers: Names of all suppler companies expected to provide equipment or to be onsite

Staging/Special Requests: List any stages and sizes to be provided by venue

Audio: List house audio to be provided if any

Lighting/Power: List house lighting and power to be provided by venue if any

Change Rooms: List any requirements for green rooms

Special Notes: Additional requests _____

_____

Note: Unless otherwise specified, any additional charges for the above are the client/sponsor's responsibility and must be authorized by the client/sponsor.

Date: _____   **Producer** _____

ABC Event Company Ltd.

ABC Event Company Ltd.,
1234 Main St., New Orleans, LA 76543, USA
Phone: 123-567-8901; Fax: 123-456-7890;
E-mail: info@abceventcompany.com

Appendix B

Example of an Actual Production Schedule for an Awards Show

Leo Awards: Production Schedule	
Date/Time	**Details**
Thursday, May 27	
7:30 p.m.–12:00 a.m.	Load-in at hotel: 7:30 p.m. – Staging company 8:00 p.m. – Lighting company 8:30 p.m. – Audio company 9:00 p.m. – Video wall company 9:30 p.m. – Decor designer Simultaneous stage construction, cable runs, rigging for truss, spiking drape positions, rigging hanging lanterns
	Hotel to have Genie lift ready at 7:30 p.m. Power hookup to be ready by 10:00 p.m.
	TD to supervise until 11:00 p.m.
Friday, May 28	
6:00 a.m.–noon	Video wall company load-in and begin set up of video wall and all A-V screens
	Audio and lighting install continues (Note to audio company – at least two 110 V power bars to be available to band on stage right)
	Preliminary lighting focus – Lighting company

Continued

Leo Awards: Production Schedule (Contd.)	
Date/Time	Details
	Drape installation – Lighting company and video wall company
8:00 a.m.–noon	Assistant TD to supervise
	Decor designer to place shoji screens and lanterns onstage
Noon–12:30 p.m.	Crew lunch break
	TD to take over supervision
12:30–2:00 p.m.	Final lighting focus – Lighting company
	Final audio checks – Audio company
	Hotel to place tables
2:00–3:00 p.m.	Video wall and A-V focus and dark time
2:00–4:00 p.m.	Decor designer to place all table centers
3:00–4:00 p.m.	Orchestra leader and 4-piece band setup, sound check and rehearse. Must be complete by 4:00 p.m.
4:00–5:30 p.m.	Presenter and Host rehearsals led by Event Manager. Will need audio, lighting and A-V
	Assistant TD to be onsite for rehearsals
5:00–5:30 p.m.	Rehearsal of show opening with Orchestra Leader and Host

Continued

Leo Awards: Production Schedule (Contd.)	
Date/Time	Details
6:00–7:00 p.m.	Reception in foyer
6:30 p.m.	Doors open
7:00 p.m.–7:30 p.m.	Crew dinner break
7:45 p.m.	Band to report to stage right
8:00–11:00 p.m.	Show – see separate running order and script
Saturday, May 29	
1:00–3:00 p.m.	Presenter and Host rehearsals led by Event Manager. Will need audio, lighting and A-V. Orchestra leader to assist as required.
	Décor touch-up as required – Decor designer
	Assistant TD onsite to supervise technical until 5:30 p.m. TD onsite at approximately 5:00 p.m.
3:00–5:30 p.m.	Final audio, A-V and lighting checks
6:00–7:00 p.m.	Reception in foyer
6:30 p.m.	Band arrives
	Technical crew standby

Continued

Leo Awards: Production Schedule (Contd.)	
Date/Time	Details
7:00 p.m.	Dinner and show begin
7:00–7:30 p.m.	Crew dinner break
8:00–11:00 p.m.	Show – see separate running order and script
11:00 p.m.–2:00 a.m. (30th May)	Technical and décor strike

Courtesy: Pacific Show Productions, www.pacificshow.ca – Copyright 2006

Appendix C

Example of a Combined Script and Show Running Order

#	Time	Ballroom/Stage	Video Wall	Music	Hotel	Front of House
104	21:50	podium) (Cue Brenda Crichlow) / Walter Daroshin speaks of Union of BC Performers and invites Brenda Crichlow, UBCP Secretary to stage to receive Outstanding Achievement Award for an Organization. (Cue Trophy model)	Live.		No host bar open. Music down.	
105	21:51	Brenda Crichlow enters back stage centre, accepts Outstanding Achievement Award and proceeds to podium to speak, then exits stage left. (Trophy model stand by and exits with Brenda Crichlow) (Walter Daroshin stands by) (Cue Ellie) (Cue Beverley Staunton)	Outstanding Achievement Award — Organization title — UBCP. Live. Lion sequence.		Music bumper. Music down. Orchestra extended music piece.	Auction open.
106	21:52	Walter Daroshin returns to podium and speaks of John Juliani and invites Donna Wong-Juliani and Alessandro Juliani to stage to receive Outstanding Achievement Award for an Individual. (Cue Trophy model)	Live. Photo montage of John Juliani		No host bar open. Music down. Music bumper.	
107	21:54	Donna Wong-Juliani and Alessandro Juliani enter back stage centre, accepts Outstanding Achievement Award and proceed to podium to speak, then exit stage left. (Trophy model stands by and exits with group) (Walter Daroshin stands by and exits with Donna Wong-Juliani and Alessandro Juliani stage left) (Cue Ellie)	Outstanding Achievement Award — Individual title — John Juliani. Live. Lion sequence.		Music down. Orchestra extended music piece.	Auction open.
108	21:57	God voice: *Ladies and gentlemen, please welcome once again, Beverley Staunton…*			Orchestra plays *Thanks for the*	

Running Script / Page **31** of 43

Prepared by SWong

Courtesy: Hamazaki Wong Marketing Group and the Leo Awards, www.hamazakiwong.com

EVENT
FOLLOWUP

This phase of the event immediately follows the end of the event itself. It is a step that is all too often forgotten by producers. A little followup goes a long way to showing one's dedication to working in the client's best interest. For a producer who is not an event manager, there is normally no need to conduct extensive attendee evaluations and analysis since that is the responsibility of the event manager. More information on overall event evaluation and assessment is given by Allen et al. (2005) and Van Der Wagen and Carlos (2005). However, especially if the event is a regularly repeated one and not a one-off, there is still a need for the producer to communicate with three key groups of stakeholders: the production team members, the venue, and the client.

9.1 FOLLOWING UP WITH THE PRODUCTION TEAM

As discussed in Chapter 5, the production team is comprised of mainly sub-contractors in the form of performers, décor designers, various technical suppliers (e.g. audio, lighting, staging, A-V, etc.), a technical director, stage managers, and possibly administrative personnel (e.g. accountant, payroll, etc.). At minimum, followup with these persons should include:

- If the event was not large and the producer was not present, at least a phone call to subcontractors to ensure that the event was executed according to their contracts and that there were no problems. If there were problems, investigation should begin immediately and resolution sought as soon as possible.
- Return of all rental items from suppliers that were not delivered and picked up by the suppliers themselves.
- For larger events, a review of the budget and individual contracts together with other team members to assess why there might have been:
  - problems with event execution;
  - changes in budgets;
  - changes in the contracted deliverables of suppliers;
  - unpredicted but necessary expenses;
  - unnecessary expenses.
- From these results, adjustment of budgets and future cost estimates as required for future repeat events.
- Final subcontractor payments according to the contracted schedule.
- Acknowledgment of the work accomplished and accolades given where due.

9.2   FOLLOWING UP WITH THE VENUE

An often overlooked step in followup is for the producer to talk to the venue where the event was held. In many cases this will be a hotel or similar location. It is a good idea to contact the catering manager or conference services manager who was responsible for the event to ascertain if everything went well from their side. In some cases, the event may have been executed flawlessly from the producer's point of view and from the client's point of view, but a minor unseen conflict between subcontractors and venue staff or hidden physical damage to the venue might have occurred during the event strike and might have become overblown depending on whose side of the story has been told. If this is not addressed through contact with the venue, the producer may never know about it. This has been known to lead to a producer becoming 'persona non grata' at that establishment in the future, without ever understanding the reason why.

9.3   FOLLOWING UP WITH THE CLIENT

At the very least, if the event is not complicated or the producer has not had the opportunity to meet the client face to face, a phone call should be made to the client the day after the event in order to receive feedback, good or bad. At the same time, and preferably before the call to the client, a call should be made to all suppliers as recommended above. Thus, if there were problems, it gives the producer the opportunity to know at least one side of the story before talking to the client. If there were major problems – and one never wants nor plans for these – then the supplier calls enable the producer to consider appropriate corrective action or at least allow the producer to provide some explanation to the client. The client call is important because it establishes that the producer is truly interested in the service being offered and is willing to do whatever it takes to make it better and to maintain a fruitful client relationship.

If the event is one that is repeated on a regular basis such as an annual awards show, banquet, or festival, then a meeting with the entire event team (other than the production team) under the direction of the client or event manager is often a necessary adjunct to the event. This usually involves a debriefing assembly in which each member at the management level, including the producer, completes a debrief of what was successful, what was unsuccessful, what could be eliminated, what could be added, and what could be improved. Budget shortfalls and problems are also addressed. Followup actions with target dates and persons responsible are usually created and monitored for completion. It is essential that the production team under the direction of the producer meets and resolves its own issues before the entire event team meets.

Followup action with the client also entails invoicing the client and receiving all payments according to the producer/client contract. Any accounts receivable should be strictly monitored on a daily basis and not allowed to go over 30 days.

Additionally, a formal thank you to the client is usually in order. This can be done best with a combination letter and evaluation sheet which can be e-mailed, faxed, or mailed back to the producer. Including a request for future business and referrals on the same form is also an excellent method of scouting new leads and determining the best time to call this client back for future event production work. A sample production company evaluation form that does just this is shown in Appendix A.

PRODUCTION CHALLENGES

1. A wonderful awards dinner that you produced went off without a hitch; however, the next morning you receive a call from the catering director at the hotel where the event was held. She is irate. Apparently, one of your subcontractors was intoxicated during the event strike and was swearing at hotel staff, causing several conflicts. Explain whom you would talk to in order to resolve this issue and how you would do it. Once you have solved the problem, write a letter to the catering director.

Continued

PRODUCTION CHALLENGES (CONTD.)

2. The lighting company that you hired for a theme event brought in 10 extra automated fixtures because they wanted to make the décor look better and the original budget did not allow for it. In addition, the strike went longer than anticipated resulting in extra labor costs for the lighting company, for which you were not charged. Compose an accolade letter for this company.

3. Write a cover letter for the evaluation form of Appendix 'A' to the client for the event in Question 2, who was 'blown away' by your dedication and enthusiasm.

4. As the producer for a large outdoor world music festival, your responsibilities include entertainment programming, audio, lighting, staging, fencing, and portable electrical power. At the end of the event, you discover that several of these suppliers had major cost overruns, some performers did not know where to report and were consequently late for their performance, and you have not been paid your final installment for your production work by the event manager. Discuss the various people you must contact, what meetings you might have to attend, and what actions you might have to take to ensure that everything is resolved and that you keep this client for future events.

5. Recommend agendas for the post-event debriefing of the production team and of the event team for the festival in Question 5.

REFERENCES

Allen, J., O'Toole, W., Harris, R. and McDonnell, I. (2005). *Festival and Special Event Management*, Third Edition. Milton: John Wiley & Sons Australia, Ltd.

Van Der Wagen, L. and Carlos, B.R. (2005). *Event Management for Tourism, Cultural, Business, and Sporting Events*. Upper Saddle River, New Jersey: Pearson Education, Inc.

Sample Event Evaluation Form

ABC EVENT COMPANY LTD.

EVENT EVALUATION

Thank you for allowing ABC Event Company Ltd. to be a part of your event. In our continuing effort to present the best shows possible, we value your opinions and comments. Therefore, we would appreciate your taking the time to complete the enclosed evaluation form and to fax or mail it back to us at the number/address below. We will keep all information confidential.

Name of Organization: _____

Event Date: _____   Event Type: _____

Please rate the following elements from 1 (poor) to 5 (excellent) by circling the appropriate number:

1. Speedy service regarding pricing and proposals		1 2 3 4 5
2. Creativity of suggestions		1 2 3 4 5
3. Competitive pricing		1 2 3 4 5
4. Entertainment (appropriate and professional)		1 2 3 4 5
5. Décor (creativity, quality, quantity)		1 2 3 4 5
6. Technical production (A-V, audio, lighting, staging, etc.)		1 2 3 4 5
7. Event execution (attention to details, communication, smoothness of show)		1 2 3 4 5

Comments: _____

_____

_____

_____

_____

_____

May we contact you or another person responsible for the next important event for your organization?

Name: _____ Phone: _____

Fax: _____ E-mail: _____

Date of Next Event: _____

City/State/Province/Country of Next Event: _____

Can you recommend us to at least two other organizations that could use our company's services?

1. Name: _____ Phone: _____

   Address: _____

2. Name: _____ Phone: _____

   Address: _____

Thank you for your feedback. Please mail or fax this form back to:

ABC Event Company Ltd.
1234 Main St. Vancouver, BC V4R 5T7 Canada
Phone: 123-567-8901; Fax: 123-456-7890;
E-mail: info@abceventcompany.com

EVENT PRODUCTION TOOLKIT

MASTER CHECKLIST FOR EVENT PRODUCTION

A   Concept and Proposal Phase

This phase begins when the potential client asks for a proposal, whatever size or type the event is.

- [ ] Set date for completion with client.
- [ ] Take time to develop concept, think of ideas, and create. ✓
- [ ] Determine overall event production budget, then set budget for each component after deducting your own profit margin. ✓
- [ ] Call suppliers (decorators/performers/sound/lighting, etc.). ✓
- [ ] Ensure all necessary taxes are included in supplier costs. ✓
- [ ] Give suppliers time to prepare their proposal and give them a target date. Stick to it.   ✓
- [ ] Ensure suppliers' creative time is included in proposal as a line item. ✓
- [ ] Include your own time for event coordination as well.
- [ ] Type up proposal in creative format. Keep budget separate on a summary page or type line by line.
- [ ] Spell-check proposal and double check for grammar.
- [ ] Check for correct client name and address.
- [ ] Put copyright page after title page.
- [ ] Include promo, tapes, videos where needed. If décor is a big part of proposal, try to use color printed or copied, customized, titled pages with pictures. At a minimum, try to include an artist rendering or sketch of new décor with the proposal. Put the sketch or rendering on a titled page. ✓
- [ ] E-mail/mail/courier/fax proposal to client.
- [ ] Call client the next day to ensure proposal was received.
- [ ] Call client every 2 weeks to check on progress.

B   Coordination Phase

This phase begins once the sale is made and usually 1 month or more before the event.

B.1 Risk Identification and Assessment

- ☐ Ensure all licenses and permits have been applied for and all insurance is in place.
- ☐ If a large public event, contact all fire, police, ambulance, first aid, and security personnel/organizations to arrange for appropriate coverage and permits.
- ☐ Prepare emergency procedures for all above areas (fire, injury and first aid, security, police) as well as for lost children and lost and found.
- ☐ Identify traffic and crowd movement patterns and assess for potential risk. Make appropriate changes to plans and site/venue layout.
- ☐ Ensure signage is adequate and well placed.
- ☐ Ensure disabled access is adequate for all event areas.
- ☐ Review and categorize all potential risks with production team.
- ☐ Ensure all supplier contracts contain compliance requirements with safety and design standards.
- ☐ Ensure adequate CGL insurance is in place and all suppliers, the venue, and the client name the producer as an additional insured.

B.2 Personnel Management

- ☐ Ensure all personnel (e.g. suppliers, venue, performers, volunteers, and other contractors) have all event details, including times, dates, schedules, location, and are aware of all the details of what they are providing.
- ☐ Ensure all personnel have proper attire and are aware of and following all regulations.
- ☐ Ensure all suppliers have contracts.

B.3 Production Management

- ☐ Reconfirm all event details with the client: date, location, number of people, demographics of guests, exact schedule, room, and any special requirements such as dress codes, performance times, speeches, and such.
- ☐ Call all suppliers and performers to confirm details of event. √
- ☐ Call all suppliers and performers who were **not** chosen to release all holds on people or equipment. ∨
- ☐ Contact venue to determine/confirm setup time, staging needs, electrical power requirements (in detail, including cost), change room needs, load-in details, potential conflicting events during setup, room layout before and during event. ∨
- ☐ Ensure function requirement sheet with all the details needed to be supplied from the venue (or site) is completed and distributed to the venue and the client. ∨
- ☐ Décor. Contact decorator and review event details. Work through the entire room/venue layout from start to finish. Ensure:
    - ☐ Decorations to be hung on walls have appropriate suspension mechanism (e.g. no nails in walls, taped items will not fall, etc.).

- [ ] Elements of décor suspended from ceiling can be hung easily, are not too heavy, and that appropriate ladders or lifts are available.
- [ ] Décor can be set up without hindering other setup of tables or room, or other changeovers.
- [ ] Scale of décor is going to be appropriate (i.e. not too big for small room and not too small for big room).
- [ ] Table centers will not interfere with sight lines.
- [ ] All three dimensions are considered equally (e.g. don't forget vertical dimension).
- [ ] Exits will not be covered by décor.
- [ ] Lighting of all décor is planned and will be appropriate, adequate, and easily accomplished. ✓
- [ ] Florals are ordered. ✓
- [ ] All props are touched up, repaired, and painted.
- [ ] All parts and tools will be ready and available (e.g. duct tape to match carpet color, bracing and enough sand bags for flats, returns for flats, complete tool kit, and sufficient electrical extensions).
- [ ] Transportation/truck is reserved.
- [ ] Staff/crew organized for setup and strike.
- [ ] Detailed floor or site plan (preferably computer-generated CADD) is completed and distributed to venue, client, decorators, performers, audio and lighting contractors, A-V contractor, and any others participating in event who need to know about it. ✓
- [ ] Entertainment. Contact all performers or their representatives and ensure:
  - [ ] All contract riders and special contract details for name acts are reviewed for possible problems or excessive costs.
  - [ ] All special requirements are appropriate and can be available (e.g. certain stage surface, certain sound needs, etc.).
  - [ ] Appropriate stage size ordered (note that a performance in a large room for large audience generally needs a 32-in. stage height or more, a dance band stage only needs a 12- or 16-in. stage height).
  - [ ] Changing room will be available and will be close to stage area if necessary.
  - [ ] Rehearsal is scheduled if needed.
  - [ ] Costuming/attire will be appropriate (e.g. no jeans).
  - [ ] All performance times, lengths of performances, and details are passed to performers.
  - [ ] Whatever power, audio, or lights needed will be provided.
  - [ ] Schedule passed to performers for setup and for entire event.
  - [ ] All necessary details are included on performers' contracts, including date, time, location, and directions to venue if necessary.
  - [ ] Performers know that prices are not to be discussed with client and that all future requests for their services are to come through the producer's company if a result of this particular event.

- ☐ Producer's business cards are made available to performers to hand out. No personal cards or phone numbers are to be given out.
- ☐ Sufficient stage managers are booked and budgeted for.
- ☐ Sound/lights/A-V. Review all initial proposals and ensure/determine:
  - ☐ Sound will be adequate for audience size. ˋ
  - ☐ If speeches will be necessary, is lectern, lectern mic, wireless, or handheld mic needed. ✓
  - ☐ Sound is appropriate for room acoustics and purpose of event (e.g. distributed or delay speakers for large room, only speakers near stage for just a band, flown speakers for best sound quality, classiness and visibility, but higher price, etc.). ✓
  - ☐ Best location for console.
  - ☐ Size of system coming.
  - ☐ Cassette/CD/DVD player available with tapes/CDs/DVDs as needed. These are useful if unexpected walk-in music or background music is requested at the last minute.
  - ☐ Sufficient cabling and mats for doorways or walkways are planned.
  - ☐ Sufficient staffing is planned.
  - ☐ Crew breaks planned into schedule.
  - ☐ Floor plan and schedule passed to audio, lighting, and A-V companies.
  - ☐ Adequate lighting for stage, room, and/or décor planned.
  - ☐ Followspots ordered if needed.
  - ☐ Location of lighting trees and/or speakers will not interfere with walkways or with sight lines.
  - ☐ If lights will be flown. If so, can they be flown with sound system?
  - ☐ Sufficient power is ordered, electrician will be available if necessary, cost is taken into consideration in budget.
  - ☐ Lighting console is co-located with audio console if possible.
  - ☐ Correct screen size(s) and type is ordered for A-V.
  - ☐ All videos and their format and PowerPoint shows are passed to A-V company in detail.
  - ☐ Adequate space is allowed for rear-screen A-V presentations if requested.
  - ☐ A-V company is given schedule and floor plan.
  - ☐ Backstage space is planned for A-V setup.
  - ☐ That an overall technical director will be present at the event to 'call the show' if needed.
  - ☐ Sufficient intercom equipment (e.g. radios, Clear-Com, etc.) is ordered for all technical personnel as needed.
- ☐ Catering. Address the following to ensure proper integration of food service with production requirements:
  - ☐ Confirm number of courses and any special requirements or needs that might affect the outcome or running of the event; for example, whether warmers will be used on a buffet which might affect the total power required if it has to be shared with lighting.

- [ ] Ensure that there is sufficient space for catering to serve diners and for event entertainment, décor, and other equipment to fit into the venue.
- [ ] Ensure that the caterer's schedule agrees with the production schedule and show running order. Avoid any potential setup interference and event conflicts by adjusting schedules to agree.

B.4 *Contracting*

- [ ] Complete all bookings and contracts for client and suppliers. Ensure contracts are signed and sent out with all details. Double check that correct deposit is requested and that client knows amount required and when it is due.
- [ ] Followup to ensure all contracts are signed and returned on schedule, and that deposits are received (or sent out to suppliers) in accordance with contract(s).

C Execution Phase

This phase usually begins approximately 2 days before the event and ends after strike.

C.1 *Risk Management*

- [ ] Ensure appropriate insurance, licenses, and permits are in place with either you or other suppliers.
- [ ] Double check event site or venue for appropriate signage and crowd control including access and exit.
- [ ] Ensure emergency procedures are written and copies are distributed to all production personnel as required.
- [ ] Ensure emergency and security personnel are in place as required.
- [ ] Ensure all personnel have appropriate safety clothing and that those who must operate specialized equipment (e.g. Genie lift) are qualified.
- [ ] Check site or venue to ensure:
  - [ ] All exits and evacuation routes are clear.
  - [ ] Stage stairs and edges are marked with safety tape.
  - [ ] Stage stairs have handrails and guardrails are in place around the back and sides of the stage as required.
  - [ ] Electrical boxes are marked with caution signs.
  - [ ] All cabling crossing foot traffic areas is securely matted and taped down.
  - [ ] Lighting is at safe levels, particularly backstage.
  - [ ] All flown trussing, audio, lighting, A-V, décor, and other equipment has been adequately secured and is safe.
  - [ ] No décor or other equipment presents any danger to guests or others.
  - [ ] The route to take personnel to and from the stage and/or their assigned performance areas is clear and easy to negotiate.

C.2 Personnel Management

☐ Ensure you have all supplier emergency contact information (work, home, and cell phone numbers).

☐ Ensure all suppliers and performers are aware of load-in and setup locations and restrictions (e.g. scheduling at loading dock, distances from load-in to event location/room, other conflicting meetings or events, exactly who to report to at venue and where to find that person).

☐ Check supplier attire for appropriateness.

☐ Ensure proper equipment is available for suppliers, either provided by them (e.g. tools) or by another source (e.g. Genie lift from the venue).

☐ Prior to start of setup and periodically throughout setup, review and monitor schedule for problem areas and to ensure everyone is on time.

C.3 Production Management

☐ Two days before event, call all performers and suppliers to ensure everything is ready and all are familiar with the schedule. Also double check contact names and phone numbers. Have them handy for the event.

☐ Dress appropriately for event (jacket/tie, suit, or dress/pant suit for women). Don't forget your nametag.

☐ Bring all event papers, especially contact phone numbers and keep them handy.

☐ Arrive at venue early or if décor, audio, lights, or A-V are first, arrive in sufficient time to check for mistakes and have them corrected.

☐ Immediately on arrival, contact client and venue to let them know you are present and available for consultation.

☐ Recheck schedule with client plus any unusual additions such as speeches or special presentations. Also determine where client will be in case you must get in touch with him/her in a hurry.

☐ Walk entire event setup several times to ensure all décor, audio, lights, A-V, staging, changing rooms, are as planned. ✓

☐ Liaise with venue staff member in charge and relay any items that will affect his/her staff such as performances or speeches in between meal courses. If possible and budget permits, try to get refreshments (limited) for crew and/or performers.

☐ Greet performers as they arrive and show them to their dressing rooms. Be friendly.

☐ On with the show!! Adhere to schedules as much as possible. Have performers or speakers ready to be onstage at least 10 min before they are scheduled. See Chapter 8 for more details about stage management and calling a show.

☐ After event, thank suppliers, performers, venue, and client. Ask client if everything went as expected and can we be of service again.

C.4 Contract Management

- [ ] Pay all suppliers and performers promptly, preferably **at the event** if possible.
- [ ] If client has not paid final installment, request immediate payment prior to event or determine and agree on the final payment method and timing.

D Followup Phase

This phase begins immediately after the event itself and ends when the client has paid the bill. The day after the event, the following should be started:

- [ ] Call all suppliers to double check that they were happy with the outcome of the event or to explain any problems they might have had.
- [ ] Call the appropriate contact person (e.g. conference services manager or catering manager) at the venue to check that they were happy with the outcome of the event.
- [ ] Call the client to ensure they were happy with the event and to double check and agree on any contractual additions or deletions.
- [ ] Send a thank you letter and Event Evaluation Form to the client within a week of the event. Include a final invoice if full payment was not made at the event.
- [ ] Make a note on your calendar to call the client 6 months prior to the event next year to request if you can be of service if the event is an annual one.
- [ ] Follow-up immediately on any leads given to you as a result of the event.
- [ ] Track accounts receivable religiously until they are paid and try to keep them less than 30 days.

GLOSSARY OF SPECIAL EVENT
TECHNICAL PRODUCTION TERMINOLOGY

Absorption: The tendency of sound waves to be soaked up by soft surfaces; the opposite of reflection.

AC (Alternating Current): Electrical current that alternates direction (positive to negative). AC is often contrasted with direct current, commonly produced by batteries for portable equipment in the special events industry. AC is what is installed in buildings.

Accent Light
1. Illumination used to make something stand out. It may be done with intensity and/or color.
2. A luminaire that provides such illumination.

Acoustic Power Output: The output, as measured in watts, of anything that generates sound.

Acoustic Treatment: Physical treatment of a room in order to change the room's acoustics, by using absorbers to attenuate the sound, reflectors to redirect the sound, and diffusers to uniformly distribute the sound.

Acoustics
1. The science or scientific study of sound.
2. The properties of a room or environment that affect the qualities of sound.

Active Matrix: LCD display that uses a solid-state device to control each pixel cell for a better quality image.

AFM: American Federation of Musicians. Union representing musicians in the USA and Canada.

Aircraft Landing Light (ACL): A high intensity, tight beam PAR luminaire that derives its name from its use as an aircraft landing luminaire. The true ACL is 28 V and 250 W, although there are many variations. Often used to add dramatic effect to stage shows.

Ampères, Amperage (Amps): Units of electrical current.

Amplifier (Amp)
1. An electronic device that increases the amplitude of a signal. The signal may be voltage, current, or both (power).
2. A combination speaker/amplifier designed for use with an instrument, as with a guitar amp or keyboard amp.

Amplitude

1. The strength of sound waves or an electrical signal, as measured against a mean.
2. That which determines loudness.

Analog-to-Digital Converter (ADC):   The electronic component that converts the instantaneous value of an analog input signal to a digital word (represented as a binary number) for digital signal processing. The ADC is the first link in the digital chain of signal processing.

Anechoic
1. The complete absence of reflected sound (echo).
2. An environment that prevents (through absorption of sound waves) all reflected sound, as in an anechoic chamber.

ANSI: American National Standards Institute.

Antenna: A metal structure or wire that picks-up or transmits electromagnetic energy through space.

Aspect Ratio: Ratio of width to height of a screen or image. Most computer and video images have an aspect ratio of 4:3, HDTV uses 16:9, and SXGA uses 5:4.

Attenuate: To make weaker. An attenuator uses resistance to reduce output voltage, as with a volume control.

Automated Fixtures (Also known as Intelligent Lights or Moving Lights): These come in several types, primarily moving yolk (or moving head) and moving mirror fixtures. In yolk fixtures, the whole instrument (light) can pan and tilt (i.e. move in the X and Y axes). In mirror fixtures, only a small mirror moves to send the beam off in other directions.

Automated Fixture Control Console: A lighting control console designed specifically for the purpose of controlling and storing/playing back cues for automated lighting fixtures. These consoles often have subsystems for controlling different features of automated fixtures such as color change, gobo, and focus position. Complex cue structures, effects, and chases are typical features of automated fixture control consoles. Three primary types of automated fixture consoles include proprietary consoles designed to work primarily with one type or brand of automated fixture; generic controllers which are programmed to control many different types of automated fixtures; and hybrid controllers which combine the functions of standard theatrical memory consoles with those of an automated fixture console.

Automatic Mic Mixer: A specialized mixer optimized for solving the problems of multiple live microphones operating together as a system, such as found in boardrooms, classrooms, courtrooms, church systems, or even hotel ballrooms. An automatic mic mixer controls the live microphones by turning up (on) mics when someone is talking, and turning down (off) mics that are not used. Thus it is a voice-activated, real-time process, without an operator, hence, automatic.

Back Curtain: A two-piece bi-parting rear curtain; part of the cyc set. Also known as a rear curtain or backdrop.

Back Light: A lighting design term referring to any light that comes primarily from behind a performer, musician, or object being lit. Backlighting is associated with strong highlights or halo effects.

Backstage: All areas related to, but not on, the stage, including dressing rooms, technical areas, and such.

Baffle: A sheet of material used to prevent a spill of light in a luminaire or in part of a set.

Balance Control: A control found most commonly on professional and consumer stereo pre-amplifiers, used to change the relative loudness (power) between the left and right channels.

Balanced Line: A pair of ungrounded conductors whose voltages are opposite in polarity but equal in magnitude. Balanced lines reduce interference from external sources like radio frequencies and light dimmers.

Ballyhoo: Followspot move in which the operator continuously moves the beam in a figure-eight motion around the stage or audience. This term is also used to describe similar movements performed by automated fixtures.

Bare Ends: An electrical term referring to the ends of a feeder cable set which do not have any permanent connector attached to them. Bare ends are often used to tie dimmer feeder cable into a house power supply or company switch.

Barn Doors: A rotatable attachment consisting of two or four metal flaps (hinged) which are fixed to the front of a luminaire to cut off the beam in a particular direction.

Bass: The lower end of the frequency range from about 20 Hz to 300 Hz.

Batten: A horizontal pipe on which luminaires, scenery, curtains, and some distribution equipment are hung.

Batten Strip: A connector strip hung from a batten.

Baud: Data transmission speed, 56.6 baud is 56,600 bits per second.

Beam:
1. Generally, the conoid, or in some cases, the pyramoid of light emanating from a luminaire.
2. In photometry, the circular area of the base of a cone-shaped beam where the intensity is at least 50 percent of the maximum intensity. The maximum intensity is ideally located at the center of the base.

Beam Angle: The angle of the cone of light produced by a light.

Beam Pattern: The complete shape of the beam, as defined in the general sense. It includes any realistic or abstract patterns introduced into the beam as well as any apparatus that alters the contour of the beam.

Beltpack: Part of the communication system (see Clear-Com) in an event, the beltpack contains the controls and circuitry to drive the headset worn by crew members.

Beta: A type of 1/2 in. tape used for editing and recording video. Very high quality.

Biamplification: The use of separate amplifiers to power woofers and tweeters. See also Crossover – Electronic, Crossover – Passive.

Blacklight: An ultraviolet (UV) light source used to create special lighting effects with fluorescent materials. UV sources can be incandescent, fluorescent, or preferably HID luminaires.

Blackout: A lighting design term referring to a light cue that takes the stage quickly into darkness. A blackout is often abbreviated as B/O.

Blinders: Luminaires arranged around the stage directed into the auditorium, used mainly for effect in rock concerts and other events.

Blocking: The process of arranging moves to be made by performers during a theatrical show, recorded by stage management in the prompt script.

Board: The main control console for the stage lighting or audio.

Boards: Slang term for the stage floor.

Border: A narrow horizontal masking piece (usually cloth), normally of neutral color (black) to mask a flown lighting rig from the audience.

Bounce: Diffuse light that has been reflected from the stage, walls, cyc, or other surface.

Box Truss: An aluminum or steel support structure often used for temporary rigging of lights, scenery, or sound equipment. As the name suggests a box truss is rectangular in shape creating a rigid structure which is easy to stack and load onto a truck. An additional advantage of box truss over other truss shapes is the ability to hang lighting instruments inside the truss, where they can remain protected while in transport.

Breakaway: Prop or item of furniture designed to break/shatter with impact. Breakaway furniture and some props are usually capable of restoration to be 'broken' again.

Breakout: A cable-connecting device that breaks a multi-circuit cable (multi-cable) into individual circuits.

Breakup: A commonly used abstract gobo that gives a textured effect to the light, without throwing a specific pattern onto the stage. Used to add interest to light beams (e.g. a leafy breakup may be used for outdoor scenes of forests or spooky woods to break up the light).

Bridle: A rigging device or method that distributes a single point of a load to more than one hanging point.

Brightness: Generally refers to the brightness of projection equipment expressed in lumens. See Lumens.

Bump Button: A momentary switch or button on a lighting control console that brings a channel to a level of full when pressed. Bump buttons allow rapid manual control over lighting control channels. On some consoles bump buttons can be put into solo mode where all channels except those controlled by the bump button go out.

Bump Cue: A lighting cue that happens instantly. Bump cues are traditionally used to emphasize similar abrupt changes in music, choreography, or to mark the end of a scene. A bump cue where all lights go out is called a blackout.

Cable: Common term describing any number of types of electrical connecting devices. All cables employ some type of conductor, usually stranded copper wire, and some type of insulation to protect it (e.g. common cable types related to stage lighting include stage cable, multi-cable, feeder cable, and control cable).

Cable (Mic or Audio):   A shielded twisted pair, usually designed for low current, high flexibility, and low handling noise. The best insulating materials are somewhat inflexible, so most mic cables use rubber, neoprene, PVC, or similar materials, with small gauge wire, and therefore, true mic cables are not intended for long runs. Unfortunately the term 'mic cable' has become synonymous with general purpose audio cable, as distinguished from speaker cable, when it can be quite different. The very best audio cable may not be the best mic cable and vice versa.

Cable (Speaker):   An unshielded insulated pair, normally not twisted, characterized by heavy (or large) gauge conductors (hence, low resistance), used to interconnect the output of a power amplifier and the input of a loudspeaker.

Cable (Twisted-Pair):   Standard two-conductor copper cable, with insulation extruded over each conductor and twisted together. Usually operated as a balanced line connection.

Cable Bundle: A group of electrical cables attached at various points by tape, rope, or other tie.

Cable Cradle: A metal sling used to support heavy stage cable as it hangs from a batten, while simultaneously preventing the cable from entering horizontal sight lines from the house to the stage. It can also take strain away from the point where the cable exits a piece of distribution equipment.

Cable Drop: An overhead electric cable or group of electric cables that extends downward for the connection of luminaires or other electrical apparatus. The cable(s) may be connected to some type of overhead support, or directly to a piece of distribution equipment.

Cable Tie: Lockable (and sometimes releasable) plastic strap used to tie a bundle of cables together.

CADD: Computer aided design and drafting. For special events, it is most often seen in two dimensions (2D) and shows a plan or top view. It can also be shown in front (elevation) and side views in 2D and in three dimensions (3D) from a number of different perspectives.

Call or Call Time
1. A notification of a working session (e.g. a rehearsal call or show call).
2. The period of time to which the above call refers (e.g. 'Your call for tomorrow night's show is 6:55 p.m').
3. A request for a performer to come to the stage because an entrance is imminent. These are courtesy calls and should not be relied on by performers (e.g. 'This is your call for the finale, Mr. Smith and Miss Jones').
4. An acknowledgment of applause (e.g. Curtain Call).
5. The technical director (TD) is said to be 'calling the cues' or 'calling the show.'

Cam Lock (TM):   A locking single contact connector commonly used to connect feeder cables and portable dimmer racks or electrical distribution panels.

Cardioid: Heart-shaped pattern exhibited by some microphones that reduces pick-up from the sides and back.

Carrier: A continuous (usually high frequency) electromagnetic wave that can be modulated by a signal to carry information.

Cast: All performers/participants in a show.

CD ROM: Compact Disk Read Only Memory. Similar to audio CD but used for data storage.

Center Stage: The middle portion of the stage, it has good sightlines to all seats in the audience.

Chain Hoist: A lifting device comprised of an electric motor and gear/chain drive system. Chain hoists are commonly used to lift portable trusses into place in order to 'fly' lights for shows.

Channel or Control Channel: A complete control path for signals in lighting or sound equipment. On manual or preset controllers this may refer to an actual fader or slider. On a computer memory console, a channel may only be represented by a number that is assigned by the system to control physical dimmers, color scrollers, or other devices.

Character Generator: (Trade name Chyron). A unit that enables the creation of letters, numbers, or other characters for use with videos.

Chase: A repeated sequence of changing lighting states. A chase can be as simple as a single string of lights flashed sequentially around a sign by a mechanical or electronic switching device (chaser or chase unit). By utilizing the chase (or effect) functions of a computer memory console, a chase can also comprise complex multi-part cues affecting large groups of luminaires.

Choppers: Two horizontal masking shutters used in followspots to shape the beam above and below.

Clearance: Message passed to the TD from the front-of-house manager (or client in the case of special events) that the house (audience) is ready for the performance to begin.

Clear-Com: Brand name of the most common type of communication equipment used for closed communication amongst technical crew members running an event. The equipment can be either wireless, enabling the crewmembers freedom of movement around the event space, or wired, requiring them to remain at a fixed position.

Clipping: Audible distortion that occurs when a signal's level exceeds the limits of a particular circuit. When an amp is 'turned up too loud,' and begins to distort, it is said to be clipping.

Closed Circuit Television: Television signal carried, usually via microwave or coaxial cable, between two or more locations, but not broadcast for general reception.

Codec: Coder/Decoder. A device that converts an analog signal into and/or from a digital signal.

Color Boomerang: A levered frame device within a followspot which allows different color filters to be introduced into the beam. Standard followspot boomerangs have space for six or seven different colors to be inserted. During a show, individual or combined frames can be quickly added or dropped from the beam as needed.

Color Changer
1. *Scroller*: A long string of up to 16 colors is passed horizontally in front of a luminaire. Remotely controlled by the lighting desk.
2. *Wheel*: Electrically or manually operated disk which is fitted to the front of a luminaire with several apertures holding different color filters that can be selected to enable color changes. Can also be selected to run continuously.

Color Filter: Color media placed in front of or within a lighting fixture to alter the color of the light produced. Filters for conventional fixtures are often made of a dyed polyester film. Since dyed filters work by absorbing unwanted colors and passing desired colors, they deteriorate from heat and must be replaced when they 'burn up.' Automated fixtures use more permanent dichroic color filters that are created by vacuum depositing thin films onto heat-resistant glass.

Color Mixing: Combining the effects of two or more lighting gels:
   1. *Additive*:   Focusing two differently colored beams of light onto the same area (e.g. cyc floods). Combining colors in this way adds the colors together, eventually arriving at white. The three primary colors of light additively mix to form white, as do the complementary colors.
   2. *Subtractive*:   Placing two different gels in front of the same luminaire. Subtractive mixing is used to obtain a color effect that is not available from stock or from manufacturers. Because the ranges of color are so wide, the need for subtractive mixing is reducing. Combining colors in this way reduces the light toward blackness. The three primary colors mix subtractively to form black (or to block all the light).

Color Rendering Index (CRI):   A single number approximate evaluation of the effect of a light source on the visual appearance of a colored surface. The number falls on a scale from below 0 to 100, with daylight at 100. Objects and people viewed under luminaires with a high CRI generally appear more true to life.

Color Temperature: The measurement of the color quality ('warmth' or 'coolness') of a luminaire measured in degrees Kelvin. A standard 1000 W tungsten halogen theatrical luminaire has a color temperature of around 3200 K.

Commando Cloth: Napped, inexpensive fabric, popular as studio backdrop and stage cyc set fabric; typically black.

Compact Disk (CD):   Trademark term for the Sony–Philips digital audio optical disk storage system. The system stores 80 min (maximum) of digital audio and subcode information, or other non-audio data, on a 12-cm diameter optical disk. The disk is made of plastic, with a top metallized layer, and is read by reflected laser light. Variations (such as the 3-in. disk) are reserved for special applications.

Complementary Colors: Colors directly opposite each other on a color wheel.

Composite Video: Combines vertical–horizontal synchronization signals, color, and picture into a single signal line.

Compressed Resolution: An electronic method of reducing the resolution of a signal to operate on a lower-resolution device. An example would be an LCD Projector that has a maximum resolution of 800×600 pixels being used with a computer that is displaying 1024×768 resolution. The image quality will be reduced when compressed.

Compression Driver: In audio, a driver, designed for use with a horn, which utilizes a diaphragm (rather than a cone) to reproduce mid and high frequencies.

Compressor: A device that reduces (compresses) an audio signal's dynamic range. Most often associated with a vocal microphone.

Computer Memory Console: A lighting console in which cues can be stored and executed electronically. Computer consoles also employ many show-editing and cue-building functions that make the cue writing or programming process easier. Computer consoles can be divided into three basic types: cue-only type consoles, theatrical 'classic' tracking consoles, and automated fixture control consoles.

Condenser Microphone: A mic that depends on an external power supply (phantom power) or battery to electrostatically charge its condenser (capacitor) plates. The power comes from the microphone pre-amp or the mixing console.

Conductor: A substance – in electronics usually a metal – that allows the free flow of electrons.

Cone: The vibrating diaphragm, employed in some speaker designs, that generates sound waves.

Connector (1/4 in. TRS): Stereo 1/4 in. connector consisting of tip (T), ring (R), and sleeve (S) sections, with T = left, R = right, and S = ground/shield.

Connector (1/4 in. TS): Mono 1/4 in. connector consisting of tip (T: signal) and sleeve (S: ground and shield) for unbalanced wiring.

Connector (1/4 in. TS): A single-conductor electrical connector with a banana-shaped spring-metal tip most often used on audio power amplifiers for the loudspeaker wiring. Also called a binding post-connector.

Connector (Cannon Connector or Cannon Plug): Alternate reference for XLR.

Connector (RCA): The standard connector used in line-level consumer and project studio sound equipment, and most recently to interconnect composite video signals. Also known as phono jack or pin jack.

Connector (Speakon®): A registered trademark of Neutrik for their original design loudspeaker connector, now considered an industry standard.

Connector (Terminal Strips or Terminal Blocks): Also called barrier strips, a type of wiring connector provided with screwdown posts separated by insulating barrier strips.

Connector (XLR): The standard connector for digital and analog balanced line interconnect between audio equipment. Also known as a cannon plug.

Console: A large or elaborate audio or lighting mixer.

Controller: A lighting control console or light board. Common types include the preset board, the computer memory console, and specialized automated fixture controllers such as the Vari-Lite Artisan II console.

Conventional Lighting Fixture: A standard lighting fixture or luminaire such as a PAR can, Fresnel, or ERS, which offers no built-in automated functions.

Convergence: Alignment of red, green, and blue video guns to combine and produce a single color video display in a CRT.

Cool Color: Generally, a color that is in the green–blue–violet range.

Cool Light: Light having a color temperature of approximately 3600–4900K (i.e. bright-white to blue-white).

Cracked Oil Fog Machine: A simple type of fog machine that atomizes oil into a fine mist, usually by introducing compressed air into a reservoir containing mineral oil. Crackers are also available which crack water into a very fine mist. Haze machines produce effects similar to oil crackers without leaving an oily residue on surfaces. It has been found to be carcinogenic.

Critical Distance: The distance from a sound source at which sound pressure levels emitted by the source equal those being reflected off other sources.

Cross Bar: A bar mounted horizontally on top of a stand. It contains two or more sliding tees for mounting luminaires, and a fixed tee for mounting the bar to the stand.

Cross Fade
1. In the lighting industry, a term referring to a cue in which one set of lights increases in intensity while another set simultaneously decreases in intensity.
2. In the audio industry, a term most often associated with DJ mixers and broadcast. DJ mixers usually feature a crossfader slide-type potentiometer control. This control allows the DJ to transition from one stereo program source (located at one travel extreme) to another stereo program source (located at the other travel extreme). It is the crossfader that becomes the main remix tool for turntablists.

Cross Talk: The unwanted leakage of signal between supposedly independent channels.

Crossover: An electrical circuit (passive or active) consisting of a combination of high-pass, low-pass, and band-pass filters used to divide the audio frequency spectrum (20–20 kHz) into segments suitable for individual loudspeaker use.

Cross-Over: Corridor formed between a back curtain or backdrop and the rear wall, so performers or stagehands may cross from one side of the stage to the other unseen by the audience, usually while a show is in progress.

CRT: Cathode Ray Tube or picture tube.

CRT Projectors: Used to project video and computer images as with LCD projectors but slightly older technology using three CRTs. Generally higher resolution but not as bright as LCD projectors. Work very well with computers of different resolutions. No zoom lens capability. They take longer to set up. Almost completely obsolete now.

CSA: Canadian Standards Association.

Cue (Q):   A point in a live show when a signal is given for some action to take place.

Cue Light: A light used to signal a cue, especially in a theater. Red usually means stand by and green usually means execute the cue.

Cue to Cue: Cutting out action and dialog between cues during a technical rehearsal, to save time.

Cueing: There is a standard sequence for giving verbal cues:
'Stand-by Sound Cue 19' (Stand-by first).
'Sound Cue 19 Go' (Go last).

Curtain Call: At the end of a performance, the acknowledgment of applause by performers (the bows).

Cut: Describes an element of the show that has been removed or deleted. Often lines, scenic items, and light cues are 'cut' from a production during the rehearsal process.

Cyberlight (TM):   Originally introduced in 1993, the Cyberlight is a moving mirror-type automated fixture manufactured by Lightwave Research/High End Systems.

Cyclorama (Cyc):   A vertical surface which is used to form the background for a theatrical-type setting, made of heavy cloth drawn tightly to achieve a smooth, flat surface. It usually represents the sky or suggests limitless space. Traditionally, cycloramas were dome-shaped or horizontally curved, but may now also be flat or vertically curved.

Cyclorama Light (Cyc Light):   A luminaire mounted at the top and/or bottom of a cyclorama in order to light it in a smooth, uniform manner.

Daisy Chaining: Connecting items of equipment together by linking from one to the next in a chain.

DAT: Digital Audio Tape recorder/player. A digital audio recorder utilizing a magnetic tape cassette system with rotary heads similar to that of a video recorder.

Daylight: Light that has a color temperature of approximately 5500–5600 K, which has been approximated to be the color temperature of ordinary sunlight during the day under normal atmospheric conditions.

dB (Decibel): A relative unit of measure between two sound or audio signal levels. A difference of 1 dB is considered to be the smallest that can be detected by the human ear. An increase of 6 dB equals twice the sound pressure.

DC (Direct Current): Electrical current that flows in only one direction.

Dead Case Storage: Area to temporarily store empty road cases used to transport lighting, audio, A-V, or performer gear.

Decoder: Device that reconstructs an encrypted signal so that it can be clearly received.

Delay

1. *Crossovers*: A signal processing device or circuit used to delay one or more of the output signals by a controllable amount. This feature is used to correct for loudspeaker drivers that are mounted such that their points of apparent sound origin (not necessarily their voice coils) are not physically aligned. Good delay circuits are frequency independent, meaning the specified delay is equal for all audio frequencies (constant group delay). Delay circuits based on digital sampling techniques are inherently frequency independent and thus preferred.
2. *Musical instruments*: Digital audio delay circuits comprise the heart of most 'effects' boxes sold in the instrument world. Reverb, flanging, chorusing, phasers, echoing, and looping all use delay in one form or another.
3. *Sound reinforcement*: Acousticians and audio engineers use signal delay units to 'aim' loudspeaker arrays. Introducing small amounts of delay between identical, closely mounted drivers, fed from the same source, controls the direction of the combined response.

Diaphragm

1. The radiating surface of a compression driver. Its vibrations emit sound waves.
2. The moving element of a microphone.

Dichroic Color Filter: Color filters manufactured by vacuum depositing thin films onto heat-resistant glass. Dichroic filters reflect rather than absorb unwanted wavelengths and so remain cooler and less subject to burn out. The process for creating dichroic filters is very precise and much more saturated (purer) colors can be created. As a result, these filters are quite expensive and are used primarily in automated lighting fixtures.

Dimmer: A device that causes connected luminaires to decrease in intensity. Most dimmers for entertainment lighting use some variation of an SCR (silicon-controlled rectifier). Individual dimmers are traditionally arranged in modules of two dimmers with modules combined into dimmer racks.

Dimmer Rack: Dimmer racks contain individual dimmer modules arranged for convenient electrical connection. Some racks are designed for permanent installation, while touring racks are designed for portable use. Dimmer racks typically contain 6, 12, 24, or 48 dimmer modules with 2 dimmers per module.

Direct Box: Also known as a D.I. (direct input) box, a device that enables a musical instrument (e.g. guitar) to be connected directly to a mic or line-level mixer input. The box provides the very high-input impedance required by the instrument and puts out the correct level for the mixer.

Directivity: The ability of a speaker or horn to direct sound to a given area that can be described by its directivity factor (Q).

Dispersion: The area throughout which the sound produced by a speaker is distributed.

Distortion: Any discrepancy between the source material and the sonic output of a sound system, a measure of unwanted signals. If a piece of gear is perfect, it does not add distortion of any sort.

Distribution Board or Panel (Distro):   System of interconnected fuse carriers and cabling that routes an incoming power supply to a number of different outputs.

DLP: Digital Light Processing or Micro Mirror Technology used in newer video/data projectors. The projection system is based on an optical semiconductor known as the Digital Micromirror Device, or DMD chip, invented by Dr. Larry Hornbeck of Texas Instruments in 1987. The DMD chip is an extremely sophisticated light switch containing a rectangular array of up to 1.3 million hinge-mounted microscopic mirrors. Each of these micromirrors measures less than one-fifth the width of a human hair, and corresponds to one pixel in a projected image. When a DMD chip is coordinated with a digital video or graphic signal, a light source, and a projection lens, its mirrors can reflect an all-digital image onto a screen or other surface. The DMD and the sophisticated electronics that surround it are known as Digital Light Processing™ technology.

DLP Projector: Uses DLP technology as described above. Extremely high resolution, compatible with most computers, very bright and compact.

Dolly: A small-wheeled platform used to move heavy items.

Down Light
1. Downward illumination, almost perpendicular with the floor.
2. A luminaire that provides such illumination.

Downlink: Signal sent from a communications satellite to the earth.

Downstage
1. The stage area nearest the audience, also containing the apron.
2. A movement toward the audience.

Drapes: Stage curtains.

Dress Rehearsal: A full rehearsal, with all technical elements brought together. The performance as it will be 'at the event.'

Dressing
1. Decorative props added to a stage setting or an element of event décor.
2. The act of adding extra props to a decorative element.

Drop: A decorative, hanging, flat fabric piece, typically built of muslin and painted. Also called a mural or backdrop.

Dry Run: A practice run, usually a technical run without performers or key people.

Dry-Ice Fogger (Fog Machine): A simple fog machine that creates thick, opaque, low-lying or ground fog by the immersion of frozen CO_2 in hot water. This type of fogger is often made from a large drum containing a heating element and some type of basket in which dry ice can be lowered into the water. The resulting fog is then forced through a hose to the desired location onstage. Dry-ice fog effects are somewhat short lived as the dry ice quickly evaporates and the water cools. Dry ice is often used to cool the fog produced by other types of fog machines making it stay close to the ground. These chiller modules or attachments are little more than insulated coolers attached to the output end of a standard fog machine.

Duct Tape: See Gaff Tape.

Duplex: Mode in which there exists two-way communications satellite transmission systems.

DVD: Officially 'DVD' does not stand for anything. It used to mean 'digital versatile disk,' and before that it meant 'digital video disk' (also once known as hdCD in Europe). A 12 cm (4.72 in.) CD (same size as audio CDs and CD-ROMs) that holds 10 times the information. Capable of holding full-length movies and a video game based on the movie, or a movie and its soundtrack, or two versions of the same movie – all in sophisticated discrete digital audio surround sound. The DVD standard specifies a laminated single-sided, single-layer disk holding 4.7 gigabytes, and 133 min of MPEG-2 compressed video and audio. It is backward compatible, and expandable to two-layers holding 8.5 gigabytes. Ultimately two disks could be bound together yielding two sides, each with two layers, for a total of 17 gigabytes.

Dynamic Microphone: A microphone design in which a wire coil (the voice coil) is attached to a small diaphragm such that sound pressure causes the coil to move in a magnetic field, thus creating an electrical voltage proportional to the sound pressure.

Dynamic Processing: The use of electronic devices to control the levels of audio signals and compress or expand their dynamic range.

Dynamic Range: The difference between the softest and loudest extremes within an audio signal as expressed in dB.

Editing: To cut, alter, correct, or revise video.

Effects Loop: Inputs and outputs that allow the sending of an audio signal to and from a signal processor such as a reverb unit, delay, gate, or limiter.

Effects Projector
   1. *Animation disk:*   A slotted or perforated metal disk that rotates in front of a luminaire to provide 'movement' in the light. Most effective when used in front of an ERS carrying a gobo.
   2. *Effect disk*:   A painted glass disk rotating in front of an effects projector with an objective lens to focus the image (e.g. flames, rain, snow).
   3 *Flicker flame*:   Irregularly slotted rotating metal disk through which light is shone onto a prism-type piece of glass that scatters the beam of light and adds the 'dancing' effect of firelight to a scene.
   4. *Gobo rotator*:   Motorized device inserted into the gate of an ERS luminaire that can be remotely controlled to rotate a gobo, usually with variable speed and direction.
   5. *KK wheel*:   Slotted metal disk that rotates in front of a luminaire to break up the light and provide movement (flicker wheel).
   6. *Lightning*:   Created through the use of either strobe sources or photoflood luminaires.
   7. *Tubular wave ripple*:   Horizontal linear luminaire around which a slotted cylinder is rotated providing a rising light (e.g. as reflected from water onto the side of a ship).

Electret Microphone: A microphone design similar to that of condenser mics except utilizing a permanent electrical charge, thus eliminating the need for an external polarizing voltage (i.e. wireless).

Elevation: A working drawing usually drawn to scale, showing the front view of a set, stage, event element, or lighting rig. Nowadays, this drawing would be in CADD.

Ellipsoidal or Ellipsoidal Reflector Spotlight (ERS) or Leko: The most sophisticated of conventional instruments. Its beam shape is uniform, and various lenses inside the changeable barrels control the size of the beam. The unit is focusable so that an image can be projected and framing shutters allow the beam to be shaped to eliminate light spill onto projection screens, the audience's eyes, and such. The lens trains available range from very wide (50°) to very small (5°). Options include irises to further reduce the beam spread, to rotating pattern holders to make the projected images spin. This is the best instrument to use with gobo patterns. Usually 100–1000 W and throw distances of 10–100 ft.

Encryption: The process of encoding or 'scrambling' television signals. Used in business and broadcast television so that unintended audiences are unable to view the signal.

Equalizer (EQ): A device that permits the precise control of specific audio frequency ranges.

Equity: American Performer's Equity Association, founded in 1913, is the labor union representing performers and stage managers in the legitimate theater in the USA.

Even Field: In lighting, a field that has a relatively uniform decrease in intensity as viewed from the center to the edge of the field (i.e. a field that does not have a noticeable hot spot).

Expander: An electronic device that increases dynamic range by reducing a signal's level any time it falls below a specific threshold.

Fade In: The gradual increase in intensity of light.

Fade Out: The gradual decrease in intensity of light.

Fade to Black (FTB): A lighting design abbreviation. It indicates that a light cue takes all channels to zero over a period of time.

Fader
1. In lighting, a vertical slider that is used to remotely set the level of a channel.
2. In audio, a control used to fade out one input source and fade in another. The fading of a single source is called attenuation and uses an attenuator.

Fast-Fold Screen: Da-Lite brand that is assembled on-site to form front or rear projection screens. See Projection Screen below.

Feedback: Feedback, the dreaded 'audio engineer's curse,' is caused by a regeneration of sound leaving a speaker and entering a microphone. This tone – a sustained shriek – is a self-perpetuating cycle that can be stopped by decreasing the volume.

Feeder Cable: The cable which feeds or supplies power to a dimmer rack. Feeder cable is usually heavy gauge cable capable of safely carrying the hundreds of amps necessary to supply as many as 96 individual dimmers in a rack. Feeder cables are usually connected via Cam Lock connectors. A bare end or tail often connects one end of a feeder to the main power supply.

Fiber Optics: Technology in which a modulated beam of light carries information through a thin glass or plastic fiber.

Fill Light

1. Supplementary illumination used to reduce shadows, preventing them from appearing black.
2. A luminaire that provides such illumination.

Filter: A device that removes unwanted frequencies or noise from a signal.

Fixed Focus: A term used to describe an optical system whereby the lenses in a luminaire remain at a fixed distance from one another, although they may move as a group within the system.

Fixture: Used to describe a type of moving light.

Flagging: When focusing lighting, flagging means waving your hand in and out of the beam of a luminaire in order to see where the beam is hitting on stage.

Flat

1. In audio, the state of an audio signal or tone whose frequency is unaltered by equalization. On most mixers and equalizers, flat is indicated by the tone controls being at dead center.
2. In stage set design, a timber frame usually covered with plywood or hardboard upon which are usually painted or designed scenic elements. Typical sizes are 4 ft wide × 8 ft high or 4 ft wide × 10 ft high.

Flood

1. The position of a movable luminaire, lens, or pair of lenses on a spotlight that produces the widest field angle.
2. To direct a large amount of light on a relatively large area.

Flood Light: A luminaire consisting of a reflector, lamp, and sometimes a single lens, used to direct a large amount of light on a relatively large area.

Floor Plan: A 2D scale drawing of the event space in plan view.

Flown or Flying: Suspending a lighting rig (trussing plus lights plus connectors and cabling) from hanging points in the ceiling using chain motors or pulleys. The truss can also support audio systems. It is the cleanest and most effective means of setting up lighting and sometimes audio gear, in that it allows more flexibility in lighting, provides better sound quality, and eliminates sight line interference. It is usually more costly than ground supporting.

Fluorescence: A process by which certain pigments or materials can be made to appear to self-illuminate when exposed to UV light.

Flyaway: A lighting design term referring to a cue in which automated fixtures move upward away from the stage in a sweeping motion.

Foamcor: A polystyrene, Styrofoam material used as a substrate for some reflector boards, or décor designs, effective because of its light-weight and ease of mounting via reflector forks.

Focus: The process by which a lighting instrument is either manually or remotely positioned to light a specific part of the stage. With conventional fixtures, focus is performed after lighting equipment is hung in place and is connected to the proper circuit. Automated fixtures can be remotely focused and may have many different focuses for a particular show. Focus presets are often created as libraries of focus points for a show.

Focus Preset: A feature of some automated fixture and digital lighting consoles that allows libraries of focus positions to be stored centrally in memory. Presets can then be accessed individually by cues to position fixtures at predetermined locations on stage. Using focus presets is a much more efficient method for cueing automated fixtures than writing positions individually into every cue in a show.

Foldback: The original term for monitors, or monitor loudspeakers, used by stage musicians to hear themselves and/or the rest of the band. The term 'monitors' has replaced 'foldback' in common practice.

Followspot: A manually operated lighting fixture specially designed for following performers as they move about a stage or room. Most followspots employ some method for manual control of iris, shutter, dowser, as well as a color boomerang. Followspots can be either long-throw or short-throw instruments. The size of the room and the distance to be projected are the factors that determine the size and intensity of the unit to be used. Usually, they are 250–3000 W in power, and throw 50–200 ft.

Framing Shutters: Thin, movable, heat-resistant metal plates that are introduced into a light beam such that a portion of the beam is blocked off (i.e. framed), affecting the beam pattern, usually forming a sharp edge in the beam. They are used in various types of luminaires, but extensively in ellipsoidal spotlights, usually four (top, bottom, right, and left), and followspots, usually two (top and bottom), always situated internally, and usually at the aperture. Framing shutters generally can be independently adjusted, but those used in followspots usually move simultaneously with a single control mechanism.

Freight Elevator: A specific-use elevator in a venue reserved for transporting technical and other equipment between floors. Typically, it is larger than a regular elevator, is located close to the loading bays, and is accessible via service hallways.

Frequency

1. The number of sound waves that pass a given point in one second.
2. The determiner of pitch.

Frequency Response: The range of frequencies that is reproducible by a speaker or electronic component.

Fresnel: A standard stage luminaire. The Fresnel produces a characteristically intense, soft-edged beam created by the pebbled surface on the back of the Fresnel lens. Excellent lighting for theaters, clubs, and TV. Beam spread can be modified from flood to spot. Usually, they are 100–250 W with throw distances of 10–40 ft.

Front Curtain: Located behind a theater proscenium and sewn with fullness, which serves as the prime closure between the auditorium and stage. Also known as proscenium curtain, house curtain, or grand drape.

Front-of-House (FOH)

1. Describes the location of the main audio mixer usually located in the audience for sound reinforcement systems. Meant to differentiate the main house mixer from the monitor mixer normally located to the side of the stage.
2. The complete area of the event space in front of the stage (i.e. the audience area).

Full Up: A bright lighting state with all lights at 'full' (i.e. 100 percent) intensity.

Fullness: Extra fabric sewn into pleats at the tops of curtains.

Gaff Tape: Ubiquitous sticky cloth tape. Most common widths are 0.5 in. for marking out areas and 2 in. for everything else. It comes in a variety of colors and good decorators and producers try to match the gaff tape color to the floor or carpet color. Used for temporarily securing almost anything. Should not be used on coiled cables or equipment. Also known as duct tape.

Gain

1. The amplification characteristic of an electrical or mechanical device.
2. The amount of volume that may be achieved before acoustical feedback occurs. Typically refers to the signal (such as vocals) going into a mixer from a microphone or other input.

Gang, Ganged, Ganging: To couple two or more controls (analog or digital) mechanically (or electronically) so that operating one automatically operates the other. Usually applied to potentiometers (pots).

Gate: An electronic device that increases dynamic range by cutting off a signal when its level falls below a specific threshold.

Gel: A term used loosely to describe expendable color filters used in stage lighting. Originally made of thin sheets of dyed gelatin, color filters are now made from polymer plastics.

Gel String: A series of color filters connected end to end and used in a color scroller.

Genie: (Trade Name) A range of mobile access platforms with either hand-cranked or compressed air lifting mechanisms.

Glitch
1. An unintended surge or brief interruption in an electrical current or signal. This can sometimes be detrimental to the integrity of the signal or to electronic equipment.
2. Any error in the execution of a cue.

Glow Tape: Luminous yellow self-adhesive tape used to mark floors and stair edges for safety and so that positions can be found in blackouts.

Go: The action word used by a TD to cue other technical personnel or stage managers.

Gobo: Short for 'go-between', it is also called a pattern, template, or cookie. A gobo is commonly an etched steel cutout placed at the gate of an ERS that produces a pattern of light and shadow in the beam of light. Patterns are commercially available from theatrical lighting dealers or can be made by hand using a number of different processes. Many automated fixtures employ a variety of gobos and gobo effects. These include rotatable gobos, gobo combinations, glass colored gobos, or even sophisticated imaging systems which combine dichroic color effects with patterns or custom designs or artwork. For special events, company logos, names, or other specific designs can be created as gobos.

Gobo Holder: A metal plate designed to hold a gobo of a particular size in a luminaire of a particular type.

Gooseneck: A small work light, supplied with some control consoles and other equipment, that has a long, narrow, adjustable support, similar in appearance and mobility to the neck of a goose. They are usually removable and dimmable.

Graphic Equalizer: A multi-band variable equalizer using slide controls as the amplitude adjustable elements. Named for the positions of the sliders (faders) 'graphing' the resulting frequency response of the equalizer. Only found on active designs. Center frequency and bandwidth are fixed for each band.

Greasepaint: Name refers to make-up supplied in stick form, for application to the face or body. Needs special removing cream.

Green Room: Changing room for performers.

Ground Lift Switch: Found on the rear of many pro audio products, used to separate (lift) the signal ground and the chassis ground connection.

Ground Loop: A voltage difference developed between separate grounding paths due to unequal impedance such that two 'ground points' actually measure distinct and different voltage potentials relative to the power supply ground reference point.

Ground Support: The truss, lifts, and towers that are set up at ground, stage, or platform level and used to support other truss or equipment above. They can be as simple as pipe and base structures (lighting tree), to large Genie lifts.

Handheld Mic: See Wireless Microphones.

Hang: The lighting rigging session.

Hanging Point: The point where rigging is attached to a truss, or piece of scenery. The location of hanging points must be determined for structural safety, but must be reconciled with available pick-up points in the building or structure to which the truss is being rigged.

Haze Machine (Hazer):   A device, similar to a fog machine, which produces a light, fine atmosphere by atomizing a special haze fluid. Since a haze machine does not utilize a heat exchange system, like a fogger, there is no warm-up time. The atmosphere produced by a haze machine is dense enough to reveal beams of light in the air, but not so dense as to become opaque.

HDTV: High Definition Television with aspect ratio of 16:9.

Head
1. A general term for a Fresnel spotlight.
2. The part of a followspot that contains the light source (i.e. not the stand, ballast, or interconnect cable).
3. The part of a metal halide luminaire that contains the luminaire (i.e. not the ballast or interconnect cable).
4. The part of an ellipsoidal spotlight that contains the reflector (i.e. not the lens barrel or the cap).

Headset
1. General term for theater/event communications equipment.
2. A headphone and microphone combination used in a communications systems with a beltpack.

Headset Mic: See Wireless Microphones.

Hertz (Hz):   A unit of frequency measurement that equals one cycle per second.

High Intensity Discharge (HID):   A type of luminaire such as a mercury or sodium vapor luminaire that produces light by causing an inert gas to discharge photons. HID luminaires find special uses in entertainment lighting and make good UV sources. HID luminaires require special ballasts and are generally not dimmable.

High Pass Filter: A circuit that discriminates between high and low frequencies and allows only the high frequencies to pass.

Hiss: Random high-frequency noise with a sibilant quality, most often associated with tape recordings.

Horn: An acoustical transformer which, when coupled to a driver, provides directivity and increases the driver's loudness.

Hot Spot: The spot of light with the highest intensity, ideally located at or near the center of a beam that has been focused for a peak field.

House Electrician: The electrician employed by a facility who is in control of house lighting and any electrical or electronic equipment owned by the facility, or for which the facility is responsible.

House Lighting: Lighting of the house or venue (e.g. hotel or convention center ballrooms) separate from the stage lighting system, typical in all but the smallest venues.

Hue: The red, orange, yellow, green, blue, violet, magenta aspect of color, without regard to other aspects such as saturation and luminance (i.e. the property of light that distinguishes it from gray of the same luminance).

Hypercardioid: A narrower heart-shaped pick-up pattern than that of cardioid microphones.

IATSE (International Alliance of Theatrical and Stage Employees): A union representing professional craftspeople in the entertainment industry. This union includes stage electricians, carpenters, and projectionists. A venue is a union house if its local crew belongs to IATSE.

Icon (TM): A moving yoke-type automated fixture distributed by lighting and sound design (LSD).

IMAG: Image magnification. Refers to the process of routing a live video image onto a projection screen.

Impedance: The measure of the total resistance to the current flow in an AC circuit, expressed in ohms, as a characteristic of electrical devices (particularly speakers and microphones). Most speakers are rated at 8 ohms. Microphones are usually classified as being either high impedance (10,000 ohms or greater) or low impedance (50–250 ohms).

Indirect Lighting: Illumination that falls on an area or subject by reflection (e.g. bounce lighting).

Inductance: A circuit's opposition to a change in current flow.

Input/Output (I/O): Equipment, data, or connectors used to communicate from a circuit or system to other circuits or systems, or the outside world.

Input Overload Distortion: Distortion caused by too great an input signal being directed to an amplifier or pre-amplifier. Input overload distortion is not affected by volume control settings and most frequently occurs when mics are positioned too close to the sound source. Input overload distortion is controllable through the use of an attenuator.

Instrument: Luminaire or light.

Intellabeam (TM): A moving mirror-type automated fixture introduced by High End Systems/Lightwave Research in the late 1980s.

Interface: Connection or isolation device such as connecting a telephone line to sound equipment.

Interlaced: Two horizontal video scans (odd, even) per video frame. NTSC is a 2:1 interlace system.

Interrupted or In-Ear Foldback (IFB): An audio subsystem allowing on-air/onstage personnel ('talent') to receive via headphones, or ear monitors, the normal program audio mixed with audio cues from the TD. Can also be used as an in-ear monitor for musicians.

Inverse Square Law: The law that states that in the absence of reflective surfaces, sound pressure (or light) falls off at a rate inverse to the square of the distance from its source. In other words, every time the distance from the sound source is doubled, the sound pressure level is reduced by 6 dB.

Iris: A device commonly used in an ERS or followspot to reduce the apparent diameter of the beam of light. Many automated fixtures also employ a motor-controlled iris that can be used to remotely adjust the beam diameter.

ISDN: Integrated Services Digital Network. High-speed Internet access, digital video, and voice.

Jack: A female input or output connector, usually for a mic or an instrument.

Jumper: An adaptor from one type of electrical connector to another.

Key Light: A lighting design term that describes a strong primary light source. Other secondary lights are often described as being fill lights. The term high key lighting describes even, bright lighting such as might be produced on a television news set.

Keystone: Trapezoid-shaped distortion usually caused by a projector being located at a non-perpendicular angle to a projection surface.

Kill
1. To switch off (e.g. a light/sound effect).
2. To strike/remove (e.g. a prop).

Laser: Light Amplification by Stimulated Emission of Radiation. A device that produces pencil-thin beams of coherent monochromatic light. Used primarily for special effects. Lasers combined with beam splitters, scanners, and mirrors, can be used to create a variety of 3D images in fog or similar atmosphere. A laser and scanning system connected to a computer controller can be used to project complex animation effects. Care is required when using lasers as this energy can cause permanent damage to the retina of the eye.

Laser Pointer: Handheld device that projects a bright red light, typically used for manually pointing at a projection screen.

Lavalier or Lavaliere Microphone: A small electret microphone designed to be worn on a person. Lavalier (the final 'e' is commonly dropped) mics are usually attached by clips rather than hung from a cord. See Wireless Microphones.

LCD: Liquid Crystal Display. The LCD consists of an organic liquid suspension between two glass or plastic panels. Crystals in this suspension are naturally aligned parallel with one another, allowing light to pass through the panel. When electric current is applied, the crystals change orientation and block light instead of allowing it to pass through, turning the crystal region dark. LCD monitors are typically found in laptop computers, or inside multimedia projectors. Most flat-panel desktop computer monitors are based on LCD technology.

LCD Projection Panel: A flat-panel LCD device that is placed on an overhead projector to display video and computer images.

LCD Projector: An electronic video/data projector for displaying video and computer images on a large projection screen. Most such current state-of-the-art projectors have excellent image quality, high resolution, zoom lenses, keystone correction, high brightness (see Lumens), and ease of set up.

Leko (TM):   A trademark for a brand of ERS currently owned and marketed by Strand Lighting.

Lens Barrel: The complete tubular front section of an ellipsoidal spotlight that contains the lenses.

Lens Holder: Any apparatus used to retain a lens.

Level

    1. An abridged version of Light Level.
    2. The position of a slider on a control console.

Lift: A height-adjustable stand or tower, sometimes motorized or operated with a crank mechanism or by gas or liquid pressure.

Light Board: A lighting control console or desk.

Light Board Operator (Board Op):   The person who runs the lighting control console, programming and executing cues as directed by the lighting designer or TD.

Light Cue: A lighting design term referring to a point in a show at which a predetermined change in the lighting is executed. The lighting director or TD 'calls the cue' usually by saying 'go,' and the light board operator executes the lighting change. A change may occur instantly, as in a bump cue, or take place as a long fade over time.

Light Leak: Unwanted light that escapes a luminaire from a location other than its intended opening.

Light Level: The average illumination on a subject, performing area, or part thereof.

Light Show: A term describing a production where the lighting takes a primary focus. The idea of a light show may have developed from the psychedelic light shows of the late 1960s, but is now used to describe a range of laser and lighting effects.

Light Valve Projector: Very bright projection system for theater-sized screens.

Lighting Control Console: The head end of a lighting system. The lighting control console sends information via control cables to dimmers or other devices instructing what they should do. Run by a light board operator, or as is common on a touring production by the lighting designer or lighting director, the lighting control console stores and executes all of the light cues for a performance. Common types of lighting consoles include the preset board and computer memory console.

Lighting Crew: A group of individuals trained in lighting skills and techniques, and collectively assembled to work on an event. The group may include any or all of the following: stagehands, electricians, roadies, gaffers, grips, operators, and lighting technicians.

Lighting Designer (LD):   The person whose primary responsibility is the visual design of the lighting for an event. In theatrical terms, the lighting designer is responsible for all aspects of the esthetic design of the show.

Lighting Plot: A scale drawing detailing the exact location of each luminaire used in a production and any other pertinent information (e.g. its dimmer number, focus position, and color number). Often drawn from the venue floor plan.

Limiter: A compressor with a fixed ratio of 10:1 or greater. The dynamic action effectively prevents an audio signal from becoming any larger than the threshold setting. It is a device that electronically controls or 'limits' the peak levels of program material.

Line Level: A signal whose voltage is between approximately 0.310 and 10 V across a load of 600 ohms or greater.

Load: Any device to which power is delivered.

Load In: The process of moving all technical gear (e.g. audio, lighting, staging, décor) into a venue and setting it up prior to an event.

Loading Bay: Parking access into a venue for unloading technical gear and décor. Usually close to a freight elevator.

Load Out: The process of moving all technical gear out of a venue following an event.

Loudspeaker (Dynamic): The heart of a dynamic loudspeaker is a coil of wire (the voice coil), a magnet, and a cone. The amplifier applies voltage to the voice coil causing a current to flow that produces a magnetic field that reacts with the stationary magnet making the cone move proportional to the applied audio signal.

Loudspeaker (Electrostatic): A thin sheet of plastic film is suspended between two-wire grids or screens. The film is conductive and charged with a high voltage. The film is alternately attracted to one grid and then the other resulting in motion that radiates sound. For pro audio applications, dynamic loudspeakers dominate.

Low Pass Filter: A circuit that discriminates between high and low frequencies and allows only the low frequencies to pass.

Lumen: Unit of light measurement (brightness) typically for projectors. For projecting in dark rooms and/or small screens, a projector with a lumens rating of 600–800 will probably suffice. For more brightly lit venues and in high ambient light conditions such as daylight, a lumens rating as high as 12,000 or more may be required. Generally, the higher the lumens rating, the more expensive the projector.

Luminaire: The international term for lighting equipment. A complete unit for the purpose of generating usable and somewhat controllable light that comprises one or more luminaires, parts designed to distribute the light, parts used to position and protect the light source, and a means to connect the light source(s) to an electrical supply.

Luminance: Video imaging relative brightness.

Lux: Unit of light measurement typically for cameras.

Marking Out: Sticking tape to the floor of the stage to indicate the location of props, people, equipment, or direction of movement.

Marley: Originally a brand name of a portable, non-slip vinyl covering used for dance performance. It has now come to be known more as a generic term for such a surface. There are several manufacturers of this type of surface.

Masking: Neutral material, curtain, or scenery that defines a performance area and/or conceals technical areas.

Microphone: An electroacoustic transducer used to convert the input acoustic energy into an electrical energy output. Many methods exist; see, for example, electret microphone, condenser microphone, and dynamic microphone.

Microphone Processor: A device that, when installed between a mic and an amp or pre-amp, allows the manipulation of the signal originating at the mic.

Mirror Ball: A lighting effect popular in discos, ballrooms, and events. A large plastic ball covered with small mirror pieces. When a spotlight (usually a pin spot) is focused onto the ball, specks of light are thrown around the room. Usually motorized to rotate.

Mixer: An electronic device that permits the combining of a number of audio signal inputs into one or more outputs. Mixers commonly provide a variety of controls (e.g. tone, volume, balance, and effects) for each 'channel.' Typically, mixers have between 8 and 64 input channels. See also Board, Console.

Monitor
1. A speaker or earphone dedicated to making it possible for a performer to hear – or monitor – his/her own performance.
2. Used for video or computer displays. Can use CRT, LCD, or plasma technology. Generally, monitors come in aspect ratios corresponding to standard video (4:3) or HDTV (16:9). 4:3 aspect ratio monitors vary in size from about 20 in. diagonal to 50 in. diagonal screens, and 16:9 aspect ratio monitors vary from 30 to 56 in. diagonals. This translates into viewing distances for the farthest person from the screens of about 8 or 9 ft for the smaller screens to about 18 or 20 ft for the larger screens. In other words, monitors are really only good for small audiences. Monitors come with a variety of features, two of the more important being direct video and audio inputs to lessen degradation in signals.

Monitor Mixer: A separate audio mixer used to create the proper signals to drive the individual musician stage monitors. Also called foldback speakers.

Moving Mirror Automated Fixture: A classification of automated fixtures, which achieve beam motion by reflecting the beam off a remotely controlled, motorized mirror. The Cyberlight (TM) by High End Systems, and the Roboscan (TM) by Martin, are examples of moving mirror automated fixtures.

Moving Yoke Automated Fixture: A classification of automated fixtures that achieve beam motion by remote motor-controlled movement of the yoke and body of the fixture. The Vari-Lite (TM) series is an example of moving yoke automated fixtures.

Multi-cable (Mult, Multi):   A cable designed to supply power from dimmers to multiple separate lighting instruments down a single multiconductor cable. Standard multi-cables can carry the equivalent of

6 or 12 standard stage cables corresponding to the same number of circuits. A breakout is used at either end to break the multi-cable apart into individual circuits. Multi-cables have the advantage of being much smaller than bundles of multiple stage cables.

Multimedia: Any combinations of video, audio, and visual presentations.

Musical Instrument Digital Interface (MIDI):   Industry standard bus and protocol for interconnection and control of musical instruments, or of other devices by musical instruments. First launched in 1983, now generalized and expanded to include signal processing and lighting control.

Neon: A type of discharge lighting generated by a high voltage across two oppositely charged electrodes at opposite ends of a long, thin glass tube filled with neon gas. As the electrical charge flows between the electrodes, electrons collide with neon atoms causing them to give off energy in the form of visible light. Different colors can be obtained by mixing other gases, or by using fluorescent coatings. For special events and advertising, the glass tube is bent to form letters and different shapes.

Noise Gate: A device that attenuates a signal when the program level falls below a preset threshold. It controls unwanted noise, such as preventing 'open' microphones and 'hot' instrument pick-ups from introducing extraneous sounds into the audio system.

Non-Interlaced: Only a single horizontal video scan per video frame.

NTSC: National Television Standards Committee. North American Television uses NTSC standards.

Offstage: Out of sight from the audience.

Ohm: The basic unit of the measurement of resistance.

Ohm's Law: The law that states the relationship between current, resistance, and voltage in an electrical circuit: amperage times resistance equals applied voltage ($V = IR$).

Omnidirectional: Capable of picking up sound from, or radiating sound in, all directions equally.

Onstage: What happens in view of the audience on the stage.

Open Face: A term used to describe luminaires that use no lenses.

Open the House: Clearance given to FOH staff by stage management that the stage is set and the audience can begin to take their seats, or that the event may now begin.

Operating Light: A work light used by the operator of a control console.

Oscilloscope: An electronic device that displays, on a video screen, a representation of an electrical signal.

Outriggers: Sturdy support legs that assist in stabilizing some stands and lifts. They are generally removable or easily folded away to assist in transporting or maneuvering the stand or lift.

Over Equalization: Adjustment of the tone controls on an equalizer to or beyond the point at which sound quality is adversely affected.

Overhead Projector: Used for displaying 8½ × 11 in. transparencies on a projection screen. These units typically sit on top of a projection cart or a table and are front projection only. The focal length of the lens determines how far in front of the screen the projector must be placed. This distance varies from about 5 ft for a 10.5 in. focal length lens, to 11.2 ft for a 14 in. focal length lens, so this space must be considered in room setup plans. Luminaire brightness of overhead projectors varies from about 2000 lumens to about 12,000 lumens. As with other projectors, larger screens and larger rooms require brighter projectors. LCD panels typically require a brightness minimum of about 4000 lumens.

Overload Light or OL Light: An indicator found on pro audio signal processing units that lights once the signal level exceeds a preset point.

PA: Public Address system. One or more speakers connected to an amplifier that may include a mixer and any combination of sound reinforcement devices.

Pad: An attenuator.

PAL: Phase Alteration by Line. This is the color television broadcast standard for the UK, Germany, and many other nations.

Pan (Panoramic) Control: A control found on mixers, used to 'move' or pan the apparent position of a single sound channel between two outputs, usually 'left' and 'right' for stereo outputs. At one extreme of travel the sound source is heard from only one output; at the other extreme it is heard from the other output. In the middle, the sound is heard equally from each output, but is reduced in level by 3 dB relative to its original value. This guarantees that as the sound is panned from one side to the other, it maintains equal loudness (power) for all positions.

Panelboard: A piece of power distribution equipment comprising a box-like metal enclosure with a hinged cover, accessible only from one side, to allow access to internally mounted circuit breakers, switches, and fuses.

PAR or PAR Can: A PAR can is comprised of a PAR (Parabolic Aluminized Reflector) luminaire and a mounting fixture and base (the can). It produces a high-intensity narrow beam of light. PAR luminaires are available in many different sizes and powers. The bigger the number with a PAR can, the bigger its size. Electric lights used in PAR luminaires are sized by multiples of 1/8 in. Therefore, a PAR8 (if such exists) would have a 1 in. diameter glass envelope. A PAR64 is 8 in. in diameter. To convert the PAR number to inches, divide the luminaire number by 8. Some common PAR luminaire types are:

1. *PAR36*: Practically all the PAR36 fittings are standard disco pin spot type with a very narrow beam 6 V, 30 W bulb. The most typical bulb used is VNSP bulb type 4515, which has 5 degrees beam and uses 6 V, 30 W. The PAR36 cans almost always have a transformer built in, and the bulb has screw terminals on the back. There are also other more rarely used special PAR36 luminaires (12 V models, up to 100 W models, etc.). The PAR36 luminaire diameter is 4.3 in. (around 110 mm). PAR36 luminaires come in a wide range of oddball voltages and powers for things like marine and aircraft (e.g. 28 V ACL version). Generally PAR36 luminaires are a bit short lived on continuous duty.

2. *PAR38*: The PAR38 luminaire diameter is around 4.75 in. (around 120 mm). These types of bulbs have typically an ES (Edison Screw) cap. Typical luminaire power levels available are 60, 75, 80, 100, 150, and 300 W. Typical beam spreads are 30 and 60 degrees (special 12 degree bulbs exist also). These types of luminaires are common in shop display fittings and security lights, also in outdoor garden lighting (special bulb version for out-door use).

3. *PAR46*: The PAR46 luminaire diameter is around 5.75 in. (around 146 mm). Typical luminaire power is around 200 W. The bulb has blade connectors.

4. *PAR 56*: The PAR56 luminaire diameter is around 7 in. (around 178 mm). Typical luminaire power is 300 W. The bulb has blade connectors. Typical beam spread is 11×25 degrees. Different beam spreads are available. PAR56 luminaires are typically available at 300 and 500 W power.

5. *PAR64*: The PAR64 luminaire diameter is around 8 in. (around 203 mm). Typical luminaire power is 500 or 1000 W. The bulb has blade connectors. Typical beam spread is 11×25 degrees. Different beam spreads are available.

   PAR cans serve many purposes in special events including décor lighting (e.g. up walls) and stage washes.

Parallel Port: Computer input/output connection that transmits data multiple bits at a time (e.g. for a printer).

Parametric Equalizer: A multi-band variable equalizer offering control of all the 'parameters' of the internal band-pass filter sections. These parameters are amplitude, center frequency, and bandwidth.

Passive Equalizer: A variable equalizer requiring no power supply to operate. Consisting only of passive components (inductors, capacitors, and resistors), passive equalizers have no AC line cord.

Patch Cord: A short electrical cable used to connect individual components of a sound system.

Patchbay or Patch Panel: A flat panel, or enclosure, usually rack-mounted, that contains at least two rows of 1/4 in. TRS connectors used to 'patch in' or insert into the signal path a piece of external equipment.

Patching
1. To cross-connect lighting circuits around the stage area to a chosen dimmer. Connecting luminaires to dimmers.
2. Using a cross-connect panel that enables any stage lighting channels at the control desk to control any dimmer or group of dimmers. Some large lighting boards have the facility for soft patching, a totally electronic way of patching.

Personal Monitor: A monitor that is small enough to be directed at a specific performer.

Phantom Power: Operating voltage supplied to a condenser mic by a mixer or external power source.

Phase: The relationship of an audio signal or sound wave to a specific time reference.

Phase Shift: The phase relationship of two signals at a given time, or the phase change of a signal over an interval of time.

Photoflood: Luminaire used by photographers that gives a bright white light. Because it has a thin filament, it gives a good flash effect (e.g. lightning), but has a relatively short life, so should not be left on for any length of time.

Pickup
1. In lighting, the action of turning a followspot on a performer.
2. In audio, a device which, when attached to an acoustic musical instrument, converts sound vibrations into an electrical signal.
3. In audio, a way of describing the directional sensitivity of a microphone. An omnidirectional microphone has equal pick-up from all around, a cardioid microphone is more sensitive from the front, and a hypercardioid has very strong directionality from the front. A bidirectional microphone picks up front and rear, but rejects sound from the sides.

Pick-up Point (Pick Point):   An architectural or structural point to which scenery or trussing can be rigged for flying purposes. Available pick-up points in a particular venue must be reconciled with necessary hanging points on the equipment to be lifted.

Pin spot: A spotlight that has an extremely narrow beam, frequently used to illuminate and isolate table centers. It is controllable only by aiming it where it is wanted. Usually 75–1000 W with a throw of 5–50 ft.

Pitch Tone: A function of frequency.

Pixel: The smallest picture element making up a computer video display.

Plasma Displays: A relatively new form of computer and video monitor. Plasma monitors work much like CRT monitors, but instead of using a single CRT surface coated with phosphors, they use a flat, lightweight surface covered with a matrix of tiny glass bubbles, each containing a gas-like substance or plasma, and having a phosphor coating. Each of the 'pixels' in this matrix is actually comprised of three subpixels, corresponding to the colors red, green, and blue.

PM: Short for Production Manager.

Polarity: A condition that has two states (in/out) and is usually described in one of three ways:
1. *Acoustical to electrical (microphone)*: Positive pressure at diaphragm produces positive voltage at pin 2 of XLR or at the tip of a ¼ in. phono plug.
2. *Electrical to acoustic*: Positive voltage into the 'plus' terminal of a speaker causes the speaker's diaphragm to move forward (produces positive pressure).
3. *Electrical to electrical*: Positive voltage into pin 2 of an XLR plug produces positive voltage at the output (pin 2 of an XLR jack), at the tip of a ¼ in. phono jack, or at the red (plus) connector of a binding post (banana terminal).

Potentiometer (Pot): A variable resistor (rotary or linear) used to control volume, tone, or other functions of an electronic device.

Power Amplifier: An electronic device that increases the volume of a signal. A basic component of all sound systems. Power amps are typically connected to a pre-amp which provides controls for individual functions (e.g. level, tone, etc.).

Pre-amplifier: See Power Amplifier.

Pre-fade Level or Pre-fade Listen (PFL): This little button on an audio mixing console allows the audio engineer to hear only that channel in the headphones when it is pressed. PFL can also be useful in identifying off-key singers so they can be turned down in the house speakers.

Pre-hung Truss: A truss or truss section which has been pre-assembled with lighting equipment and connecting devices in the shop prior to installation at load-in. Using a pre-hung truss saves many hours when loading a show in/out, and makes for an efficient method of storing equipment on a truck.

Preset Board: A lighting control console comprised of banks or 'scenes' of redundant sliders each controlling one channel of the lighting system. Individual looks can be set up on banks and by using scene

Short Throw: A term used to describe a luminaire that has an effective intensity at a relatively short distance. This term is very subjective and dependent on the type of luminaire used.

Shutters
1. An abridged version of Framing Shutters.
2. A rectangular, metal apparatus that resembles a venetian blind in form and function, generally used as a mechanical dimmer or blackout mechanism on large spotlights.

Sibilance: A hissing sound, usually coming from vocals into a microphone.

Side Light: Light which comes primarily from the side of a performer or object being lit. Strong side lighting is associated with the emphasis of the edges or sides of performers or objects, tending to enhance their dimensionality.

Sight Lines: Imaginary lines drawn from the most extreme seats in the house to the performing area to determine what portions of the performing area will be visible to all of the audience.

Signal: An electrical impulse.

Signal-to-Noise Ratio: The ratio, expressed in dB, of an electronic device's nominal output to its noise floor.

Simplex: Transmission in only one direction.

Slap Echo (Slapback):   A single echo resulting from parallel non-absorbing (e.g. reflective) walls, characterized by lots of high-frequency content. So-called because you can test for slap echo by sharply clapping your hands and listening for the characteristic sound of the echo in the mid-range.

Slide Projector: Used for displaying 35 mm and 2 in. $\times$ 2 in. slides on a projection screen. Now considered obsolete technology for events.

Smoke Machine: A smoke machine or fogger is an electrically powered unit that produces clouds of white non-toxic fog (available in different flavors/smells) by the vaporization of mineral oil. It is specially designed for theater and film use, but often finds its way into special events.

Snake: A cable, usually running between the stage and FOH mixer, that combines multiple lines used to connect mics, instruments, and monitors to a mixer.

Socapex (TM):   A multi-pin connector that can carry a series of lighting or sound circuits. Very robust and designed for touring. Available in 19-pin (6 circuits) and 37-pin (12 circuits) configurations. Sometimes shortened to SOCA.

Soft Light
1. Illumination that produces shadows with a soft edge.
2. A luminaire that provides such illumination.

Soft Patch: A term used to describe a patch system whereby the dimmers can be interchangeably assigned to any one of any number of channels. This type of patch system is usually found on memory boards.

Solo: On a lighting console, solo mode kills all other channels except the single dimmer you're working with. It can be useful for identifying a channel in a large rig, but can be dangerous during a show. Some consoles allow you to assign flash buttons to solo mode that will turn off all channels except those loaded into that flash button or submaster.

Sound Level Meter: A device that measures, in dB, the amplitude of sound waves.

Sound Pressure Level (SPL): The measurement of the loudness, or amplitude, of sound, expressed in dB.

Sound Reinforcement: The use of electronic devices to reinforce, alter or increase the level of sound.

Source Four: (Trade Name) (Also known as S4) Range of luminaires manufactured by ETC.

Special: A luminaire within the lighting rig that is required for a specific moment or effect within the performance, and is not part of the general cover lighting.

Spike: To mark the position of an item on stage, such as musical instruments, lectern, and microphones. Spike tape is normally thin gaff tape, although other weaker tape (e.g. masking tape) is used on precious floors.

Spill: Unwanted light onstage.

Splitter: An audio device used to divide one input signal into two or more outputs. Typically this type of unit has one input with 6–16 (or more) outputs, each with a level control, and often is unbalanced.

Squawker: A common nickname for a mid-range driver.

Stage Left: The left side of the stage when facing the audience.

Stage Light: A luminaire intended to illuminate any portion of, or anything on, a stage or similar performing area, exclusive of practical lights and work lights.

Stage Manager: Person who assists with moving performers and equipment on and off stage.

Stage Right: The right side of the stage when facing the audience.

Stage Wash: See Wash.

Standby: Audio cue for 'Get Ready.'

Star Cloth (Drop):   A piece of scenic canvas, painted or plain, that is flown or fixed to hang in a vertical position, usually black, and has a large number of small low-voltage luminaires sewn or pinned through it which gives a magical starry sky effect.

Strike: To remove all technical equipment and décor for storage and/or transport when an event is over.

Strobelight: A special lighting effect that produces multiple rapid bursts of high-intensity light. Strobe lighting is almost always produced by a compact xenon strobe luminaire activated by a power supply and timing circuitry. Strobelights can be simple low-power devices with fixed flash rates, or sophisticated devices triggered by a lighting control console at specific intervals.

Subwoofer: A large woofer loudspeaker designed to reproduce audio's very bottom end (e.g. approximately the last one or two octaves), from 20 to 80–100 Hz.

Suppression, also Gain Suppression: The term used to describe the technique of instantaneous reduction of a sound system's overall gain to control acoustic feedback, and thus reduce echoes.

SVGA: Super Video Graphics Array. Resolution = 800 × 600 pixels.

Sweet Spot: Any location in a two-loudspeaker stereo playback system where the listener is positioned equidistant from each loudspeaker. The apex of all possible isosceles (two equal sides) triangles formed by the loudspeakers and the listener. In this sense, the sweet spot lies anywhere on the sweet plane extending forward from the midpoint between the speakers.

Switcher, Data: Takes a video signal from any number of sources and adjusts it before sending it to a projection system. The source can be a camera or playback unit. Adjustments include raising or lowering the scan rate, boosting the line resolution to the highest possible level (e.g. SVGA to SXGA), and splitting the signal to send it to multiple projectors.

Switcher, Video: Allows for switching between video sources (e.g. two or more cameras, different video standards, computer playback) and effects. The latest technology is seamless with no obvious picture interruptions during switching.

SXGA: Super Extended Graphics Array. Resolution = 1280 × 1024 pixels.

Sync: Synchronization. Scanning signals that are used to keep the video display generator locked to the source.

Talent: Any and all performers.

Telescoping Stand: A height-adjustable stand that has two or more concentric tubular sections that slide inside one another and lock into place.

Three-Fer: A circuiting device that allows three lighting instruments to be joined into one cable or circuit.

Three-Phase
1. A term for an AC electrical supply that has three hot legs, with each leg at a phase that is 120° apart from the other, with or without a neutral leg.
2. A term used to describe something that requires a three-phase electrical supply to operate.

Throw Distance: The effective distance between a luminaire and the area or subject to be illuminated.

Tie-In: To connect the line side leads of power distribution equipment, dimmer racks, and such to the primary electrical supply for a location, such as a venue circuit breaker panel or other piece of power distribution. This is generally done with feeder cables.

Tie-In Set: A set of feeder cables or other necessary connecting devices (e.g. Cam Lock) needed to tie-in a dimmer rack. A standard tie-in set includes a ground, neutral, and three hot cables with bare ends in one end for connection at the venue disconnect panel.

Toe-In: The degree to which the inside front edges of a pair of speakers are angled toward each other.

Transducer: A device that converts sound into electrical energy (e.g. a microphone), or electrical energy into sound (e.g. a speaker).

Transformer: Device that transfers electrical energy from one alternating current circuit to one or more other circuits, either increasing (stepping up) or reducing (stepping down) the voltage.

Travelers or Traveler Drape: Curtains or scenic pieces moving on horizontal tracks.

Trim
1. To finely adjust the height of battens, curtains, or any item whose exact height is critical.
2. To finely adjust the voltage output of some electronic dimmer at the lowest control setting.
3. To finely adjust the focus, beam direction, shutter positions, and other variables, for a group of luminaires set up for a production.

Truss: A framework of alloy bars and triangular cross-bracing (usually of scaffolding diameter) providing a rigid structure, particularly useful for hanging lights where no permanent facility is available. Very often box-shaped in cross-section, so known as Box Truss. This type of truss is useful for touring as luminaires/speakers can be hung inside the truss which protects them when loading and takes up less space in a truck. Also comes as triangle truss but this has the disadvantage over box truss that instrumentation must be struck from the truss before it can be loaded into a truck.

Tweeter: A speaker (driver) that reproduces only frequencies above a certain range, usually about 3–5 kHz.

Twist-Lock Connector: A commonly used type of locking blade connector that requires a twisting action to lock the mating connectors together, manufactured by Harvey Hubbell, Inc. The name 'Twist-Lock' is trademarked.

Two-Fer: An electrical connecting device that allows two lighting instruments to be combined into one cable or circuit.

Ultraviolet (UV):   A UV light source is used to create special lighting effects with fluorescent materials. UV sources can be incandescent, fluorescent, or preferably HID luminaires.

Unbalanced Line: Cable that consists of one-conductor and a shield.

Unidirectional: A mic that picks up sound primarily from one direction.

Union House: A venue that is a union house holds a collective bargaining agreement with its union employees guaranteeing such things as pay scale, working hours, and conditions. If a theatrical venue is a union house it is most likely covered by IATSE.

Up lighting: Cost-effective way to highlight décor pieces, accentuate given attributes of a venue, or just add color to an event space. Typically used to light walls from floor-mounted luminaires.

Upstage: The part of the stage furthest from the audience.

Vari-Lite (TM):   A company that manufactures, rents, and supports a complete automated fixture and control system. A pioneer in automated fixture technology, Vari-Lite supplies its own console operators and repair technicians for most applications.

VGA: Video Graphics Array. Resolution = 640 × 480 pixels.

Video In: Input video connection for an electronic device such as a VCR, female RCA jacks, or BNC.

Video Out: Output video signal from a device such as a VCR or camera, female RCA jacks, or BNC.

Videoconferencing: Linking of two or more groups via closed circuit satellite television.

Videotape Formats: There are several different formats for videotapes:
1. *VHS or SVHS (1/2 in.):*   Inexpensive and popular, used extensively for movies and home recording prior to DVDs.
2. *Hi 8 (8 mm):* This is better quality than VHS and designed for low-cost industrial use.
3. *Mini DV:*   New high-quality digital format gaining popularity for industrial use. Very small.

4. *Betacam/Betacam SP*: The professional standard of extremely high quality but expensive.

5. *Digital Betacam*: Higher quality than Betacam SP. Current standard for quality in digital video production.

Videowall: High-end image display systems consisting of multiple monitors (cubes) placed in various configurations such as 2 × 2 (e.g. 4 monitors with an overall aspect ratio of approximately 4:3), 3 × 4 (e.g. 12 monitors with an overall aspect ratio of 16:9 or HDTV size), and almost any other combination desired. The monitors are especially constructed for this type of display, typically vary from 2 to 4 or 5 ft in depth, and are designed to be stacked together. The monitors use the same technology as found in other projection systems (e.g. CRT, LCD, or DLP). The technology basically takes video, digital data, and/or computer graphics input and feeds it into a processor that manipulates and splits the signal to allow it to go to one or more monitors. Almost limitless possibilities are available for uniquely displaying the image or combinations of images. The advantages of a videowall include constant resolution and brightness no matter to what size the image grows.

Visual Cue: A cue taken by a technician from the action on stage rather than being cued by the stage manager or TD.

Voice Coil: Wire, usually copper, wrapped around a former (tubular core). When attached to a cone or diaphragm, surrounded by a magnetic field, and set into vibration by an AC, a voice coil causes a speaker to emit sound waves.

Voltage: The electrical pressure (electromotive force) of a current within a circuit.

Voltage-Controlled Amplifier (VCA):   An amplifier whose output is controlled by varying its voltage rather than by direct resistance (as with a potentiometer).

Wash

1. An even, overall illumination over a large area, typically a stage.

2. To create such an illumination. Can be a variety of things from three-color to one-color, color-corrected, or video level lighting wash. Three-color or four-color is a basic wash for entertainers. It has different colors to set the mood for the performance. Video level lighting is a diffused white wash used for TV applications. Often described in terms of 'K.' 'K' refers to thousands of watts of light. Thus, a 12 K, three-color wash is 12 instruments total in three groups of color, four instruments each, with each one rated at 1000 W.

Watt

1. A unit of measurement that equals about 1/746 horsepower or enough electrical energy to perform one joule per second. A joule

describes the energy of 1 Newton displaced 1m in the direction of the applied force. A Newton is the amount of force needed to accelerate 1 kg 1m/s.

2. 1 V multiplied by 1 amp.

Wattage: The measurement of the amount of power used by an electrical device. Stage lighting equipment is rated in watts (or kilowatts – 1 kW being equal to 1000 W). This refers to the amount of power required to light the luminaire. A higher wattage luminaire requires more power and gives a brighter light output. Dimmers are rated in terms of their maximum load capacity in wattage. Wattage = Amperage × Voltage.

Wedge: A monitor speaker, in the shape of a wedge, designed to sit on the floor and be directed toward the performer(s).

White Noise: Analogous to white light containing equal amounts of all visible frequencies, white noise contains equal amounts of all audible frequencies (technically the bandwidth of noise is infinite, but for audio purposes it is limited to just the audible frequencies).

Wing: The areas to the left and right of the stage or performing area not visible to the audience. Often set up as temporary areas and delineated with drape.

Wireless Microphones: Also known as radio mics, they operate as handheld, lavalier, or headset (e.g. forehead, over the ear, or boom) types. They all incorporate a microphone, battery, transmitter, and antenna. The handheld types incorporate all components in the body of the microphone. With the other types, the microphone is placed near the mouth but the transmitter, antenna, and battery are in a separate small box that must be affixed to the performer somehow, such as on a belt. Wireless mics operate on two different signal frequencies, VHF (very high frequency), which is cheaper, prone to signal dropout, and of lower quality, and UHF (ultra high frequency), which is more expensive but has a higher-quality signal.

Woofer: A speaker (driver) that reproduces only frequencies below a certain range, usually about 800–1000 Hz.

WYSIWYG: Acronym for 'What You See Is What You Get.' Mainly used in the context of a software tool for lighting design and production administration. Capable of stunning 3D rendering of lighting states, and direct connection to a lighting control desk. Enables accurate previsualization of lighting designs and greatly increases the understanding between the producer and LD in the early stages of a production.

Xenon: High-output discharge luminaire commonly used in strobe lighting. Some followspots also use xenon luminaires. Xenon luminaires have a color temperature of between 5600 and 6500 K.

XGA: Extended Graphics Array. Resolution = 1024 × 768 pixels.

Y-Connector or Y-Cord: A three-wire circuit that is star connected. Also spelled wye-connector. It is okay to use a Y-connector to split an audio signal from an output to drive two inputs; it is not okay to use a Y-connector to try and sum or mix two signals together to drive one input.

Yoke: A sturdy, U-shaped metal bracket that attaches to opposite sides of a luminaire (or video and film industry reflectors, butterflies, etc.) such that it allows either to tilt freely. A locking mechanism is provided to prevent slippage when the desired position has been achieved. Also provided at the center of the yoke is a hole, stud, or receiver for mounting the yoke.

Zoom Focus: A term used to describe an optical system whereby the lenses in a luminaire adjust such that a beam pattern with a hard edge can be attained at various sizes at various distances without sacrificing beam lumens.

Index

A

Accolades, following event, 186
Accounts payable, 47
Accounts receivable, 47, 109, 187, 197
Additional named insured(s), 100, 148
Agenda, meeting, 85–6
Alternate Dispute Resolution (ADR), 103, 107–8
American National Standards Institute (ANSI), 100, 143
Analogies, 34–5
Anamorphism, 26
Antenna, 167
Arbitration, 103, 108–9
Assembling, the production team, 80–1
Atmospheric perspective, 26
Audio engineer, 107, 163, 166
Autocratic, style of leadership, 83
A-V director, 163, 166
Award shows, 7, 141

B

Banquet seating. *See* Seating, banquet
Battle of the forms, 104
Belt pack, 167
Binocular disparity, 25
Body language, 91
Brainstorming, 36–7

Breach of contract. *See* Breaking a contract
Breaking a contract, 106–7
Briefing, 93, 171, 176
Budget:
    adjustments to, in event follow-up phase, 15, 186, 187
    as judging criterion in brainstorming, 36
    as part of event proposal, 62, 66–8, 81
    as part of initial event design, 12
    producer's role in formulating event budget, 17
Budget layouts, 52–5
Budgeting, 41–59
    accounts payable, 47–8
    accounts receivable, 47
    budget layouts, 52–5
    cash flow, 47–8
    contingencies and unexpected expenses, 46
    deposits, 47
    employee/contractor decision, 56
    event insurance, 56–7
    expense categories, 44
    hourly fee, 49–51
    line of credit, 48
    making a profit, 48–52
    markup of supplier costs, 48–9
    preparing the production budget, 42–6
    researching and categorizing expenses, 44–5

Budgeting (*cont'd*)
  supplier terms, 47–8
  taxes, 57
  tracking and updating expenses, 45–6
  Workers' compensation, in budget, 58–9

C

CADD:
  as in skill required by event producer, 10
  as part of event proposal, 71
  as used in production management, 152,
    157, 160–2
  example in risk management scenario,
    138
Calling the show, 81, 152, 166, 170–6
Canada Labour Code (CLC), 93
Canada Occupational Health and Safety
    Regulations (COHSR), 93
Canadian Electrical Code (CEC), 143, 145
Canadian Special Events Society (CSES), 7
Canadian Standards Association (CSA), 143
Canadian Tourism Human Resource
    Council (CTHRC), 7, 64
Cancellation policy, in contracts, 102
Capacity, for venues and sites, 152, 154–7
Capacity, formula for, 155
Care-based thinking, 76
Cash flow, 47–8
Categories of special events, 6–8
  celebrations, ceremonies, and
    spectacles, 7
  expositions and trade shows, 7
  meetings, incentives, conventions, and
    exhibitions (MICE), 6
  meetings and conferences, 7
  private events, 7
  public events, 7
Catering Director, 153
Catering Manager(s), 87, 89, 153–4, 186
Celebrations, 2, 7
Celebrity worship, 5
Ceremonies, 2, 3, 4, 7
Certified in Exhibition Management
    (CEM), 7
Certified Festival and Event Executive
    (CFEE), 7
Certified Meeting Planner (CMP), 7
Certified Special Event Coordinator
    (CSEC), 7, 64

Certified Special Event Manager (CSEM),
    7, 64
Certified Special Events Professional
    (CSEP), 7, 64
CGL insurance, 100, 145–9
Channel, communication, 168
Characteristics, of creative person, 20–1
Classroom seating. *See* Seating,
    schoolroom
Clauses, in contracts, 102–4
Clear-Com, 167–8
Cognitive process, 21–9
  depth perception, 25–6
  experience and context, relationship to
    perception, 26–7
  illumination phase, 29
  incubation phase, 27–8
  motion perception, 26
  perceptual constancy, 24
  perceptual organization, 22–4
  preparation phase, 22–7
  translation phase, 29
Comm. *See* Communications equipment
Commercial General Liability (CGL)
    insurance. *See* CGL insurance
Communication channel assignment, 168
Communication protocol, 169–70
Communications equipment, 167–68
Competent parties, in a contract, 98
Compliance, with standards and
    regulations, 100, 142–5
Computer aided design and drafting.
    See CADD
Concept and proposal phase, of event
    organization:
  definition of, 12
  preparing the budget in, 41–5
  site inspection and venue liaison in, 152,
    154
  working with the production team in,
    83–4
  writing a proposal in, 61
Conceptual combinations, 33–4
Conciliation, 108
Conference Services Manager, 153
Conferences, 5, 7
Conflict resolution, 88–91
  body language in, 91
  interest-based approach to, 90
  language of, 90–1

positional approach to, 90
spoken language in, 91
Congresses, 7
Consideration, in contracts, 98
Consumer shows, 7
Contact information, for parties to a
    contract, 99
Contact lists, 164
Content, of proposal, 65–8
Contingencies, in budgeting, 46
Continuous talk, 167
Contract management, 97–136, 197
    alternate dispute resolution (ADR), 103,
        108–9
    arbitration, 103
    breaking a contract, 106–7
    cancellation policy, 102
    clauses, 102–4
    competent parties, 98
    conciliation, 108
    consideration, 98
    contact information, 99
    deadline date, 104
    definition of a contract, 98
    elements of a contract, 98
    event details, 99–100
    financial information, 101
    force majeure, 102
    indemnity and limitation of liability,
        102–3
    independent contractor status, 103
    intellectual property, 103
    issuing contracts, 104–5
    items to include in a contract, 99–104
    legal jurisdiction, 103
    litigation, 109
    mailbox rule, 104
    mediation, 108
    meeting of the minds, 98
    negotiation, 108
    performing organizations and unions,
        103
    resolving disputes, 107–9
    riders and rider information, 101–2
    rights of assignment, 103
    sample contracts and riders, 109–110,
        112–36
    signing authority, 105
    signing contracts, 105
    small claims court, 109

special clauses, 103–4
termination policy, 102
terms and conditions, 99–102
Convention Industry Council (CIC), 7
Convention Services Manager, 153
Conventions, 6–7
Coordination phase, of event organization:
    contract management in, 98
    definition of, 13
    production management in, 152–64
    risk management in, 137–8
    working with the production team in,
        84–7
Copyright and intellectual property, 74–5,
    103
Copyright statement, 74–5
Corporate dinners, 7, 141
Creative cognition, 28
Creative fee, for proposal, 74
Creative perception, 28
Creative person, 20–1
    characteristics of, 20–1
    intelligence, 20
    personality, 20–1
Creativity, 16, 19–38, 62–3
    analogies, 34–5
    classical brainstorming, 36
    cognitive process, as applied to.
        See Cognitive process
    conceptual combinations, 33–4
    external environment for, 29–32
    lateral thinking, 36–8
    lifespan development of, 21
    reversals, 35–6
    social environments for, 21
    techniques and methods for, 32–8
Cue(s):
    depth, 25
    in running a show, 163–4, 166–75

D

Dead case(s), 158
Deadline date:
    for contract signing, 104
    for submission of proposal, 63
Debrief, with event team, 187
Democratic, style of leadership, 83
Deposits, on contracts, 47
Depth perception, 25–6

Destination Management Company (DMC), 9, 80
Dimensions, of venue or site, 157, 160
Disputes, resolving, 107–9
Distance, between tables and/or between chairs, 154–7

E

Earpiece, 167
Electrical power, 44, 66, 87, 141, 153, 157–9, 165
Elements of a contract, 98
Emergency exits, 158
Emergency vehicles, 159
Employee/contractor decision, 56
Ends-based thinking, 76
Ethics, 73–6
Evaluation, from client, 187
Event coordinator, 1, 8–9, 153–4
Event details, needed in contracts, 99–102
Event followup. *See* Followup phase, of event organization
Event manager(s), 1, 8–9, 16, 41–2, 52, 80, 103, 142, 164, 185, 187
Event marketing, 8
Event organization, 11–15
  concept and proposal phase, 12
  coordination phase, 13
  execution phase, 13
  followup phase, 13–15
  initial event design, 12
  marketing and sales phase, 13
  preliminary research, 12
  responsibility areas, 15–17
Event planner(s), 1, 8
Event planning, 10, 15, 105, 160
Event producer(s):
  definition of, 9
  habits of effective, 10–11
  skills required by, 9–10
Events, private, 7
Events, public, 7
Execution phase, of event organization:
  definition of, 13
  production management in, 164–76
  working with production team in, 87–93
Expense categories, for budgeting, 44
Expenses, tracking for budgeting, 45–6
Expositions, 7

F

Fee, creative, for proposal, 74
Fee, hourly, 49–51
Fencing, 65, 87, 151, 159
Festivals, 4, 7–8, 141, 164
Fixed station, communication, 167
Followspot operator, 166
Followup phase, of event organization:
  budget review following, 186
  definition of, 13–15
  event evaluation from client, 187
  final subcontractor payments, 186
  following up with the client, 186–7
  following up with the production team, 185–6
  following up with the venue, 186
  meeting with event team, 187
  thank-you letter to client, 187
Force majeure, 102
Format, of proposal, 68–72
Freight elevator, 157, 165, 176
Fundraisers, 7

G

GANNT chart, 15
Genie lift, 139, 158
Gestalt psychology, 22
Go, command in show calling, 174–5
Graduations, 4
Green rooms, 66, 102, 153, 158, 167, 174–5
Guidelines, for the operation and/or use of equipment, 143

H

Habits, of effective event producers, 10–11
Hands-free, communication, 167
Hanging points, 157
Headset, 167
Health, of production team, 93–4
Hierarchy, of production team, 81, 87
Hold harmless agreement, 148
Hourly fee, method of making profit, 49–52
House lighting control, 157

I

Idea generators, 37–8
Illumination phase, of cognitive process, 29

Incentive events, 7
Incubation phase, of cognitive process, 27–8, 33
Indemnity, 102–3
Independent contractor status, 103
Industrial shows, 7
In-ear fold-back (IFB), 167
In-ear monitor. *See* In-ear fold-back
Infrastructure, 159
Inspection, of site and venue, 152–60
Insurance, 17, 42, 56–7, 63, 66, 100, 103, 138–41, 145–9
Intellectual property. *See* Copyright and intellectual property
Intelligence, of creative person, 20
Intercom, 167–70
Interest-based approach, to conflict resolution, 90
International Association for Exhibition Management (IAEM), 7
International Association of Theatrical Stage Employees (IATSE), 153
International Electrotechnical Commission (IEC), 143
International Festivals and Events Association (IFEA), 7
International Organization for Standardization (ISO), 143
International Special Events Society (ISES), 7, 64
Interposition, 25
Issuing contracts, 104–5

J

Janusian thinking, 33

L

Laissez-faire, style of leadership, 83
Language:
    body, 91
    spoken, 91
Laser distance measuring device(s), 160
Lateral thinking, 36–8
Leadership, 83–4
    autocratic style of, 83
    democratic style of, 83
    laissez-faire style of, 83

Legal jurisdiction, 103
Liability insurance. *See* CGL insurance
Licenses, 13, 17, 66, 140, 164
Lighting director, 163, 166
Limitation of liability, 102–3
Line of credit, 48
Linear perspective, 26
Litigation, 109
Live presentation, of proposal, 73
Loading dock, 157, 165, 176
Logistical limitations:
    of indoor venues, 157–8
    of outdoor sites, 159–60

M

Mailbox rule, 104
Management, of site and venue, 152–4
Marketing and sales phase, of event organization:
    definition of, 13
    in GANTT chart, 15
    producer tasks in, 17
Markup, method of making profit, 48–9
Master of Ceremonies (MC), 163
Mediation, 108
Meeting of the minds, in contracts, 98
Meeting Professionals International (MPI), 7
Meetings:
    as in type of event, 5, 7
    of production team, 84–6
    safety meetings, 94
Meetings, Incentives, Conventions, and Exhibitions (MICE), 6
Mega-events, 4
Microsoft Project, 15, 164
Monocular cues, 25
Motion parallax, 26
Motion perception, 26

N

National Electrical Code (NEC), 100, 143–5
National Fire Code (NFC), 100, 144
National Fire Protection Association (NFPA), 143, 145
Negotiation, 108

Non-standard setups, for indoor venues. *See* Setup, non-standard, for indoor venues
Non-traditional standards development bodies, 143

O

Occupational Health and Safety (OHS), 93
Occupational Safety and Health Administration (OSHA), 93, 142
Occupational Safety and Health Standards (OSHS), 93, 100, 145
Oral contract, 98
Overhead, 49–51

P

Payments, subcontractor, 186
Perception, 22–8
Perceptual constancy, 24
Perceptual organization, 22–4
Performing organizations and unions, 103
Peripheral drift, 26
Permits, 13, 17, 66, 140, 157, 164
Personality, of creative person, 20–1
Portable power, 159
Portable toilets, 159
Positional approach, to conflict resolution, 90
Power, electrical, 44, 66, 87, 141, 153, 157–9, 165
Preparation phase, of cognitive process, 22–7
Presets, 171, 172
Press-to-talk, 167
Product launches, 7, 8
Production book, 164
Production management, 17, 151–84
  CADD, as used in, 160–2
  calling the show, 170–6
  communications equipment and protocol, 167–70
  determining indoor venue capacity, 154–7
  during event coordination phase, 152–64
  during event execution phase, 164–76
  establishing logistical limitations, of venue or site, 157–60

production schedules, running orders, and scripts, 162–4
  running the event, 166–76
  site and venue layout, 160–2
  site inspection and venue liaison, 152–60
  staffing the show, 166–7
  supervising event setup, 164–6
  supervising event strike, 176
  understanding site and venue management, 152–4
Production Manager, 166, 167, 175, 176
Production schedule, 152, 153, 162–4, 165, 171
Production team, 11, 17, 79–94, 185–6
  assembling the team, 80–1
  conflict resolution within, 88–91
  health and safety issues of, 93–4
  hierarchy of, 81
  organizing the team, 81–3
  producer's tasks, 86–7, 91–3
  running efficient meetings of, 84–6
  working with the team, 83–93
Productivity, 50–1
Professional Convention Management Association (PCMA), 7
Professionalism, 63, 144, 145, 176
Profit, making a, 48–52
Proposals, 17, 61–77
  bidding against oneself, 76
  budget, 66–8
  CADD, 71
  CDs and DVDs, 71–2
  company background, 65
  content, 65–8
  copyright and intellectual property, 74–5
  cover and binding, 70
  creative fee, 74
  creativity, 62–3
  delivering a winning proposal, 73
  description of services and products, 65–6
  ethical considerations, 73–6
  experience, 64
  font, 68
  format, 68–71
  graphics and photos, 66, 72
  Internet, use of, 72
  live presentation, 73
  mail, courier, or e-mail, 73

obtaining supplier contacts, 76
preparing a winning proposal, 64–72
professionalism, 63
size and design, 69–70
technology, use of, 71–2
timing and followup, 73
uniqueness, 71
using other people's ideas in a proposal, 75
what wins business, 62–4
Protocol, communications, 169–70

R

Radio code alphabet, 170
Radio code numbers, 169
Radios, 165, 167
Random input, 37
Reasons, for special events, 3–6
   commercial, 5–6
   educational, 5
   political, 4
   religious, 3–4
   social, 4
Receiver pack, 167
Regulations, 143–5
Rehearsal(s), 93, 99, 139, 167, 171–4
Relative height, 26
Rendering:
   three-dimensional, 160–2
   two-dimensional, 160–2
Request for proposal (RFP), 65, 81
Retreats, 7
Reunions, 4, 7, 8
Reversals, 35–6
RFP. See Request for proposal
Rider(s), contract, 100–2
Rights of assignment, 103
Risk assessment, 17, 140–1, 144, 148
Risk management, 17, 137–50
   assessment and evaluation of risks, 140–1, 144, 148
   assessment checklist, 148
   avoidance, 140
   completing insurance applications, 149
   compliance, 142–5
   consultants, 148–9
   controls, 140
   general guidelines for the operation and/or use of equipment, 143

general standards for the safe design and use of equipment, 142–3
general standards for workplace safety, 142
identification of risks, 140
industry initiatives, 147
insurance, 145–9
monitoring, 140–1
policy, 148
process of, 139
realities of insurance and its relationship to event production, 146–7
reduction, 140
regulations, 143–5
retention, 140
risk management policy of individual companies, 148–9
theory, 139–42
theory versus reality, 138–42
transfer, 140, 148
Ritual, 2–5
Robert's Rules of Order, 85–6
Rule-based thinking, 76
Running order, 91, 152, 162–4, 165, 166–7, 171–6
Running the event, 166–76
Run-through, 172

S

Safety, of production team, 93–4
Schoolroom seating. See Seating, schoolroom
Script, 151, 162–4, 165, 167, 171–6
Seating:
   banquet, 154–5
   classroom. See Schoolroom
   schoolroom, 154
Seminars, 7
Setup(s):
   non-standard for indoor venues, 156–7
   standard for indoor venues, 154–6
Sewage, 159
Show caller, 168–76
Show calling, 152, 168–76
Showbook, 164
Signing authority, 99, 105
Signing contracts, 104–5
Site, as in outdoor event location, 12–13, 91, 144, 152–4, 159–62, 176

Site lighting, 160
Skills, required by an event producer, 9–10
Small claims court, 109
Software, project management, 10, 15, 164
Special events:
    categories of, 6–8
    definition of, 2
    reasons for, 3–6
Spectacles, 7, 8
Spreadsheet, 43, 45–6, 52
Staffing, the show, 166–7
Stage management, 44, 167
Stage managers, 80, 139, 163, 166–8,
    174–5, 186
Standard setups, for indoor venues, 154–7
Standards, for the safe design and use of
    equipment, 142–3
Standards, for workplace safety, 142
Standards Council of Canada (SCC), 143
Standards development bodies, non-
    traditional, 143
Standards Development Organization
    (SDO), 142
Standby, command in show calling, 174–5
Standup reception, 154
Supervision:
    of event setup, 164–6
    of event strike, 176
Supplier terms, for contract payments,
    47–8
Surveyor's measuring wheel, 161, 166
Symposia, 7

T

Table layout, 154–7
Talk-through, of event or show, 167
Tasks, of producer, 86–7, 91–3
Taxes, 52, 57, 101
Technical direction, 80, 81, 151, 165
Technical Director (TD), 151, 163–76
Technical riser, 157
Technology, use of in proposals, 71–2
Telephone lines, 159

Termination policy, 102
Terms and conditions, 99–102
Texture gradient, 26
Thank-you, letter to client, 187
Theater, 4, 167, 171
Theater seating, 154
Theme events, 7, 28
Three-dimensional rendering, 160–2
Toolkit, onsite, 165–6
Trade shows, 5, 7, 8
Translation phase, of cognitive process, 29
Trompe l'oeil, 26
Two-dimensional drawings, 160–2

U

Underwriting, 146–7
Union house, 153
Unions, 103, 153
Useable area, of venue, 155–6

V

Vectorworks, 10, 160
Venue, as in indoor event location, 8,
    12–13, 33, 36, 67, 71, 87, 89, 92, 99,
    106, 139, 141, 148, 152–9, 160–1,
    172, 176, 185–6
Vivien, 10, 160

W

Waivers, 91, 140, 148–9
Warranties, 99
Waste and refuse, 160
Water mains, 159
Weather clause. See Contract management,
    items to include in a contract
Wheelchair ramp, 157
Workers' Compensation or Workers'
    Compensation Board (WCB), 42, 56,
    58–9, 87, 103, 142–3, 145
Workshops, 7

masters one look can be faded to the next. The two-scene preset is the most common preset board. Cues are manually set on alternate scene banks and faded from one to the other.

Programming: The process by which light cues are set up, written, and recorded into memory on a memory console. Programming on contemporary control consoles may involve complex manipulation of functions and software, but rarely involves actual program coding.

Projection Screen: Projection screens come in two main forms:
1. *Tripod*:   These are for front projection only. The fabric pulls up and out of a metal cradle. The base is a three-legged tripod. They are available only up to 8 ft × 8 ft in size and are best used for presentations in small rooms/spaces with audiences under 150 people.
2. *Fast-Fold*:   These consist of a fabric that snaps to a rigid aluminum frame. The screen can be used for front or rear projection depending on the type of fabric used. Legs can be adjusted to various heights and the screens can also be flown if required. They are available in sizes up to 30 ft in width.

Props: Short for 'properties,' these are furnishings, set dressings, and all items large and small generally used as part of event décor. Usually separate from linens, murals, and all technical gear.

Proscenium Arch: The opening through which the audience views a performance, usually found only in permanent theaters. Usually just called the proscenium, it is seldom actually arched in modern construction.

Protocol: The specific type of analog or digital signal (AMX or DMX 512) used by a lighting control console and the equipment it controls.

Proximity Effect: An increase in the bass response of some mics as the distance between the mic and its sound source is decreased.

Punch Light: A high-intensity luminaire that floods an area with light whose color temperature is approximately that of daylight.

Quad Box: A piece of power distribution equipment comprising a small, metal enclosure housing four, flush, female connectors, and a permanently installed power cord whose conductors are electrically connected to the female connectors.

Rack: An abridged version of Dimmer Rack or Power Distribution Rack, or an apparatus that is a combination of the two.

Radio Frequency Interference (RFI):   Radio signals from external sources (e.g. cell phones) that invade and can be heard through, sound systems.

Rated Luminaire Life: The total length of time that a luminaire should operate effectively, as set by the manufacturer.

Real Time: A term used to describe any system which operates such that input, processing, and output take place over a short period of time and without any long delays, or without storage of input or of intermediate or final results.

Rear-Screen Projection: Locating the projector behind a translucent screen to be viewed from the front.

Reflection: A term that describes the amount of sound 'bouncing' off hard surfaces.

Reflector
1. Generally, anything that causes reflection.
2. A metal or glass apparatus, usually curved in some manner, used in most luminaires for the purpose of directing light rays from a light source.
3. In the film and video industries, a metallic or reflective fabric panel, used for bounce lighting, or simply to redirect light, with the light source being a luminaire or sunlight. They are available in a variety of sizes, shapes, and materials of varying reflectance.

Rejection: A microphone's ability to selectively exclude sounds coming from outside its pick-up pattern.

Resolution: For computers, this refers to the number of pixels contained in the maximum screen viewing area, in other words the amount of detail that is seen in an image. For video, it refers to the number of lines per inch.

Response Time
1. The time it takes for a dimmer to reach its intended level from the initiation of an input control signal.
2. The time it takes a luminaire filament to react to a change in voltage.

Restore: A cue to resume or return to any previous state, setting, or function (e.g. lighting).

Reverb: Any electronic or acoustical device designed to simulate, or capture, the natural reverberation of a large, hard-surfaced (echoic) room, and mix it back with the original recorded sound.

RF Signal: Signal sent via RF.

RGB: Red, Green, Blue are the basic light components that make up color TV and computer displays.

Rider
1. Also called a technical rider, this is information sent to a venue or producer by a performance group detailing lighting, audio, staging, and dressing room requirements. Ideally arrives before the group.
2. A supplement to a written contract that spells out specific details of services or products to be provided.

Rig or Rigging
1. A complete structural assembly for hanging or supporting luminaires, scenery, and/or other production equipment comprising some or all of the following: truss, motors, support cables, luminaires, pulleys, pipes, and other hardware, for the purpose of creating a temporary performing area.
2. To set up and connect support items, such as cables, ropes, pulleys, hoists, motors, chains, or slings between the points and the items to be flown.

Rigger: A technician responsible for the rigging of flown equipment for an event.

Risers: Flat platforms or stage sections of various sizes, usually portable, used for building stages or for supporting production equipment. Standard sizes are 8 ft × 4 ft and 8 ft × 6 ft. Heights generally vary from 12 to 48 in.

Road Case: A sturdy, rugged box, often supplied with handles, and castors or wheels, used to transport and protect production equipment such as control consoles, dimmer racks, luminaires, and musical equipment.

Road Crew: Technical crew members who travel with a production on tour.

Roboscan (TM): A moving mirror automated fixture manufactured by Martin.

Rolling Rack: A portable dimmer rack on castors for ease of transportation.

Router: An audio device used to selectively assign any input to any output, including the ability to add inputs together. In this way, one input could go to all outputs, or all inputs could go to just one output, or any combination thereof.

Runway Lights: Footlights that are used on stage runways.

Safety Cable: A steel cable that has a clip on one end and a loop on the other. It is intended to be threaded through a piece of hanging equipment and around a support structure, such as a batten or truss, and then clipped to its loop. It then acts as a safety support should the primary support, such as a pipe luminaire or hanging arm, fail.

Sandbag: Canvas bag used for weighing down scenery supports, especially flats.

Scan Rate: Horizontal and vertical scan speeds, usually specified in kHz or Hz.

Scanning: The electronic process of moving an electron beam across a CRT surface.

Scene or Scene Preset
1. A set of predetermined light levels that can be set up on a lighting control console in advance of need, and to which the operator may fade or go when desired.

2. A term used to describe a lighting control console that has such a capability.

Scoop: Named for its scoop-like shape, an open-face flood light with a large, diffused reflector that is essentially the body of the luminaire. The reflector is parabolic, spherical, or ellipsoidal, and is generally made from unpainted aluminum.

Scrim: In the theater and special events industry, a thin, gauze-like curtain. When illuminated from the front, it appears opaque, and when illumination is present behind it but not on it, the scrim becomes almost transparent. It can also appear translucent when there is some illumination directly on it, and some illumination present behind it, in the proper proportions.

SCSI: Small Computer Systems Interface (scussy). Connection interface for computer peripheral equipment.

Sealed Beam Luminaire: A luminaire with an integral light source, reflector, and lens, all of which are either sealed within, or are part of the envelope.

SECAM: Systeme Electronique Couleur Avec Memoire, the television standard used in France and throughout the Eastern Block Republics. It has 625 scan lines and 25 frames per second.

Segue (Pronounced 'Segway'):   Musical term for an immediate follow-on. Now often used as jargon for any kind of immediate follow-on in entertainment or event segments.

Sensitivity: The sound pressure level directly in front of a loudspeaker (on axis) at a given distance and produced by a given amount of power.

Serial Port: Computer input/output connection that transmits data one bit at a time (e.g. used for a computer mouse).

Set: A complete stage setting for a show or a complete piece of décor.

Sharktooth: A material used for fabric scrims used in theater or events.

Shelving: The setting of the on-axis output of complementary drivers (woofers, mid-range, tweeters) to provide the desired frequency response.

Shield: A metal enclosure that prevents electronic components from being affected by unwanted interference. Shielded speakers may be placed near a TV, for instance, because their magnets cannot affect the picture tube.

Shin Buster
1. A luminaire placed as close to the stage floor as possible. It is focused such that no light shines on the floor, thus giving the illusion that the subject is floating.
2. Generally, any luminaire mounted close to the stage floor.